MONTSÉGUR
AND THE
MYSTERY
OF THE
CATHARS

MONTSÉGUR
AND THE
MYSTERY
OF THE
CATHARS

JEAN MARKALE

Translated by Jon Graham

Inner Traditions

Rochester, Vermont

Inner Traditions
Rochester, Vermont
One Park Street
Rochester, Vermont 05767
www.InnerTraditions.com

Originally published in French under the title *Montségur et l'énigme cathare* by
Éditions Pygmalion/Gérard Watelet, Paris
First U.S. edition published by Inner Traditions in 2003

Library of Congress Cataloging-in-Publication Data

Markale, Jean.
   [Montségur et l'énigme cathare. English]
   Montségur and the mystery of the Cathars / Jean Markale ; translated
by Jon Graham.
      p. cm.
Includes index.
   ISBN 0-89281-090-4 (pbk.)
   1. Montségur (France)—History. 2. Heresies,
Christian—France—Languedoc—History—Middle Ages, 600–1500.
3. France—Church history—987–1515. 4. France—History—13th century.
5. Albigenses. I. Title.
   DC801.M832M3713 2003
   272'.3—dc21
                                                    2003013529

Printed and bound in the United States at Lake Book Manufacturing, Inc.

10 9 8 7 6 5 4 3 2

Text layout by Priscilla Baker
This book was typeset in Sabon

Contents

Part 1

THE SITES

1

A Long March to
Montségur

The name Montségur has been singing in collective memory since the
time in the year 1244 when the pyre was lit on the side of a mountain
reputed to be sacred in order to burn 205 miscreants who had been con-
victed first of heresy and then of persisting in their error. It seems that
the flames of this pyre continue to illuminate not only the deep vales of
the Ariège Pyrenees but also the torturous folds of humanity's guilty conscience. An event that occurred under the rule of good King Louis (later
Saint Louis) and that could have passed for a simple police operation—
which it effectively was—or a regrettable chance mishap has taken on a
universal dimension, deliberately evoking intolerance, fanaticism, and
man's inhumanity to man. We no longer accept this kind of injustice,
whether motivated by political or religious reasons—at least when it
involves events in the distant past—and we now condemn depriving
people of their deepest beliefs as well as their political independence.

The crusade against the Albigensians was undoubtedly motivated
as much by political as religious reasons, though both incentives were
combined in perfect harmony beneath economic motives. The "injustice" at Montségur has become a crime, and crimes are not so soon forgotten. In fact, they tend to decisively promote those who have been
their unfortunate victims. The blood of the Christian martyrs will forever stain the Roman circuses, and the cross of Jesus will always stand

on Golgatha. But the Latin cross is not the same as this one. Jesus' true cross was in the form of the *tau*, while the Latin cross most often displayed as his symbol is a solar sign that has come down to us from the dawn of time.

It so happens that any event worthy of figuring in human memory, rather than being stripped of its original significance, is charged and enriched with new resonance in accordance with how it has been filtered through time. It even happens sometimes that the place where the event has taken place comes to be considered as the essential element of its memorialization, thereby giving such a place a symbolic value that enhances as well as deforms it. Such is the case for Montségur, the mecca of Cathar resistance against both the Church and Capet power. We would have greatly astonished the two hundred *perfecti* who were hurled into the flames by asking them where they had hidden the Grail. Although the word *grail* is of Occitain origin, it is not an established fact that the Cathars knew of it or that they shaped the confused notions that cloak it today. It is only since the end of the nineteenth century, and especially since Richard Wagner's *Parzival*, that Montségur became associated with the Grail. Again, it needs to be said that Richard Wagner himself grumbled quite loudly when learning of this association because he was deeply convinced—could he have been otherwise?—that the Grail Castle had been located in Bavaria, on the banks of the Rhine. It is true that Wagner was a zealous promoter of all things German and that he somewhat forgot the earlier Celtic and Occitain texts on the Grail theme.

Whatever the case may be, one observation must be made: Montségur was either a Cathar fortress or a Cathar temple and is also—perhaps—the castle where the Fisher King preciously guarded what Chrétien de Troyes (the first to speak of it) prudently named *a* grail, without giving any additional details about just what it may have been. This only added to the mystery, and Montségur, the eagle's nest where all the clouds in the world converge, gained an incontestable legendary aura from it.

In my memory Montségur is first several lines and a drawing in a violently anti-Albigensian school textbook from which emerged Simon de Montfort, vigilant protector of the orthodoxy, cloaked in heroism. This was a time when it was impossible for me to doubt whatever people were trying to teach me. After all, Montségur and the Cathars were quite far away, both in time and space. My world was located between Paris and Brittany. It was only later, when I was in the tenth grade, that the shadow of Montségur suddenly appeared through a Brocéliande Forest that was already a reality to me because it formed part of my childhood landscape and was revitalized by my study of French medieval literature.

We did in fact have a literature professor, Jean Hani, who had a passion for both the tales of the Round Table and contemporary poetry. I was thus given the opportunity to familiarize myself with the legends of Tristan and Iseult, Merlin, which I already partially knew, and Perceval's quest for the Holy Grail. But in tandem with this plunge into the past, we studied poets of the twentieth century, among them Maurice Magre, who was not only the key to my discovery of contemporary literature but also to the Grail at Montségur.

Of course I had no preconceived notion of the Grail. It was as abstract to me as the fortress of Montségur. I was surprised that the land of the Pyrenees could serve as the context for an adventure that I could consider only as Breton. This was during the darkest hours of the Occupation. The German-controlled radio gave abundant play to the *Prelude and Death of Isolde* by Wagner as well as the *Prelude of Parzival* or the *Enchantment of Good Friday*. I loved this music and I still do because I instinctively use it as the theme music when I imagine scenarios based on Arthurian tales. I had seen Marcel Carné's film, *Les Visiteurs du soir,* which awoke my enthusiasm and convinced me once and for all that my destiny lay in fishing in the deepest depths of the Middle Ages for what nobody else had yet perceived there. A short while later I saw Jean Delannoy's *L'Eternal Retour,* which provides a perfect and magnificent transposition of the myth of Tristan by Jean

Cocteau. The unusual combination of cinema, music, medieval litera-ture, and contemporary poetry made me what I am today: an ageless knight in quest of a Grail that flees my grasp each time I believe myself to be on the verge of possessing it. The Grail crops up before me when my path takes a detour through the dark forests populated in my imag-ination with fairylike beings and those strange women of the mounds who appear before travelers to point out a direction that may actually be the wrong way.

In all of this Montségur played the role of a beacon, but one I saw no need to reach, for I firmly believed that the Grail castle could exist nowhere but in Brittany, or actually in Great Britain (I knew the origin of the Arthurian romances was to be sought on the other side of the Channel). I had of course read the commentaries inspired by the resem-blance between the names Montségur and Montsalvage, where the wounded King Anfortas awaited Parzival's arrival. I had even made sure to verify this connection in the Wolfram von Eschenbach text used by Wagner to construct the libretto for his lyrical drama, but I found scant relationship between Muntsalvasche (the name used by Wolfram) meaning the "mountain of salvation" and Montségur, which means the "secure mountain." When I visited Montsûrs in Mayence, I knew that this name, like that of the Ariegeois castle, derived from the same Mons Securis. Ultimately, because the Grail Castle in the French romances is Corbenic and because my visceral anti-Germanic sentiments were nat-urally quite strong at that time, I deliberately dropped Montsalvage from my field of vision regarding legend.

Of course Montségur still remained there. But I viewed it as an Albigensian citadel, for the word Cathar was unknown to me then. At that time I regarded the Albigensians as square pegs in round holes, people with bizarre beliefs who assumed the existence of a god of evil opposed to a god of good. I saw nothing in common between these oth-erworldly heretics and the Celts, who I, even at that early age, was beginning to suspect possessed annoying heretical tendencies—but it could not be the same heresy. And if, when reading the poems of the troubadours, I wondered about the identity of that inaccessible and never seen mysterious lady whom they sung about with so much love, it did not remotely occur to me that she might be an image indicating in veiled terms the church of the Believers and the Perfects. Because of my profoundly monist bent and systematic denial of the absolute opposition between good and evil, I found it impossible to feel any kinship with the Albigensians, these dualistic heretics. And besides, Occitania was far away and the strong focus of my imagination was concentrated on the Armorican shores.

Montségur was thus buried deep in my memory and emerged only toward the end of the 1960s. The occasion was the French television showing of a Stellio Lorenzi dramatic series on the Cathars. Besides being interesting, this series had the merit of explicitly revealing to a large audience the principal events of the tragedy experienced by the Occitanian people of the thirteenth century, a history that could not to be found in textbooks. But what attracted me most strongly was the sumptuous and magnificent image shown during the series credits. It was a shot probably taken from a helicopter: The fortress was perched atop an apparently inaccessible mountain, and in the camera's play, it seemed literally to be spinning, like a comet seeking a spot to land amidst the center of a tormented world. In addition, the musical accompaniment, borrowed from Serge Prokofiev's *Alexander Nevsky*, gave this image a fantastic quality, making it seem almost like a hallucination. Overall, the image and music gave me a strong sensation of dizziness that I still feel when I think about it, even after all this time.

I felt as if I was confronted by an absence, an emptiness, not only by the play of the poetic image, in itself quite strong, but also by the background of this image. These mysterious Cathars, about whom I knew nothing and who had entered history the same way in which the Celts had—by legend—were the only thing capable of filling the emptiness I felt. But where could I pick up their trail? How could I discern it among the creations of the mind, literature, the plastic arts, architecture—those vestiges that the Inquisition had desperately sought to remove forever? I had read certain works by René Nelli, but the Cathar thought he unearthed seemed so far from my own concerns that I renounced any intention of following it further in a direction that could easily be labeled theological. In contrast, I found the poetry of the troubadours spellbinding, and I strove to discover among their words the path that would lead me to the true Montségur, the one to be found nowhere and everywhere, the ideal and secret lair of what I imagined to be the Grail.

I owe much to René Nelli. He introduced me to one of the most important texts of medieval Occitania, the *Roman de Jaufré,* of which he published a magnificent translation. This archaic Arthurian epic, thanks to an author of genius, provided me with almost all of the keys opening the mysteries of the legend of Arthur and the Grail. It is a fundamental work that preceded the now-classic tales of Chrétien de Troyes and the *Prose Lancelot.* It revealed to me the subtle relationship that exists between medieval Occitain civilization and Celtic traditions. Further, I admit to seeing several times within this text the shadows of the Believers and the Perfects.

But it was especially through his study on the eroticism of the troubadours that René Nelli set my foot on a road from which I would not swerve. I was desperately seeking to establish a connection between Celtic concepts of love—as seen in the legend of Tristan and the Irish epics—and the famous *courtly love* that I prefer to call *fine love,* for that term appears to harmonize more closely with the profound sense of the expression. In the light of this study, what I'd once considered only a game of the court that had been refined in accordance with the rules of Christian morality became an entanglement of archaic rituals that hardly conformed to the customary norms of Christian orthodoxy. Fine love suddenly took on a strange appearance and gave off an aroma that clearly smacked of fire and brimstone. I had read repeatedly that the poetry of the troubadours had been influenced by Islam, but it was certainly not Arabic civilization that I found there. By all evidence it involved a pre-Christian, pre-Islamic initiatory path, and I began to believe that the Cathars had some role to play there. As we will see, this intuition was not so far from the truth. This initiatory path incontestably led to the fortress of Montségur. The difficulty lay in tracing the history of the Cathars from this outline. Montségur still seemed extremely remote.

Other signs appeared, among which was one that threw me off the trail: the strange work by Otto Rahn, *The Crusade Against the Grail*. It was not the content of the book that disturbed me; I had already read, regarding the Celts and the Grail in particular, even more unlikely ravings than the visions of Otto Rahn, which were merely echoes of those of the enigmatic Antonin Gadal. Neither was I disturbed by the fact that a German had taken an interest in the questions of the Grail and the Cathars.

I knew nothing precise about Otto Rahn, and the research performed by Christian Bernadac in this regard had not yet been published. It was easy, however, to understand that during the 1930s, from the time the power of the Nazis increased, "official" (rather than dissident) German intellectuals, acting in accordance with Nationalist-Socialist ideology, were looking for *something* among the Cathars in the Pyrenees, more precisely at Montségur. Once again we find the Montségur/Montsalvage comparison. I knew that Adolf Hitler planned to celebrate the ultimate victory of the Third Reich with an exceptionally grandiose performance of Wagner's *Parzival*. I also knew that the birth of Nazism in Germany had been surrounded by strange fairy godmothers labeled *polars* that were more or less secret associations having clearly occult tendencies, such as the Thule Group, and that claimed to be working toward the restoration of an Aryan Nordic Order opposed to Mediterranean and Semitic cosmopolitanism. Further, I was perfectly aware that the grail of Wagner and Wolfram von Eschenbach, but not the Celtic Grail, could be interpreted as a symbol of racial purity. The ambiguous nature of von Eschenbach's text allows for the most insane interpretations. But where did the Cathars fit into all of this? The word Cathar means "pure." Not to mention any names . . .

Under these circumstances, seeing that all investigation regarding the Cathars would lead me to formulate theories I was loath to support, for I was totally opposed to the National Socialist ideology out of deep personal conviction, I decided to abandon the road to Montségur. I would not visit the Pyrenees, which I knew nothing about and which held no attraction for me. I would leave the Cathars undisturbed; it didn't matter if anyone could establish a connection between them and the Grail. My Grail was elsewhere and I was at great pains to demonstrate that fact, if only by pointing to an enigmatic engraving on a granite support stone inside the Gavrinis Mound, located by the Gulf of Morbihan.

I was unable to conceal my irritation each time anyone mentioned Montségur and the Grail to me, and I gave many erudite lectures demonstrating the incompatibility of the Cathar's dualist mentality with the monist system of the Celts. The Cathars were simply heretics as were many others who did not have the fortune to be protected by princes as powerful as those who aided Luther and Calvin, and Montségur was merely a fortress perched atop a rocky peak, like so many others that can be found in France, especially in the Pyrenees and the Central Massif. In Brittany, though the Bretons call their hills mountains, there are no fortresses on the summits. Instead there are sanctuaries, usually fairly modest fortresses, and it was these that compelled my attention. It was in their substructures that I found traces of the druids, and I have to admit that the druids spoke more deeply to me than the Perfects.

In 1978 I made a series of radio broadcasts entitled "A Small Anthology of Popular Beliefs" that consisted of giving the floor to the last witnesses of folk beliefs in the various regions of France. Having just finished the series on Brittany with my old accomplices Pierre-Jakez Hélias and Charles le Quintrec, I made the decision to next visit the Languedoc region. I already had in mind the perfect interview subject: René Nelli. But time was short, and because Nelli was not available, I had to change my plans at the last minute. This was how I arrived one morning in Toulouse from Belgium, where I had just done a live radio broadcast and where an engineer from the FR3 was waiting to escort me and to record my show. I started by setting up an interesting discussion with Daniel Fabre, one of the top specialists of Occitan oral tradition, who was then teaching at the University of Mirail.

We then left for Verniolle, a small town near Pamiers, where I had arranged to meet with Adelin Moulis, a memorable figure who was one of the most faithful artisans of the post-war Occitan intellectual renaissance. This was the first time in my life that I had truly set foot in Cathar country. The Foix road vanished into peaks half hidden in the snow-covered clouds. The Pyrenees appeared to me to be a kind of submerged world into which I was almost scared to venture. The impression of vertigo that possessed me as I watched the credits roll for the Cathar television program came to me again. But in passing by Saverdun I could not help thinking, with my mania for etymology, that I was still in Celtic country, for this name clearly included the Gallic term *duno* meaning "fortress." What fortress? The image of Montségur returned to haunt me.

We recorded hours of discussion with Adelin Moulis. He spoke on everything and digressed often, surrendering to the passion he had for his land and the "observances" he had discovered. When he spoke to me about Esclarmonde de Foix, sister to the count of Foix who became a Cathar perfecti in 1206, he gave the impression of knowing her well and of having met her countless times on the twisting paths at the confluence of two rivers. However, in the small bungalow where he lived, everything was serene and peaceful. There were no Cathars there—though they remained close by. I felt their presence as familiar shadows pointing at me.

We shared an odd meal in a Pamiers restaurant. Adelin Moulis was an agnostic, the engineer was Jewish, and I was what I had always been, born a Christian though ensnared in the traps of druidry. We talked long into the evening, and it was there that I realized I was truly somewehere else, in a land that carried within it all the seeds of heresy, a land unlike any other, where the Cathars still live in utter anonymity among people who neither speak nor think about them. The smallest stone seemed to me like a vestige of them. The smallest roof suggested it housed mysteries. I would have loved to have gone further. It was then that I realized I would make the journey to Montségur. Adelin Moulis had led me to the border; the rest depended on me.

But this time I was there on a specific errand that did not allow for any variation in approach. Following a final day of wandering the streets of Toulouse, where I attempted to unravel the inextricable knots of the relationship between Count Raymond VII and the king of France, I left to return to Paris, where I had a good deal of trouble getting the Adelin Moulis broadcast to fit into the framework of the program for which it had been recorded. But the Cathar poison was now in my blood. It was no longer a remote and somewhat abstract world that opened before me, but something more tenacious, like a revealed truth that we accept without being able to find any arguments to gainsay it.

One essential observation I made was that a permanent Cathar presence must exist. A doctrine of that kind, intensely lived by people who did not hesitate to die rather than renounce it, is worthy of interest, even if we do not share belief in it. It is unthinkable that, despite the persecution and the prejudice of annihilation, such a doctrine could be lost entirely. I felt the Cathars around me even though I was incapable of recognizing their face as it had evolved in southern French society of the twentieth century. I sensed that this land was permeated with a *different* spirit—which led me to a second observation: I knew nothing about the Cathars except the generalities that can be found in history textbooks and tourist guides. Perhaps there was something more to this doctrine than the primal duality of good and evil, in the guise of the devil and the Good Lord, opposed in a merciless battle. Surely it concealed a reality that was more nuanced and original. But was I ready to face such a reality?

The answer at that time was no. I had not shed all my instinctive suspicions. To go to Montségur was perhaps an act motivated by curiosity, an act of opening, but it was also a dive into a somewhat alarming unknown. I had heard too many tall tales about the Celts and druidism in particular to be fearless of finding more of the same at Montségur. The shadow of Otto Rahn told me nothing worth hearing. While there is no Ragnarök, no "twilight of the Gods" in Celtic mythology, the Germanic eschatology I saw in the background of Otto Rahn's venture contributed to discouraging any basic research on my part. I also told myself that the Cathar region was situated in that Visigothic Septimania that has left numerous traces on Occitain soil. The Visigoths came from Sweden. The Grail of Montségur was that of Wolfram von Eschenbach. This was a Germano-Persian Grail guarded by knights who resembled the S.S. I had no desire to write the story of the Third Reich, even in a symbolic form.

However, that year of 1978 was an important one for me in the various maneuvers of fate that eventually led me to the Cathar citadel, and I owe it all to Marie Môn. Part Breton, part Catalan, but especially Languedocian and furthermore a Huguenot, she had everything necessary to lead me straight to heresy's heart. She had dived into the cold, bubbling waters of the Barenton Fountain and claimed, rightly in my view, that the Occitain Calvinists were remote descendants of the Good Men pursued by the Inquisition. She had gone behind the walls of Montségur to gather her thoughts in solitude, sheltered from the cold wind, which, snatched from the heights by the valley below, rolled off the surrounding mountains like an anguished scream from the depths of the ages. She had, however, sensed that the site lent itself to all ambiguities, that nothing was clear-cut or definitive, and that sometimes disturbing shadows emerged at sunset in the tufts of scrawny trees and along the splintered rocks.

It was Marie Môn who dragged me up to the *pog* (peak) of Montségur. Coming from Toulouse, where I had again been speaking of the cursed gold that legend claims was brought from Delphi by the Gaul Brennus and was profaned by a Roman proconsul, I rediscovered

Saverdun and the plane trees on the square of Pamiers. But this time, I traveled further. Reassured by the tutelary mass of the Foix château, vigilant guardian of a land that both disconcerted and fascinated me, I could see rising the peaks of those Pyrenees whose name evoked "fire" and "purity" to me. Hercules, we are told, strayed there, and it is there he encountered the young Pyrene. This story is pulled from countless variations. Another version informs us that this same Hercules, wandering at the other end of Gaul, fell in love with a young princess named Galathea, and with her founded Alesia, where they had a son named Galates, from whom the Galatians and Gauls descended. We know that this Hercules, who bears scant resemblance to the Greek demigod of the same name, is an incarnation of the folklore figure Gargantua, who in turn is an avatar of the Celtic god Ogmios or Ogma, the guardian giant of roads who enslaves humans through the charm of his speech.

The Pyrenees are worthy of such a giant and we should find out why, not far from Montségur, on the other side of the Frau Gorges, there is a Gargante Pass. In addition, to the south of Montségur, at an altitude of about five thousand feet, the Rock of Gourgue dominates the landscape, even seeming to protect the pog upon which the Cathar castle was built. The name Gourgue is incontestably related to Gargantua.

All of this implies that my approach to Montségur was surrounded by a particularly complex mythological atmosphere blending Cathar elements with underlying Celtic and Germanic realities. Without going so far as the ultimate aggravations of the imagination, it was permissible for me to raise questions and seek answers to them.

We arrived by way of the road from Mountferrier that twists and turns at the whim of the foothills of Mont d'Olmes. Further on, beneath a peak among so many others, there were ruins. But were they really ruins? In this land where rocks are shattered by winter ice and the burning sun of summer, it is hard to tell if the destruction we see is due to men, time, or nature constantly in motion. The earth is crenellated, as if to defend itself against invasions from outside, but the guards who once patrolled this inextricable line of fortifications are now vanished. Today, roads violate the mountainsides, passing through the pine woods and barren expanses where only greenish bushes grow, their color easily confused with that of faded stone. The vegetation here is that of both mountain and scrubland. I did, however, encounter the familiar dimension of certain moors in Brittany, those that are set apart from the human world, as if haunted by the memory of mysterious, supernatural inhabitants who would have once prowled around them. In Brittany these moors are the domain of the Korrigans, those nocturnal beings who lead travelers astray when the wayfarers have not given the sign of recognition that allows them to cross into forbidden zones. What is the story here? What might be hiding behind the bushes, looking for a sign from me that might be either accepted or rejected?

This was how we arrived beneath the pog. Seen from below, it took on an even more fantastic appearance than I dared hope. It was larger, higher, and more inaccessible than it looked to be in photos or engravings and was even more savage than in the skillfully framed image that played behind the documentary credits, leaving such a great impression on me. I was now ready. I had to set off toward the top of the pog, for it was there that I would find the light.

I don't think I ever climbed a mountain before with such speed and ease. Regardless of stones shifting under foot or grass slipping beneath my feet, I climbed and climbed. I was reminded of the episode in Victor Hugo's *The End of Satan,* in which the poet depicts the hunter Nimrod flying through the air in a cage built from the wreckage of Noah's Ark, pulled by four eagles. And the eagles climbed . . . Why would this have reminded me of eagles? To describe Montségur as an eagle's nest is a cliché of frightful banality. So? Eagles can climb higher than men in their attempt to wrest secrets from heaven.

It was in this spirit that I reached the walls. With no further reflection, I passed through them by the south door, having noticed, beneath the paving stone that serves as a doorsill, a small, pliant branch that someone had twisted clumsily into the shape of a pentagram and left there. Why not, after all? I told myself that the pentagram was a symbol commonly used by the Cathars. The visitors to this high place must have performed a symbolic gesture before entering this "holy of holies." Anyone spending the night on a Breton moor should hold a forked stick in hand to dispel the Korrigans. At Montségur the "golden bough" could well have been a pentagonal shape. Nothing would surprise me.

The wind was blowing inside the walls as if furious at my intrusion. I could hear it groaning along the ramparts, seeking to penetrate the smallest hole or the smallest shadowy corner. Just what was this place where I found myself?

In truth, I felt as if I was in a prison located halfway between Heaven and Earth, and I was afraid that I would not be able to get out, that I would be obliged to remain there eternally. This fleeting impression, lasting a few tenths of a second, seemed inexplicable to me. Was it based on my remembrance of the countless folktales that involve a castle suspended in the air, mysteriously tethered by four golden chains to something higher and invisible, something not described? Or could I have been thinking of that crystal chamber in the very beautiful story of Tristan's madness, the place to which the hero, disguised as a madman, declares that he will bring Queen Iseult? Could this crystal chamber be the same as the chamber of the sun in Irish legends, that place that will rejuvenate by its heavenly light whoever stays there? Or might this even be the invisible castle, the prison in the air where the fairy Vivian imprisoned Merlin the magician? Could this be the *éplumoir Merlin* as it's described in a thirteenth-century text?

All these thoughts flooded my mind so quickly that I could not put them into any order. They struck me in the same rhythm as the wind. The imagination is a beautiful thing. Getting something out of it is what's most important, and to do this, it is necessary to master it. I persist in my belief, even today, that these were only extremely brief images washing through me, and that when entering the fortress of Montségur, I was merely making connections between these familiar legends and the often-voiced hypothesis that this structure was, in reality, a solar temple. I was content to experience the moment.

But it quickly turned into a bad experience.

In the courtyard there two men taking measurements with a surveyor's chain and feverishly jotting down figures in a notebook. Another man was hugging the walls and trying to determine their alignment. On the eastern platform, which can be reached by a staircase, a woman was reciting a poem in German. I climbed up to this platform. Beyond, in the distance, I could see only peaks, nothing but peaks. The voice of the woman reading the poem was carried off by the wind.

Then I looked down.

I have never experienced such intense and painful dizziness as I did then. In looking over these jagged slopes and ravines opening beneath me like an infernal abyss, I was unable to combat the strong terror that invaded me. All attempts to deal with my fears reasonably were in vain; nothing worked. Somewhere Pascal describes, or rather imagines, that if someone were to place a very sturdy but very narrow plank between the two towers of the cathedral of Notre Dame in Paris, and then were to order the bravest philosopher in the world to cross it, the philosopher would begin and then experience such fear that he would refuse to take another step. Pascal was seeking to demonstrate the visceral truth that intellectual conviction is impotent when confronted with the power of the imagination. It is true that Pascal did not suffer from vertigo; it was he who performed the famous experiment with the mercury column on the Puy-de-Dôme. But as for me, I did suffer from vertigo, and this was an atrocious attack that forced me to return inside the walls. There, at least, despite the sensation of imprisonment, I had the illusion of security.

But when it came time to go back down the mountain, it was even worse. I do not think I have ever experienced such a void within myself, inspired here by the steep incline I hadn't noticed in my casual ascent but which now leaped to my eyes in all its immensity. I had to crawl, sometimes threading my way on all fours through the brush, having no confidence in the pebbles on the path that I could envision rolling out from beneath my feet and causing gigantic avalanches that would carry me off with them. Jean-Jacques Rousseau, who took a certain pleasure in suffering, spent hours perched over dreadful precipices and would even go so far as to throw stones down them while imagining he was those stones falling into the darkest abyss of fear. Every precipice is an open maternal womb. Are we scared that we might be swallowed up, are we scared to travel in the direction opposite it and thus snap the continuous line of the future and dissolve into the primordial ocean of nonexistence? I am tempted to say yes. But was my vertigo only fear?

Human thought seems to travel faster than its verbal expression. What did this insurmountable vertigo hold? The imaginary was splayed beneath me and I could grasp it: It was not unreal and it was not the material void that haunted me that afternoon as I descended as best I could the slopes of the pog of Montségur. I wonder if I may not have had a fleeting vision of the tragedy that took place there in 1244, when 205 Perfects perished in the flames at the base of the pog. And beyond this sacrifice, the smoke of which is still not extinguished, I think there was the immense void of the Cathar mystery. Mystery always causes fear. But it also attracts us. There is a certain pleasure to be found in vertigo; to enter the abyss of shadow is an act that is as exalting and exciting as soaring toward the flames of the sun, no doubt because shadow and light are two apparently contradictory aspects of an essentially unique reality.

Could the dualism of the Cathars be a false dualism?

I returned to Montségur four years later. There was no reason for me not to return and climb back to the top. But this time, as I climbed I did so slowly and cautiously, stopping at every landing and every odd feature of the terrain to turn back and view the leg I had just traversed, to note how it looked and what distance separated me from the bottom.

There was no wind in the castle this time. And there were no people. On this autumn morning the sun was sweet, caressing, familiar. A little mist was floating in the north. Toward the south the huge mass of the Pyrenees was melting into a still-pale sky. The stones of the walls were the same colors as before, and above, from the platform, I could see the horizon and the huge ravines, and I had no fear of being swallowed by them. The space unfolding beneath me was my own. The village of Montségur offered its red roofs to me as an invitation to life's calm and peaceful repose, far from the torment and tempests that shake the world. I knew that somewhere in these mountains a haven of peace existed where I could find the sleep of the traveler.

But I also realized that we should always look back when venturing onto unknown paths. It is by carefully marking off the road traveled that one benefits from any quest, because what really matters, when all is said and done, is not the mysterious object gleaming behind a curtain of mist, but the quest itself that led there.

2

The Castle of Montségur

The spell induced by Montségur, no matter how intense, is caused by two basic facts: On the one hand, the fortress bearing this name is located in an extremely remarkable setting and, on the other, it was the theater of a historical tragedy whose shadowy areas are substantial enough to inspire the most delirious fantasies. Added to these are the specific motives of everyone who has taken an interest in Montségur and the Cathars, most of whom, in all likelihood, are not looking for the same thing.

The fortress of Montségur is located on a pog, meaning on a *puy* (*pech* or *puig*), a term thought to have come from the Latin *podium* (elevated place) but actually stemming from a much older provenance, seemingly from the pre-Celtic era and found as well in the French *pic* (peak).

That said, the fortress does not occupy the entire pog of Montségur, which itself is an enormous mass of limestone rock about a mile and a half long and varying from nine hundred to fifteen hundred feet in width. With its highest altitude being about 3,900 feet, this rocky block is a detached part of the Tabe Massif (which some insist on calling Thabor) formed by the Olme Mountains, the Frau Mountains (whose average altitude is 6,000 feet), the Saint-Barthélémy peaks (whose average altitude is 7,500 feet), and the Soularac (7,563 feet). The summit provides an unimpeded view in every direction—thus it is easy to understand why this site has been occupied since ancient times. It is a privileged observation post that offers a commanding view of the entire countryside surrounding it.

But its height is not the only element in its favor. Its geographic layout, quite exceptional in its own right, makes this pog a natural fortress upon which the castle was but one of many developments. In fact, the mountain is close to inaccessible except from the southern slope, where there is an incline that rises to a platform surrounding the summit in an irregular fashion some five hundred feet below. Furthermore, the cliffs, ranging in height from 195 to 255 feet, form fortifications that are just as effective as constructed walls. To the east of the fortress, which is the most impressive side, the platform of the summit is extended by a very narrow ridge—only a few yards in width—that required no additional protection because surrounding it are formidable sheer cliffs some three hundred feet in height, providing a natural shield. It was at the extreme end of this ridge where an advance position of the Montségur defenses was located, the famous barbican taken (though not without huge losses) by the Inquisition's hired Basque mercenaries during a midnight assault during the siege of 1244. It was from this occupied barbican that these troops then bombarded the walls and interior of the castle with a stone thrower, thereby bringing about the capture of the garrison and the subsequent tragedy we are familiar with today.

Though it is the Cathar history that stays in mind, this site originally had nothing to do with heretics; in fact, the Cathars had control of Montségur for only about forty years. The excavations that have been carried out on the pog on a regular basis since the beginning of the twentieth century, but especially since 1956, have revealed traces of the very different eras during which this site was occupied. First of all, I must correct a common misconception: The ruins of the castle that can be seen today are not those of the castle besieged by the Inquisition—at least they do not correspond exactly to that fortress. Following the siege of 1244, in fact, the fortress was occupied by a royal garrison and was renovated, as were all the so-called Cathar castles of the region, at the end of the thirteenth century. They constituted such strategic strongholds in a very unstable territory, close to the Catalan frontier, that it would have been unthinkable not to use them after they were modified to make them even more secure.

While it is important to point out that the overall plan of the fortress dates from the very beginning of the thirteenth century (this is an incontestable fact, though there are anomalies allowing for various speculations), it is absolutely impossible to say what the building looked like before the year 1200. We do, however, have at our disposal a very interesting piece of information: During the twelfth century, Montségur was not included on the list of fortresses in the fiefdom of Mirepoix, which was then attached to the count of Foix. This proves that before the Cathars settled there in about 1206 there was no longer anything but ruins on the pog of Montségur.

However, the occupation of this piece of land goes back much further. To the north of the fortress but still on the platform, excavations have unearthed the ruins of a veritable village, but because this site is cramped for space, its occupation was vertical, with newer civilizations building their structures on top of those that had been there previously. It is difficult to define with any precision what belongs to which era. However, prehistoric remnants have been discovered: a sharp-sided arrowhead typical of the Chasséen period (from 3000 to 2000 B.C.), as well as small blades, a percussion tool, and a piercing arrowhead of the Chalcolithic type (2000 to 1800 B.C.). It is known that the region of Montségur was much frequented by prehistoric peoples. Important remnants of civilization have been discovered, in particular, in the caves of Las Morts, Tuteil, and the chain of Morenci, not to mention the group of caves in the upper Ariège valley around Ussat-les-Bains, a favored site and an important population center because of its thermal springs. Evidence of the Celtic Bronze and Iron Ages can also be seen in the remnants of shelters and sepulchres that are fairly numerous in the vicinity.

There was probably a Roman presence on this site, but apart from a bronze coin from about A.D. 300, documentation is lacking. It is true, though, that the Romans rarely settled on high ground, preferring instead to establish their camps and surveillance posts in the valleys, where they could easily monitor the roads, which are quite rare in the mountains. In fact, it was toward the end of the Roman Empire, at the time of the arrival of the Visigoths, that the Montségur region appears to have taken on a certain importance.

We know that the Visigoths left an indelible stamp on a large part of Occitania. They occupied a wide swath of territory stretching between Narbonne and Agen, the Rouergue and the Perigord, and the Pyrenees minus Cerdagne and the Comminges. Emigrating from Sweden in several waves, they were no more cruel than other peoples of that time, and while they sometimes destroyed cities, they rebuilt others and were responsible for the reign of a brilliant civilization to which archaeology can bear witness. This was how the famous Septimania was formed that later became the Razés, which itself was divided into three earldoms: Carcassonne, Narbonne, and Razés proper (in other words, Rennes-le-Château or Rennes-les-Bains). The design for the future domain of Mirepoix, which would encompass Montségur, was already sketched out in the framework of this Visgothic administration. Following the Muslim invasions and the reconquest of this land by the Franks, the feudal system made its appearance and the earldom of Foix emerged to which the domain of Mirepoix, thus Montségur, was attached.

During the early medieval era, the life of the inhabitants of Montségur must have been similar to that of all others living in the mountains. Outside of tending livestock and working at some rudimentary crafts, what else could they have done in this poor and somewhat inhospitable land, which in truth was more favorable for hiding in than for pursuing lucrative activities? If a Cathar community had not settled on the pog in search of either refuge or solitude for meditation and observing their rituals, no one would speak of Montségur today and the ruins of the castle would not be lifting their enigmatic appeal toward Heaven as they do now, in a language we cannot even comprehend.

It was thus, at the beginning of the thirteenth century, that the Cathars began to frequent the pog of Montségur. Small houses were built on the northern face, forming a veritable village. One of these was owned by a certain Forneira, mother of the local lord, Ramon de Perella, one of the vassals of Raymond-Roger, count of Foix. This was a time when heresy was gaining ground throughout the Languedoc region, which was under the protection of the count of Toulouse, Raymond VI. But the Cathars guessed that danger would come from the north. The king of France's claims on Occitain territory were becoming more explicit, and they knew that Philip Augustus would need only the smallest excuse to send in his troops and begin the annexation of a land that was an irritant to the Capet monarchy. The pretext was quickly found in the Albigensian heresy, which was making great inroads against official preaching and, most important, was causing injury to the local ecclesiastics, whom the faithful were abandoning. Philip Augustus sought authorization from the pope to mount a crusade to halt the growth of this heresy.

This prompted the Cathar leaders to ask Ramon de Perella to fortify the ruins of Montségur, and the fortress was subsequently rebuilt, for Ramon also knew a trial of strength was inevitable. In 1206 Esclarmonde, sister to the count of Foix, received the *consolamentum,* the supreme Cathar sacrament (in truth, the only Cathar sacrament), thus declaring her adherence to the perfecti among the *credenti* (Believers). At this same time a Spaniard, Dominic de Guzman, who later became the famous Saint Dominic, settled in Fanjeaux, in the center of a country whose conversion to orthodox doctrine had been entrusted to him as his personal mission, and, also in 1206, the papal legate Pierre de Castelnau was assassinated, which served as a pretext for Pope Innocent III to preach the crusade.

The die was cast. Simon de Montfort, at the head of the royal troops, ravaged the countryside with unquestionable success. But while Cathar Occitania seemed lost, the fortress of Montségur was not attacked and increasing numbers of credenti moved there. In 1213 the defeat of Muret sounded the death knell of free Occitania as well as any hopes the Cathars had of being left in peace. Henceforth, to survive they were forced to hide and evade the formidable agents of the

Inquisition, that enormous machine for oppressing conscience and burning people that had been entrusted to the members of Saint Dominic's Order, who worked under the responsibility of the Holy See. Simon de Montfort died in 1218, Saint Dominic in 1221, and Raymond VI of Toulouse in 1222. His son, Raymond VII, was excommunicated in 1226 for displaying too much tolerance toward the Cathars and for showing signs of his desire to wrest back the majority of the domains stolen from him by the northern crusaders. But in 1229 the count of Toulouse was forced to submit under the terms of a treaty he signed in Meaux with Louis IX (or rather, in reality, with Blanche de Castille, who was holding the reins of government during her son's minority).

The Meaux treaty dealt a harsh blow to Catharism, for even though Raymond VII was obviously playing a double game, he was forced to sacrifice the most visible Cathars in order to save the others. Though generally well accepted by even the Catholic populace because they were a symbol of resistance to the French occupation, the Cathars were now forced to organize. In 1232, under the impetus of the deacon Guillabert de Casteres, they held an important synod. During this meeting, they officially requested of Ramon de Perella—not a Cathar himself but protective of them—that he accept all the Cathars who wished to relocate to Montségur in search of refuge and that he strengthen the defenses of the fortress. Ramon de Perella hesitated. He knew that in accepting, he risked incurring the wrath of the Church and the French king. But he had confidence in the pog of Montségur, for it was deemed impregnable. He eventually accepted and ordered the reinforcement of the site and garrison.

It must be pointed out that the Cathars had the means of paying their fair share for these defense preparations. They possessed an immense treasure, the origin of which still remains somewhat mysterious, and they stored it in the castle cellar. They paid Perella liberally and contributed to the upkeep of the garrison.

Thus Montségur became the veritable beacon of Catharism, "Satan's synagogue," as certain chroniclers of the time put it. Numerous pilgrims flooded there from all over Occitania to hear the sermons of the Good

Men. What is surprising is that the king's seneschals made no attempt to take Montségur before its defenses were strengthened, nor did they mount any serious attacks against the pilgrims. It seems that Blanche de Castille, for reasons that escape us, wished to handle the Cathar situation carefully while at the same time speaking aloud of the necessity to destroy them. The attitude of the regent toward Raymond VII is far from clear.*

However, Raymond VII was in the uncomfortable position of having to supply pledges of loyalty to royal authority as well as the papacy. Of course, he made regular protests against the actions of the Inquisition in his domains, for he knew full well that the Dominican brothers were far more harsh in their fight against the heretics than were the bishops and priests of the local clergy, and thus his protests aided the Cathars. Furthermore, he obtained the suspension of the Inquisition in his territories for four years, from 1237 to 1241, which constituted a relative success. But in return he had to show proof of his own harshness against certain overly visible Good Men. He thus ordered the Albigensian deacon Johan Cambito brought from Montségur to Toulouse along with three other heretics and had them condemned to be burned at the stake.

It was around this same time, in 1240, that Guillabert de Castres died. This noteworthy Cathar figure who has entered into legend was said to have administered the consolamentum and preached in hundreds of localities right under the very nose of the Inquisition, and no doubt with the protection of the count of Toulouse. One year after Guillabert de Castres, veritable leader of the Cathar religion, was replaced by Bertrand d'en Marti, Raymond VII, his back even closer to the wall, was compelled to promise King Louis IX that the castle of Montségur would be destroyed. He besieged it, but of course, this siege was of no consequence. It was purely a matter of form and show, and the fortress did, after all, appear impregnable.

---

* For more on Blanche de Castille's odd indulgence of the count of Toulouse, see Jean Markale, *Le Chêne de la sagesse: un roi nommé saint Louis* (Paris: Hermé, 1985).

We can gather an idea of what Montségur was like at this time from written documentation, in particular from the narratives of the chroniclers and also from a systematic study of the terrain as it appears in the light of the most recent excavations.

The castle itself formed only a portion of the defense system and takes up only a small area with respect to the overall size of the pog. It was simply the essential part of a vast complex that included the entire rocky spur it sat upon, bordered on all sides by more or less sheer cliffs. When we carefully study this spur from the top of the walls, it can be seen that the entire plateau has been reworked. Obviously the military constructions are the easiest to discern. In addition to the castle, which is the highest point, defenses on the southern slope can be noted. As we can see today, this slope is the most exposed and offers relatively easy access. There were also advance defense positions on the northern slope that can hardly be seen today, buried as they are beneath vegetation. On the eastern side, an advance post for surveillance of the exits from the Carroulet gorges has a counterpart a little to the north in the lookout post of Tower Rock, which allows entry into these same gorges to be monitored.

The Cathar village was located between the castle and the northern slope, where twisting and turning paths offered it protection. To the east and west the mountain itself provided enough isolation for the settlement. This village was home to the community of the perfecti and the credenti. It is in fact unthinkable that these individuals, given to meditation and intellectual speculations, could have lived inside the castle. This was where Ramon de Perella's mercenaries were housed, and the Cathars sought shelter within its walls only when danger threatened.

The castle is almost 2,250 square feet in surface area. In the center there is a small open-air paved courtyard of about 330 square feet. Built around this courtyard and arranged in three stories were structures of various purposes: workshops, smiths, arms rooms, and storage sites. Three staircases gave access to the wall walk and the defense openings in the walls. This was the part of the castle in which Ramon de Perella's soldiers lived, who at the time of the siege were commanded by Pierre-Roger de Mirepoix. These soldiers are generally estimated to have numbered about 150, but because the majority had brought their families, as was customary, the total population was somewhat larger. There were also stables for the mules and horses—small and perfectly suited for the steep paths of the mountain—that could be brought up to the castle by a tended road. Excavations have revealed that the men in the garrison were fully equipped with spears, javelins, knives, daggers, slingshot, and arrows. Huge stone balls weighing from 130 to 175 pounds have also been found. These were manufactured on site and served as projectiles to be thrown by trebuchets.

The occupations of the men at arms were quite varied. They ensured the surveillance of the defenses, manufactured and repaired the armaments, accompanied the convoys that replenished the provisions, or were assigned to guarding various people leaving or returning to the site. When not on duty they must have passed their time playing dice; the excavations have unearthed numerous dice made from bone and ivory.

The eastern platform of the castle constitutes the thickest portion of the wall, about 15 feet, which is quite considerable. This point, entirely covered with hoarding, wooden galleries mounted on the tops of the walls to defend the approaches, was both the best site for surveillance and the very heart of the defense system.

The keep and a huge cistern are located on the west, or actually the northwest, side. This cistern was replenished with water collected from the roof tops of the castle by means of stone or baked clay gutters. An overflow provided water for the village below. It is estimated that this cistern could hold 180 cubic feet of water.

The room in the ground floor of the keep was pierced with five openings for light. Four of these openings faced each other in pairs and were oriented to the summer solstice sunrise. This particularity, as can be imagined, has provided an argument for those who view the Montségur fortress as a solar temple, but it is still only an argument.

There are many other buildings whose architecture takes the solstice sunrise into account with no religious motivation of any kind. However, because the Montségur construction also takes the winter solstice sunrise into account, we cannot automatically eliminate the hypothesis of a solar temple that included a remarkably effective defense system.

In this room a door provides access to a helical staircase that leads up to a second floor lit by four large windows. This is where the lord's lodging was located, complete with a large chimney that abutted the south wall, allowing only one access to the dwelling area.

The entire castle was covered with terraces and tile. But there is nothing truly specific in this complicated architecture; the construction primarily took into consideration the characteristics of the terrain, and the renovations undertaken after the siege of 1244 have distorted the vision we might have of the castle as the Cathars knew it.

Carved into the rock path leading to the castle on the pog's south slope were three hairpin turns. This path as a whole forms a kind of staircase of some twenty "donkey-sized" steps. The southern door was particularly large, 6 feet by 10 1/2 feet, and was protected by hoarding set on corbels, projecting stones that served to anchor the ends of the beams. These corbels are still visible today. The approach to the threshold passed over a group of wooden landings that were partially removable, demonstrating that this door, the most vulnerable, was configured to provide the best defense possible.

Protected by this imposing mass, the inhabitants of Montségur, the Cathars, lived in an agglomeration that spread out at the foot of the fortress and over a portion of the pog. During the first part of the thirteenth century, the most important quarter of the village girded the keep. Recent excavations have unearthed, from a surface of 1,890 square feet in five levels, three dwellings with their outlying buildings, their communication networks, and a cistern annexed to one of these buildings to provide water to the structures. These stone and wood structures could be accessed from one another by means of narrow stairways that overlapped each other. Every flat surface of this village area seems to have been used. It is even likely that additional surfaces on which to build homes were manufactured from fill or by carving out rock. There are about fifty dwellings from this time period in this former Cathar village. Following the siege of 1244, the few remaining inhabitants, perhaps along with some newcomers, moved farther down toward the foot of the pog, to the site known as Prat de la Gleiso, below the current parking lot. It wasn't until after the Religious Wars* that the current village of Montségur was established above the Carroulet Gorges, sheltered from the north wind and closer to the fertile valley land.

On the Montségur pog, life still had to be lived. In winter each of the homes was heated by a simple fire among stones, the smoke escaping through a hole in the roof or a door. The wall chimney, which had appeared in the eleventh century, was not yet widespread and the only one in Montségur was located in the large hall of the keep.

The furnishings in these homes were quite rudimentary, consisting of pallets, some chests, stools, and benches. Wooden doors with iron latches allowed rooms to be closed off. Lighting was provided by candles or oil lamps of the *calèlh* type, having four burners and made of iron. Plateware consisted of jugs, different kinds of terracotta containers, glasses for drinking, and knives. Each dwelling had at least a small cistern.

But what did these people dwelling on an isolated and barren mountain live on? In fact, subsistence was essentially assured by grazing livestock, which was possible on the slopes, and the growing of a few crops. Hunting and fishing in the nearby streams should not be overlooked,† and it was always possible at Montségur to get supplies from outside, even during the most difficult periods of the siege. Likewise, communication could be maintained with the outside world.

---

* [These ended in 1598. —*Trans.*]

† [While the perfecti were vegetarian, the credenti, who had yet to be entirely purified, could eat meat of all kinds. —*Trans.*]

All that remained was the problem of water, and it was this problem that ultimately led to the Cathars' defeat.

Based on archaeological discoveries, their basic diet consisted of cereal grains, wheat, and rye. The bones of a large number of cattle, sheep, roe deer, wild boar, geese, and chicken have been found, as well as remnants of fish bones. It is likely that meats were preserved by either smoking or salting them, and there was always an abundant amount in storage. If the subsistence was not top grade, it was by and large sufficient, and the chronicles concerning the siege never mention famine.

The Cathars on Montségur did not spend all their time meditating or engaging in religious exercises. Their pastoral and agricultural duties demanded a great deal of physical activity. In addition, they made clothing from sheep's wool (which was spun on spindles) and animal skins and even manufactured their own vegetable and mineral dyes. Iron scissors were available for cutting and bronze needles were used for knitting. They also crafted belt buckles and studs. Decorative accessories were not overlooked and included pendants, rings, and pectoral crosses as well as toiletry articles, namely tweezers, which were indispensable for pulling out splinters and thorns. And of course we cannot forget religious and symbolic objects such as the famous lead tokens that most likely served as identification badges for admission into secret meetings, or the mysterious pentagrams whose exact meaning is still far from being known.

There is a tendency to consider Montségur as a kind of monastic establishment. Protected by the fortress and its occupying garrison, the Cathars, in the village, would have led a life similar to that led by orthodox Catholic monks. First, however, a distinction must be made between the two categories of Cathars, the perfecti and the credenti. The perfecti were those who had attained a high level of not only initiation but purity. Having received the consolamentum on request, they could be regarded as the only true Cathars. Practicing austerity, sexual abstinence, and vegetarianism, they were, according to Cathar belief, ready to return to the kingdom of God with no need of reincarnating again to purify and free themselves of the slavery of matter, a satanic creation. They could not bear arms or perform tasks considered degrading, and they devoted themselves to meditation, preaching, and cultural practices. The credenti were not held to the same austere standards because they had not attained the same degree of wisdom and purity. They knew they would have to live again in order to complete their initiation and become entirely purified. They did not have the same prohibitions, particularly concerning food and sex. But out of respect for life, no Cathar—theoretically—whether perfecti or credenti, had the right to bear arms and wage war.

The obvious military aspect of Montségur leads us to assume, then, that the majority of the castle's occupants were not Cathars. Furthermore, the discovery of animal bones leads us to think that not all the inhabitants were vegetarians. The perfecti and credenti alike lived active lives and there was no fundamental distinction between the daily activities of one group and those of the other. All of this indicates that on Montségur at the beginning of the thirteenth century there was a heretical Cathar community closer in spirit to the earlier Celtic Christian monasteries of Ireland than to the Cistercian abbeys of that time. Furthermore, the religious significance of their community was absolutely connected to its political significance. While it is possible that Montségur in 1240 was considered to be the Cathar capital, it is absolutely certain that it was regarded as the mecca, the veritable symbol, of Occitain resistance to Capetian colonization. Hence the events that led to the tragedy of 1244.

We know that in 1241 Raymond VII of Toulouse was forced to reaffirm both his allegiance to the monarchy of France and his intention of engaging in the struggle against heresy. He even put the pog under siege, though not emphatically, which made it possible for him to declare to the king's envoys and the agents of the Inquisition that it was a waste of time to try to capture Montségur. He was waiting only for an opportune moment to drive out the French troops and restore the integrity of his domains. Further, because he had no legitimate male heir, he was using all means at his disposal to have his marriage to the barren Sancha of Aragon annulled so that he could wed a woman who would give him a son. But Louis and Blanche de Castille pursued maneuvers meant to prevent him from contracting a new union. Their scheme had been laid in advance: Raymond's daughter, Jeanne de Toulouse, would wed Alphonse de Poitiers, the brother of Saint Louis, a move that would sooner or later bring the earldom of Toulouse within the royal family's sphere of influence.

Raymond VII was thus stalling for time. Without a doubt he used the Cathars by protecting them, for they were enemies of the king of France and they represented to the local populace, the majority of whom were Catholic, resistance to northern oppression. In fact, Raymond VII would have helped any heretical sect, provided they displayed his own unhappiness with royal policy. In 1242 he was the mastermind of a vast plot that included the counts of Foix—Comminges, Armagnac, and Rodez—as well as the viscounts of Narbonne and Béziers against Blanche de Castille; Hugues de Lusignan, count of la Marche; and Henry III Plantagenet, king of England and duke of Aquitaine. Almost the whole of Occitania was involved in this secret coalition, and the emperor Frederic II, who delighted at the prospect of causing difficulty for the Capet monarchy, was a knowing accomplice.

Unfortunately for the Occitains, and of course for the Cathars themselves, the rebellion erupted too soon because of a drama that, while it seemed to be a minor incident, was perhaps the result of an intentional provocation by the royal government. In fact, Louis IX and Blanche de Castille had informers, not to mention spies, throughout the earldom of Toulouse, and these servants did not neglect to inform their masters that a serious plot was in the works. This suggests a hypothesis: Paris, from its perspective, determined that the rebellion should break out as soon as possible, before the conspirators could fine tune their efforts. This would then justify rapid intervention by royal troops, which would be all the more effective because royal adversaries would not have time to truly prepare. Actual proof for this theory is lacking, but the hypothesis holds up in view of the events that followed. During the month of May in 1242, two Inquisitors, Brother Armand Guilhem of Montpellier and Brother Étienne of Narbonne, set up their tribunal in Avignonnet, a small township of Lauragais, located in the lands of the count of Toulouse. They were staying at the castle of Avignonnet, which was commanded by Ramon d'Alfaro, the *bayle* (bailiff) of Raymond VII. Ramon d'Alfaro sent a messenger to Pierre-Roger de Mirepoix, informing him of the presence of the two Inquisitors, who were both noted for their fanaticism and cruelty. In the fortress and village complex of Montségur, reaction was quick in coming, for a good number of Cathars and soldiers in the garrison had relatives who had been mistreated or burned by these two Inquisitors. A group of about fifty knights and men-at-arms converged and made their way toward Avignonnet. While en route, their ranks were swelled by sympathizers who also had kinfolk to avenge. This expedition was in fact far from secret—everyone knew that the men were determined to murder the Inquisitors—but oddly enough, nobody alerted the future victims. This only reinforces the theory that the rebellion was deliberately provoked.

Ramon d'Alfaro himself greeted the conspirators and guided them through the castle to the rooms where Brother Arnaud and his companions were sleeping. What resulted was a massacre, for everyone wanted to participate in this "weeding": Every member of the tribunal including the notary and the bailiffs were killed. In case Inquisitors might succeed in escaping, groups of mounted soldiers waited on every road leading out of Avignonnet. None could escape "Cathar" justice. The men of Montségur began the journey back to their fortress, and once the news traveled, the entire region rose up in revolt. Raymond VII occupied Albi, which had been taken from him by the king of France.

The royal authority's reaction was extremely violent. The papacy demanded that someone be punished as an example and the king took advantage of the situation to definitively crush anything that stood in the way of his plans to annex the earldom of Toulouse. A series of battles for which they were poorly prepared revealed how premature the

Occitains' actions were. Additionally, following some shady dealings, the count of Foix defected to the side of the king and Raymond VII, defeated on the battlefield and abandoned by his allies, was once again forced to sue Louis IX for pardon. The king did not believe a single word of the count's repentance, but Raymond had taken the precaution of addressing the Queen Mother, Blanche de Castille, rather than directly addressing the king. Although irritated by the behavior of her Occitain cousin, she forced Louis IX to make up with Raymond and allow him to keep his earldom.

Blanche de Castille's attitude remains inexplicable and prompts a number of questions. It could well be asked if Raymond VII might not have had secret means of applying pressure in order to receive such indulgence when, as an excommunicate and declared rebel, he was liable to the confiscation of his domains. In any event, we know that Queen Blanche has left a strange imprint in the popular memory of Cathar country, particularly in Razés, where a mysterious treasure is attributed to her. It is true that her name is also associated with the widespread belief throughout the Pyrenees in the existence of the White Lady;* in other words, a female fairy who rules over the underground world of caves that are quite numerous in this region.

Ultimately, the massacre of the Inquistors at Avignonnet provoked a bloody repression. Montségur, the home of the assassins, then became "Satan's synagogue," and it certainly appears that from this moment on, both the Catholic clergy and the royal power set in motion the capture of the fortress and the physical and symbolic destruction of everything it stood for. Louis IX had hopes of "rehabilitating" Raymond VII, all the more so because he needed brave and experienced knights in the Holy Land. He had come to share the opinion of Blanche de Castille, who sought to deal with the count of Toulouse tactfully. But while the king could forgive, or at least display his magnanimous nature, the Church had no reason to forget the murder of its Inquisitors. Because

---

* ["White Lady" = *dame blanche.* —*Trans.*]

of this, Montségur was destined to be destroyed. But Raymond VII would not be relied upon to do the job. It was preferable to let him go to Rome, where he could plead his case before the pope and obtain a reversal of his excommunication. In fact, his absence was beneficial. The king could then entrust to a reliable man the mission of "chopping off the dragon's head," which was how Hugues des Arcis, the seneschal of Carcassonne, was chosen.

In the treaty of Lorris signed in January 1243, Raymond VII of Toulouse acknowledged both his defeat and that of all of Occitain. He was pardoned, but under very strict conditions: In particular, he had to commit in writing to punish the assassins of Avignonnet, cease all relations with the Holy Roman Emperor, and invest all fortresses giving shelter to the Cathars. The count of Toulouse signed.

In May 1243, an army consisting of ten thousand men, a surprising number given both the time and the mountainous nature of the region, took position around Montségur under the direction of the seneschal of Carcassonne and the theoretically spiritual authority of Pierre Amiel, archbishop of Narbonne. This marked the beginning of what would become a year-long siege.

The army took its time and constructed its quarters, forming a kind of ellipsis around the circumference of the mountain except for the eastern side, where a deep gorge dug by a torrent from the Tabe Massif presented terrain that was too steep to be used. The different camps were scattered at various levels, and a slope of twelve to fifteen hundred yards might exist between the camps on the southeast side of the mountain and those on the opposite side. In front of every position there were vertical cliffs that defied any attempt at climbing and also represented a risk of surprise attacks because they could so easily conceal enemies. Above, on the pog, the fortress and village complex was enclosed by a wooden stockade that twisted at the edge of the abyss, leaving here and there a way out that the most experienced among the besieged used to communicate with the outside. The front line of the royal troops was never airtight, and how could it have been in that uneven, torturous landscape?

The uncontested master on the pog was Bertrand d'en Marti, the Cathar bishop who had succeeded Guillabert de Castres. In addition, there was Pierre-Roger de Mirepoix, who was not a Cathar but had final say on all the defense operations. The garrison included both knights and men-at-arms who had brought their families with them. Because there may have been about fifty women perfecti, an equal number of male perfecti, and almost two hundred credenti, the population on the Montségur pog at the time of the siege was about five hundred.

At first the siege seemed perfectly futile. No advances had been made six months after its commencement in May 1243. Several engagements had taken place on the slopes that were less steep, but with no results, for the nature of the terrain was such that a handful of men could easily resist forces far superior in number. It was at this point that the besieging forces received reinforcements: the Albi bishop, Durand, and a group of military strategists with expertise in war machines. At the same time, the other side welcomed a choice recruit, Bertrand de la Beccalaria, himself an expert in machines who came from Capdenac and who placed his scientific knowledge in the service of the Cathar cause. Both sides, in short, were evenly balanced. But the leaders of the royal troops, convinced that no attack could be made unless devised by specialists and those who know all the mountain's secrets, made an appeal to Basque mercenaries.

In November 1243, a group of these Basques managed to set foot on the southern slope of Montségur, some five hundred feet below the fortress. It was a precarious position, but it would allowed other operations to be put into action, especially if the position could be held. A trebuchet was fired continuously and, despite its lower position, managed to send several stones into the eastern barbican of the castle. It was in this direction that the royal troops now trained their efforts.

During a night at the end of December, a group of lightly armed volunteers worked their way up the eastern cliffs beneath the rocky spur of the pog's eastern end, led by a guide who knew the secret paths and who, in all likelihood, was a Cathar renegade. They made their way to the ridge and massacred the guards on the barbican. It was then the turn of the Basques, who were waiting in their sheltered positions, to burst into the barbican and take possession of it, which they did despite the defenders' stiff resistance. It is said that when daylight came, the volunteers on the mission of the night before trembled in fear at the sight of the precipice along which they had crawled in the darkness with no idea of the danger they were running. It is also said that they swore to their comrades that they would never have dared such a venture if they had seen the precipice.

The taking of the barbican changed the tide of the battle and considerably reduced the length of the siege. In fact, from the barbican, which allowed them surveillance of their enemies, the bishop of Albi's men began assembling an enormous stone thrower only some three hundred feet from the castle ramparts. This trebuchet allowed stone shot weighing sixty to eighty pounds to be fired toward the inside of the fortification, where it caused great damage to both the roofs and the walls. Thus the situation, which until that until that time favored the besieged who had mocked the royal forces over the years, turned to the advantage of the king's troops.

Pierre-Roger de Mirepoix, head of the Montségur garrison, did not delude himself about the future. He succeeded in convincing the bishop Betrand d'en Marti to evacuate the Cathar treasure. Thanks to the complicity of some royal army sentinels, who were simply bought, it was possible to transport a large quantity of gold and silver to a fortified cave in the upper Ariège Valley and from there to the castle of Usson in the Donnézan. There the treasure bearers tried to recruit an elite troop who would charge the crusaders and throw their ranks into disarray. They could then race into Montségur by the eastern ridge after having destroyed the stone thrower or turned it against their assailants. An agreement was reached with a Catalan leader, more or less a highway bandit, named Corbario, who assumed charge of this operation. The attempt failed, however, mainly because Corbario's men lost their way in the Lasset Gorge during the dark night. The bishop of Albi's stone thrower, then, continued to do considerable damage.

On March 1, 1244, the Cathars and garrison troops, well-prepared and ready for any eventuality, attempted to mount a sortie. They were repulsed, and Pierre-Roger de Mirepoix realized that the situation could not go on much longer, though it was not for lack of provisions or the inability to maintain contact with the outside. At night groups of armed Cathars ran the royal blockade and, led by trustworthy men, made their way to the fortress. Others brought messages to Bertrand d'en Marti. There was thus no problem getting either provisions or weapons. But water had become a great concern. The cisterns were polluted by the large number of rats that had fallen into them, which, rather than an accident, seemed to be an act of betrayal by a member of the garrison who had been bribed to do this work. It was high time to make some decisions in an attempt to stave off the worst.

Everyone was informed of the actual state of affairs, after which the Cathars gave Ramon de Perella and Pierre-Roger de Mirepoix all authority for negotiating an honorable surrender. The two leaders sent a message to the seneschal of Carcassonne, asking what conditions were acceptable for surrendering Montségur.

The siege, lasting nearly a year, left the leaders of the royal troops exasperated with the length of time it had endured. Because they knew they could never take Montségur by assault, Hugues des Arcis, Archbishop Pierre Amiel, and Inquisitor Ferrier agreed to the majority of requests of the besieged: All those who surrendered would have their lives spared and be left alone if they made sincere confession of their sins; they could leave with arms and baggage, and no punishment would be demanded for participation in the Avignonnet assassination. The besieged were given a deadline of fifteen days and their surrender would be expected on March 16.

All of this raises a question: Why this leniency? One theory suggests that perhaps it was to allow the Cathars time to celebrate one last solar festival, probably of Manichean origin, on the spring equinox. But it seems surprising that the victors, bitter foes of any heresy, could display such tolerance. The seeming leniency of setting free all who confessed their sins was in reality a dreadful trap. The victors knew full well that the true Cathars, particularly the Perfects, would not deny their faith, preferring instead to die upon the pyre.

On the night before the surrender, four perfecti who he had separated from the others and hidden in the cellars of the fortress were aided in their escape by Pierre-Roger de Mirepoix. They made their way by cable down the long western face of the mountain. Who were these four men? They were probably Cathars who knew certain secrets, perhaps the location of the treasure, or who were at least "missionaries" charged with keeping the doctrine alive. Or perhaps they were carrying documents to be stored in a safe place. In any event, it is easy to see why this escape at the final moment, in the most unlikely conditions, and with all the mystery that surrounds such an event, inspired so many interpretations and theories without any proof. There was also talk of an underground glacier in the mountain facing Montségur where the fugitives may have buried documents or a treasure. Because the glacier recedes every year, so the theory goes, only patience is required for the time when the ice will give back what has been entrusted to it. But this could be a long wait.

On March 16, 1244, the occupants of Montségur left the pog. Two hundred five Cathars refused to confess their errors and persisted in their faith. Among them, of course, was the bishop Bertrand d'en Marti, but also some women, in particular Esclaramonde de Perella, the daughter of the regional lord; her mother, Corba de Perella; and her grandmother, Marquésia de Lantar. A pyre was immediately erected, perhaps on what is called the Prat del Cramates (meadow of the burned ones), where a commemorative monument is located today, but no one is sure of the exact location. The pyre was lit and the "heretics" hastened to it, singing like people who were assured of returning to the original purity of a time when evil had not yet troubled the progress of the world.

Several weeks later in Paris, King Louis IX, whom we know as Saint Louis, was informed of the capture of Montségur and the *auto-da-fé* that ensued. He was also told that Gui II of Levis had taken possession of the area in the king's name and established a garrison of loyal men there. This was what was important to Louis IX, ownership, in the heart of a dubious land, of an impregnable fortress where his authority could be exerted. The rest, meaning the burned heretics, was only a police operation; it was not the first time such a thing had happened. Furthermore, his conscience was at peace. The heretics had been given a choice and if they had chosen to die, well, that was their responsibility. This was the hard law of the time, and no one took offense, not even the Cathars, for whom disdain of the world constituted a rule of life.

This aspect of the matter is one that is often overlooked. It was normal in this time to burn people for their religious opinions, the golden rule being to eliminate all that was unorthodox for the greater good of the majority. Such action was simply an application of the words from the Gospel: When a branch is rotten, cut it off and burn it so the rest of the tree will survive. Notwithstanding the actions of some fanatics, whose sadism and neurosis do not need to be displayed here, the Inquisitors never had a sense they were committing an injustice by sending men and women to the pyre after having tortured them. Other times, other mores. Furthermore, if the Cathars had prevailed in Occitania, they probably would have acted in the same fashion to those Catholics who refused to abjure their own faith. The wars between Catholics and Protestants have shown what such attitudes can inspire; tolerance existed on neither side. Violence, on the other hand, was plentiful in both camps.

The Montségur pyre seems ignominious to us. But do not overlook the fact that the Cathars who died there were happy. The flames permitted them access to the perfection they had been seeking all their lives. Is this remark so shocking?

It is true that the pyre still burns, as André Breton says in one of his poems. And it is not close to being extinguished in our smoke-filled minds. It was the means by which Montségur entered into history— and also into legend. But where can the line be drawn that separates history and legend?

3

The Castle of Quéribus

Montségur was not the only Cathar citadel and, while the pyre set ablaze there on March 16, 1244 dealt a harsh blow to Occitain resistance, it did not denote the end of Catharism. Another equally impressive Cathar fortress held out for eleven years following the capture of Montségur. This was the castle of Quéribus, located much farther east, at the very border of Catalonia and Occitania—a frontier region whose history has always been as torturous as its landscape.

Here they are no longer the Pyrenees but the Corbière Mountains, an arid massif bordered on the north by the Aude Valley and on the south by the Agly Valley, forming a kind of transitional zone between the Central Massif and the Pyrenees. Though a Mediterranean climate prevails here, it does not preclude some harsh winters. A land of vineyards, at least on the highly exposed slopes sheltered from the tramontane winds, it is however a "wasteland" to borrow the expression used in medieval text *The Quest of the Holy Grail* to designate the desolate area that surrounded the castle of the Fisher King: Loose stone and shrubs predominate as if the wind and sun were united in common cause to slowly and patiently destroy the rocky hills no longer tolerated by the sky.

It is on the summit of one of the limestone peaks of the southern Corbières Mountains that the castle of Quéribus rises up like a petrified ghost overlooking both the mountains and the sea. The rocky ridge that supports it, tracing the border between the Aude Department and the

Pyrenees Orientales Department, stretches east to west from Tautavel to Bugarach, in the earldom of Razès, another strange place in which memory of the oldest Cathars still lurks. At present, the crest of the ridge can be traversed using one of three crossings, among which is the Grau de Maury, the former Grau de Quéribus, dominated on one side by the Roque de la Poucatière, which rises some 2500 feet, and the Roc du Courbas, rising to 3000 feet and on the other side by the powerful mass of the castle, which acted as a lock on the entrance to this region. This southern barrier of the Corbières is difficult to cross from north to south, which is the reason it was long considered a frontier between Languedoc and Catalonia, or between France and the Roussillon, as the history books call Catalonia.

Toward the north, the slopes of this rocky ridge—sometimes a completely barren expanse of rocks baked by the sun and split by the frost, and sometimes a garrigue with the scattered growth of pine trees, thyme, and rosemary—are bordered by the Cucugnan, a tributary of the Verdouble. This is in fact the location of the village of Cucugnan made famous by Alphonse Daudet—or rather by his "negro" Paul Arène, who wrote his *Letters from My Mill* for him. There is a tendency to think of this village as being located in Provence, but those who assume this forget that Daudet was a native of Languedoc. And after all, isn't the well-known sermon of the Cucugnan priest in the tone of the Inquisitors and preaching friars who promised hell to the sectarians of the dualist heresy?

The cliff on the south of this ridge is reminiscent of the abyss surrounding Montségur. The slope plunges steeply toward the Maury River, a tributary of the Agly, which has also lent its name to a village and to a vineyard that produces some reputable wines. The landscape is grandiose, perhaps less epic in proportion than that around Montségur—less lofty, less snow-covered, but equally impressive, more chaotic and fragmented, and in fact much more secret. A traveler through the mountains here can discover scattered in small valleys and sheltered parts of the slopes abandoned or ruined sheepfolds that attest to significant pastoral activity in centuries past. And of course there are the grapevines that climb as high as possible, the sole source of wealth today in this underprivileged land.

However, humans have always inhabited the Corbières Mountains. Archaeological excavations have revealed the former presence of a superior Paleolithic people along the Verdouble Valley, in Tautavel and in the caves of the Grau de Padern, quite close to the Quéribus site. There were also settlements here during the Megalithic Age, and some remnants have been noted, such as a menhir near Cucugnan, which, like so much similar evidence, is no longer there today. During the Iron Age, the region was occupied by the Gallic people known as the Volques Tectosages, the likely originators of the famous Celtic cross that was later adopted by the Cathars and then the Huguenots.

During the the time of the Romans, when this land had become a province—the Narbonnaise—the heights of the Corbières were recognized as excellent belvederes for keeping watch on what was happening on the littoral far below. It should not be forgotten that the Languedoc coast was an important migratory route. Hannibal and his Carthaginians passed this way en route to Italy from the southern tip of the Iberian peninsula, and the Romans built the Domitian Way here, which gave them mastery over Iberia. Because the Romans, in addition, had discovered metal deposits in the Corbières, many secondary roads were created to exploit them, and numerous Gallo-Roman villas were built along these roads, one of which passed through Cucugnan from Tuchan to Bugarach. Substantial remnants of these villas have been discovered.

The Domitian Way also became the invasion route for the Visigoths, who supplanted the Romans here in 419 A.D., subsequently scattering throughout what would become Septimania before being defeated by the Franks in 507. At that time, the Corbières range became the northern border of the Visigoth kingdom. But Septimania soon fell into the hands of the Moors, who were not dislodged until 759 by Pippin the Short.

In the beginning of the ninth century, the land of Peyrepertuse, which encompassed the site of Quéribus, was part of a significant parcel of territory given by Charlemagne to his cousin Guilhem as a reward for his victory over the Saracens. But the land was hostile to Carolingian domination. The population was, in fact, quite disparate and the different peoples settled there had each left a profound impression. The Merovingian influence survived in some spots and troubles erupted, causing Charles the Bald to divide Septimania in two to establish better control over it. In 865 it was divided into Gothia proper and the Spanish Marches, which became the prerogative of Wilfred the Hairy, count of Barcelona, who shared sovereignty with the lord of Carcassonne over the Sault, the Donnezan, and the Fenouillède regions, that of Peyrepertuse, and the earldom of Razès.

The name Quéribus was cited for the first time in a written document in 1020, and in 1066, Béranger, viscount of Narbonne, paid homage to Guilhem, the count of Bésalu, for the castle of Quéribus, the revenues of which his wife had received as a dowry from her father, Bernard Taillefer. In the twelfth century, as the result of a series of various successions and marriages, the castle of Quéribus became part of a great territorial expanse dependant on four noble houses: Bésalu, Cerdagne, Barcelona, and Provence. But because of the particular situation of this area, always in a contested and disputed zone, it had gone to ruin and almost nothing remained of its past grandeur. It was thus a country emptied of both inhabitants and resources and became a place in which numerous Cathars sought refuge, fleeing the onset of their persecution at the end of the twelfth century.

It was not until 1209, however, that the famous crusade against the Albigensians began. On July 22 of that year the inhabitants of Béziers were all massacred. The strongholds of the rebel heretics fell one after the other under the assault of troops commanded by Simon de Montfort. In August Carcassonne capitulated. The following year, in July 1210, 150 Cathars were executed in Minerve. In November the castle of Termes was taken after a four-month siege. In 1211 systematic massacres took place around Lavour. The defeat of Muret on September 12, 1213, marked the end of the first crusade. The entire

Cathar region was now occupied except for Fenouillèdes and the Peyrepertuse, which included Quéribus. The minor lords of the region were all Cathar sympathizers, but because of this, all were officially stripped of their fiefdoms, thereby becoming what are called the *faidits*.

The military crusade was definitively ended by the Meaux Treaty, signed in 1229. Henceforth the struggle against heresy—and for French control over Occitania, which was inseparable from heresy—was entrusted to the Inquisitors, who could, at any time, request that French troops and vassals rally to the king of France. What could then be seen in Corbières was a patient nibbling away at the last strongholds occupied by the Cathars or their sympathizers.

Quéribus was at that time the responsibility of the knight Chabert de Barbaira, a former military engineer for the king of Aragon, who, at the death of the vicount Pierre de Fenouillet in 1242, was invested with complete military authority over all the remaining independent castles in the region. He was quite well informed about Cathar ideas and sought to protect the fugitives from the pyres and battles of the crusade.

In 1230, the Cathar bishop of Razès moved into Quéribus to live until his death in 1241. In fact, a document of the time specifies that a number of major heretical figures could be found at Quéribus, particularly the deacon Pierre Paraire, Raymond de Narbonne, and a man by the name of Bugaraig. This last name seems related to one of the stranger places in Razès, Bugarach, which is both the name of the western peak of the southern Corbières and a probable reference to the Bulgarians, or Bougreans, who seem to have been the ancestors of the Occitanian Cathars.

Of course, the day following the fall of Montségur, Quéribus, which was an equally impregnable fortress, took on considerable importance and became a second "synagogue of Satan," but no attempts were made to take Quéribus. The seneschals of Carcassonne were content to capture those castles that were less protected and less well situated, such as Padern and Molhet in 1248, and Puylaurens and Saint Paul of Fenouillet in 1250. Nevertheless, the vise was inexorably tightening on Quéribus.

On his return from the Crusades in 1255, Louis IX, who wished to be assured that Carcassonne was encircled by a top-rate defense system, decided to go all out in his efforts to bring Quéribus under royal control. He appointed Pierre d'Auteuil seneschal of Carcassonne and entrusted him with carrying out this mission.

We are ill informed about the ensuing events, which remain fairly obscure, for the texts concerning the siege of Quéribus are quite vague and often contradictory. One thing is known for certain, however: In May 1255, Pierre d'Auteuil began to surround the castle.

This was a task no easier than the encircling of Montségur. Quéribus is built on a kind of rocky peak that itself overlooks a steep ridge. It has very impressive natural defenses: Surrounded by a great void, it is effectively protected on the least steep side of the ridge by a massive keep, ensuring that the fortress could hold off a large army for some time. Adding to the difficulty was the fact that the seneschal had trouble recruiting the necessary troops for this action. It appears that the prelates of Languedoc refused him their aid, no doubt from motives of pure blackmail, for the regional clergy of that time were in conflict with the king's seneschals due to sordid reasons of material interest. Pierre d'Auteuil then requested assistance from the archbishop of Narbonne, but received no answer. He sent a letter of protest to Louis IX, but the all the king could do was order the seneschal of Beaucaire to lend assistance to his colleague in Carcassonne.

The help requested by Pierre d'Auteuil was not, in reality, explained by the siege, which required only about a thousand well-placed troops, but by the threat hanging over him from the king of Aragon, who had let it be known that he would not hesitate to cross Languedoc with his army en route to Montpellier, where Aragon's subjects were in rebellion. It so happened that the Aragonese king had always maintained excellent relations with the defender of Quéribus, Chabert de Barbaira. Finally, after much shilly-shallying, the archbishop of Narbonne sent aid "because the castle of Quéribus is a refuge for heretics and scoundrels and thus a matter of concern to the Church."

But the conditions in which the siege took place were not favorable to the seneschal of Carcassonne. On the one hand, he understood that he could never put an end to the resistance of Chabert de Barbaira in his fortress because, unlike Montségur, it could not be approached to install a stone thrower. On the other hand, he was troubled by what was transpiring on the other side of the Catalonian frontier: In being stuck beneath Quéribus, he was leaving the king of Aragon a free hand in his undertakings. Because this seemed the principal danger, Pierre d'Auteuil lifted the siege in September 1255, thoroughly determined never to begin again such a futile venture. However, at the end of the year, the fortress of Quéribus was officially restored to the king of France, who had purchased it—theoretically—from its owner, Nuno Sanche, in 1239. How did this happen?

There is one hypothesis that has every chance of presenting the correct version of the facts: It places on the scene Olivier de Termes, one of those who, along with Raymond Trencavel, had unleashed the revolt of the faidits in 1239 in order to recover the lands that had been confiscated from them. Because of Raymond VII's hesitations, the revolt had been stopped short of its goals and Trencavel and Olivier de Termes had been forced to surrender. Olivier then definitively reconciled with the king of France and accompanied him soon after on the Crusades, where he became a hero. Thanks to the king's favor, and probably well paid for his efforts to boot, he had somewhat forgotten that he was the son of the Raymond de Termes, who had died in the dungeons of Carcassonne after the capture of his castle in 1211, during the first crusade against the Albigensians. He had also forgotten that he was the nephew of the Cathar bishop Benoit de Termes, who had taken refuge in Quéribus, where he died in 1241.

Regarding Quéribus, in all likelihood Olivier de Termes, who knew the Corbières Mountains quite well from having given royal troops a hard time there, had caught Chabert de Barbaira in an ambush. The captured de Barbaira won back his life and freedom in return for the surrender of the castle, which were the conditions set upon him "under penalty of a thousand silver marks held as surety by Philippe de Montfort and Piere Voisins." Subsequently, Chabert de Barbaira is mentioned three times in official agreements, including the September 12, 1278 agreement between the bishop of Urgel and the count of Foix concerning the division of Andorra, which suggests that he had returned to grace.

As for the Cathars who had found refuge in Quéribus, nothing is known of their fate, nor does any document mention it. It is likely, however, that because the fortress of Quéribus had not been taken or surrendered under the constraints of a siege, that the Cathars naturally scattered, seeking anonymity, and perhaps emigrated into northern Italy. The "last boulevard of southern independence" had fallen without glory, but also without any fruitless massacres. This may be the reason why Quéribus does not share Montségur's reputation. For such a legacy to be won, heretics must be burned.

Under the authority of the king of France, the fortress subsequently became the pivot of the entire defense system between Roussillon and France. Significant renovations were made in 1258, which, as at Montségur, considerably distort the picture we might imagine of the Cathar building. In 1260 the fairly undermanned but efficient garrison consisted of a lord and ten sergeants-at-arms. In 1321 the walls were refinished and strengthened. In 1473 the castle was taken by Aragonese troops come to free Roussillon from French occupation, but it was recaptured by the French in 1475. Finally in 1659, Quéribus lost all importance when the Peace of the Pyrenees Treaty confirming the annexation of Roussillon by France was signed. Occupied until 1789 by the Castéras Sournia family, the fortress soon fell prey to the wind and memory.

It must be acknowledged, though, that Quéribus is impressive, not only by virtue of its site, equally astonishing as Montségur's, but also for the enigmatic circumstances surrounding its history. For instance, as with Montségur, it may not have been only for reason of its "security" that the Cathars gathered there. But it is difficult to draw any solid conclusions about its past because of both a lack of written documentation and the transformation the original castle has undergone since the time of the Cathars. Questions nonetheless arise: The Cathar desire to live on the peaks—where they were able to touch the sky even if the living conditions were difficult—reinforces the controversial and contestable theories regarding the Cathar "solar temples."

Quéribus is obviously an "eagle's nest" and, as has been said, "a falcon tightly clinging to a clenched fist of a rock." This expression, coined by Gaston Mouly, is both absolutely accurate and eloquent. On the approach to the fortress, we may feel both powerful and reckless, but at first sight the architecture seems to be of an exemplary sobriety. A wide path climbs steadily up the north slope of the mountain (which is the side that is least steep) until it reaches a terreplein defined by a wall that has eroded significantly. A stairway, in some places hollowed out of the rock and in others built of carved stone, crosses the first threshold from there and zigzags to the entrance of the fortress. Here, in contrast to Montségur, are three successive enceintes arranged as landings and shadowed by the keep.

The lowest enceinte consists of three separate parts: The first, formed by a wall running north to south, is intended to defend the stairway. The second, running from east to west, protects the entrance, which has a "slaughterhouse," or hiding place, configured into the inner facing of its groined-vault architecture. A third wall climbs eastward, enclosing the lowest enceinte. On the inside is a staircase that hugs the structure and ends in the second enceinte formed by a gigantic wall. Within this wall the remnants of a large rectangular room, probably a guard post, can be seen, and facing it is a cistern the insides of which were made waterproof by a pink coating known as tiler's mortar.

Beyond this is the third enceinte, built of limestone and by far the most important, for it protects several rooms in addition to the imposing mass of the keep. To the left on entering is a long vaulted room illuminated on the south side by an arrow loop and extended on the northwest by a watchtower that most likely served to protect the first cistern. To the right a three-story dwelling place can be seen that receives light from numerous openings on its southern side. There are exterior courtyards on two different levels and a second cistern located beneath a small hall. The keep sits in back toward the south and is one of the most remarkable of its kind in all of Occitania.

What can be found there is everything necessary for an effective defense of both the castle and the entire eastern slope of the mountain. But what is truly surprising is the presence, at the very heart of the keep, of an architectural gem, the famous "hall of the pillar," which has been the subject of hypotheses that are as audacious as they are varied.

The first impression upon entering this hall is of having entered a sanctuary. It is a single room, though it appears larger to us than it did to the castle's original occupants because it was once divided into two stories. What makes it so astonishing is its one immense pillar that soars toward the ceiling. There it breaks into four vaulted sections with intersecting ogives, an unusual construction given the severity of the site. The light in the room comes from a curious double bay window, which is in fact a single bay whose cruciform transom demarcates two lower rectangular windows and two upper windows that form a broken arch. The entire bay window sits within a recessed portion of one wall, and two rows of stone benches, known as *coussieges,* run the length of the walls, which are each about twenty-two feet long.

It is not known if this hall served as a chapel, though the majesty of the room, with its central palmlike pillar, tends to give that impression. But where might the altar have been located? And would it have been a Cathar sanctuary, the site of some esoteric worship? There are so many questions that cannot be answered. But it must be said that wherever the Cathars spent time, they left strange remnants that are ambiguous enough to fire the imagination.

Montségur and Quéribus were not the only Cathar castles, nor were they the only ones labeled as such. Not far from Quéribus, deep within the Corbières region, on the other side of Cucugnan, is Peyrepertuse. The very name attests to a bumpy scrubland full of holes, for it means literally "pierced stone." The road that leads to the fortress is narrow and rough, and from it can be seen the outline of a curious monument that anyone would hesitate to call a castle. It looks more like a natural fortification carved out of the stone by severe weather conditions. But on drawing nearer, it is more difficult to distinguish between what is natural and what is not, which is accentuated by the fact that Peyrepertuse, in contrast to compact Quéribus, stretches out in such a way that it merges with the rocky ridges beneath it. Unlike both Montségur and Quéribus, it is not a building with a courtyard; instead it is a veritable village, "a celestial Carcassonne," in the words of Michel Roquebert who was haunted by these "citadels of vertigo." The castle proper is only the centerpiece of a large ensemble perched on the rock, overlooking the entire region.

Peyrepertuse leaves a very different impression from the other castles because of its site. But history has left few truly visible remnants there. It is even quite possible that the Cathars never settled there and that Occitain resistance never found any support there. Poorly prepared to follow the 1239 uprising, Peyrepertuse fell after only several days' siege, when the royal troops, following their triumph over Trencavel, surged through the Corbières. In fact, the only illustrious figure known to have stayed at Peyrepertuse is the famous Henri de Trastamare, the Spanish grandee and pretender to the throne of Castille. He found refuge at the castle in 1367, before succeeding in his undertaking and becoming Henry the Magnificent. But the Cathars were long forgotten by this time.

The somewhat romantic ruins of Aguilar Castle, also in the Corbières region, still stand above Tuchan. Truthfully, all that remains of it are pieces of the large enceinte wall and the keep, with a Roman chapel. There is a strong possibility that during the beginning of the Albigensian crusade, numerous Cathars fleeing the neighboring villages or escaping the massacres took refuge in Aguilar Castle for a while. But documentation of this is lacking.

More information is available about the castle of Termes, also in the Corbières, but a bit farther to the northwest, in the neighborhood of Razès. Termes was, in fact, one of the most important castles in the region, and it lent it name to the local area, the Termenès. During the first Albigensian crusade its defenders showed ferocious resistance to the royal troops. In 1210 the fortress held for four months despite being bombed incessantly by stone throwers. Finally, Simon de Montfort prevailed over this desperate resistance and captured the castle's lord, Raymond de Termes, who, though not a Cathar, had always shown tolerance toward the heretics and was not disposed to look kindly on the invasion of Occitania by men from the north. His brother was a Cathar bishop and his son Olivier was an active participant in the 1239 revolt before being forced to cede his fortresses of Aguilar and Termes, make amends, and, as we saw earlier, betray the last defender of Quéribus. Simon de Montfort had Raymond de Termes imprisoned in a dungeon in Carcassonne, where he died. Termes remains a name that is definitively linked to Catharism, but its castle is now only a pile of ruins.

Ruins are also found in Puilaurens, midway between Quillan and Saint Paul de Fenouillet, but here they are lavish ruins that rise out of the wooded mountains in a landscape more reminiscent of Montségur than Quéribus. The path leading to the fortress is a mere passageway bordered by enormous broom trees before it literally plunges into a fissure broken up by a series of defensive walls. The entrance to the fortress opens onto a mousetrap, for it is, in fact, false—a roofless cubbyhole in which it was impossible to escape the arrows that were fired from the convergent loopholes of the true entrance and the stones projecting from the top of the curtain wall. The farmyard is a simple enclosure bordered by high walls that extend into a rocky spur. The wall walk is almost sufficient defense on its own, for the precipice that opens directly beneath the walls drops off steeply. There are only two towers in the structure to assist in the defense. The keep itself dates from the twelfth century.

Everything is small in scale at Puilaurens, even the vaulted hall with its intersecting ogives that occupies the interior of the main tower. But this scale, which excludes the castle's skyward construction, gives the entire edifice a strange, almost disturbing appearance. The fact that its surroundings are wooded makes the fortress seem like a lair for ghosts, or even vampires like those fabled to roam the Carpathians.

But it was not vampires who frequented Puilaurens—though it is true that to some northern Catholics the Cathar heretics who stayed there during the first half of the thirteenth century could have passed for bloodthirsty demons! Unfortunately, documentation concerning this period is lacking, and while it is certain that Puilaurens, like Quéribus and Montségur, was one of the last Cathar refuges, nothing is known of the events that prompted its capture or the circumstances under which this capture took place. The Cathars who were there left behind nothing but legends, such as that of the White Lady regarded by some as Queen Blanche de Castille. Belief in the White Lady was still strong in 1880, as is recalled by Louis Fédié, patient historian of the Razès earldom and the diocese of Alet:

> The White Lady, a deathless souvenir of the Gallo-Celtic era, personification of the druidesses who, two thousand years ago, devoted their efforts to the mysteries of their fierce rituals, still lives in the countryside. The White Lady of the castle of Puilaurens appears at certain times during winter nights lit by the waxing crescent moon, and traverses, while trailing her phantom veils behind her, the incredibly imposing towers and ramparts of the ancient fortress.

We must not forget that we are in the Pyrenees facing the Corbières Mountains. As is well known, the White Lady haunts all the valleys of the Pyrenees, right up to where mountain slopes meet the Atlantic. She was even spotted at Lourdes, in the Massabielle Grotto. She is not at all hesitant to show her face in the Corbières region either, especially in the Razès earldom, where she has been seen on numerous occasions.

Certainly the image of Châteaubriand's Velléda weighs a bit too heavily on the memory, for, historically speaking, there is no proof that druidesses ever existed. On the other hand, fairies are of Celtic origin, or Gallo-Celtic, as Louis Fédié would say, and it is true that in 1880 the Cathars were not mentioned in the region because it was fully in the grip of Celtomania. Everywhere people were marking "druidic" monuments that actually dated from at least two thousand years before the druids. Similarly, it was claimed that the Breton language was the oldest in the world—spoken even in Eden, and that Jesus was not a Jew but, being Galilean, was actually Gallic.

These details concerning the state of mind found in the region of Puilaurens, Montségur, and the Razès earldom at the end of the nineteenth century are not gratuitous. Actually, they contributed to a reality that would play a great role in the decades to follow with respect to the rediscovery of Catharism. We can note the reemergence at that time of strange traditions concerning Jesus and Mary Magdalene—a White Lady in her own right—connected to Razès. The Cathars were strangely linked to the Templars as Grail guardians and heirs of the ancient druids, and like them, were victims of Roman Catholic repression. Meanwhile, in the shadows, a certain Father Boudet, soon to become priest of Rennes-les-Bains, was preparing a work on the "true Gallic language," a work as farfetched as it is fascinating and assuredly no work of chance.

4

The Upper Ariège Valley

In our minds Cathar country is Occitania. This is, however, not accurate. Catharism was associated with fairly precise regions in the French Midi;* moreover, it has been forgotten that it also manifested sporadically in the north, specifically in Champagne, not to mention in northern Italy, where it seems it first appeared. We must also recall that their contemporaries did not call them Cathars; this was the name a certain number among them chose to call themselves. They were actually known theologically as dualists, and commonly by the term *patarins,* which by all evidence derives from a deformation of the name Cathar. Most generally, especially after 1209, they were known as Albigensians.

Does this imply that the very center of the heresy was the city of Albi and its immediate environs? Absolutely not, for the Cathars were no more numerous in Albi than in the other cities of Languedoc. It fact, Albi may have been less affected by the heresy than other cities, and a great number of its inhabitants were quick to enlist in the militias participating in the armed struggle against the heretics. It is possible, then, that the name derives from the memory of a characteristic incident: At the beginning of the twelfth century, Sicard, the bishop of Albi, sought to have the heretics burned, but the local populace, respectful of freedom of speech, liberated them. Likewise, the name could be viewed as related to the theological discussions between the archbishop of

---

* [The French midi refers to the central portion of Southern France. —*Trans.*]

Narbonne and the heretics that took place in Albi in 1176, which were a prime example of the deaf talking to the deaf, and thus ended in a stalemate. In reality, the Occitanian common man was in the habit of actually calling the Cathars the Good Men, which acknowledged their moral values but did not carry any kind of geographical connotation.

It is difficult to place accurately Cathar settlement patterns in medieval Occitania because actual settlement was very uneven and often the result of social and economic conditions or was determined by the presence of Cathar deacons, who were more or less effective as preachers or exemplars. An additional difficulty in arriving at conclusions concerning their settlement is the fact that all social classes were represented among the Cathars. For example, Benoit de Termes and Raymond de Mirepoix were the heirs of rich, noble families, and Esclarmonde de Foix was a vicountess. But alongside them were bourgeois individuals, both rich and poor: peasants; artisans; professional soldiers, all of whom abandoned their activities, which were incompatible with the Cathar doctrine of respect for all life; vagabonds; and of course, renegade clerics—in short a very heteroclite and heterogenous mass. In some villages, everyone was Cathar. In others, there might not be even one Cathar, or simply a few who may have been obliged to conceal their activities. The population center of Toulouse, with its university, was nonetheless a city profoundly—and more or less secretly—Cathar. Finally, there were sympathizers who were quite accepting of the presence of heretics in their midst and who assisted them to the best of their abilities when need arose. How many Cathars were thus spared from the Inquisition's jails and pyres by authentic Catholics?

It is possible to find a loose correspondence between the Cathar zone and the region belonging by blood to the counts of Toulouse. In that era, the earldom of Toulouse led the way as one of the best organized and most flourishing states. Before the 1209 crusade, this earldom spread over what is now some fifteen French departments, among which are Haut-Languedoc, Armagnac, Agenais, Quercy, Rouergue, Gévaudan, Comtat Venaissin, Vivarais, and Provence, the latter having

been transferred from the control of the Holy Roman Empire. To these
it is necessary to add the domains of the vassals of the counts of
Toulouse, or in other words, those of the viscounts of Carcassonne,
Béziers, Albi, and Razès (Trencavel Dynasty) and those much reduced
domains of the viscounts of Narbonne, especially the lands of the count
de Foix. The distribution of heresy over this vast region was obviously
quite uneven. It was very weak in Provence, for instance, and in the
Vivarais, but reached its maximum concentrations in the regions of
Toulouse, the Razès, and the earldom of Foix.

Questions can be raised concerning this success of Catharism in the
Toulouse counts' zone of influence, questions that are connected to the
peculiarities of Occitanian civilization.

Common sense alone shows that everything Occitain has a strong
Latin influence and reveals the imprint of the Mediterranean spirit. The
earldom of Toulouse was based on statute law, in contrast to the northern states, which were based on customary law. Further, this statutory
and Roman-influencd law was balanced by local customs that were
quite different from those German-influenced customs of the north. The
Roman influence likewise seems obvious linguistically. The Occitain language, or rather the various Occitain dialects, are closer to Latin than
the dialects of the *langue d'oil*.* This, however, is something of a false
impression; the Occitain language underwent the same evolution as the
langue d'oil, but what is forgotten is that it suffered less mixing than the
language of the north. It remained purer, meaning that it generally
evolved from the dog Latin spoken by the populations who originally
spoke Gallic for some time into the Middle Ages. The Celtic reserve is
important in the *oc* dialects, much more so than in the *oil* dialects.

In fact, the Occitania of the counts of Toulouse at the close of the
twelfth century constituted a harmonious synthesis of Latin and Celtic

---

* [The language of northern France was known as the *langue d'oil,* as opposed to that
spoken in the south, the *langue d'oc. Oc* and *oil* are different forms of the word *yes.* Part
of southern France is still known as Languedoc. —*Trans.*]

civilization, a crucible in which the germ of another civilization was growing, one that could have buried Western Europe had it not been systematically and knowingly crushed, broken, and destroyed by the royal Capetian authority and the lords of the north with the complicity of the Roman Catholic Church, under the guise of a crusade to defend the true faith.

Occitania was no monolithic bloc; quite the contrary. The numerous domains that were more or less held by vassals of the House of Toulouse belonged to the House in only a very elastic sense. The vassal status was dependent on each party's good will. Even within their own domains the great feudal lords were on mutual ground with their vassals, who were for the most part owners of impregnable fortresses and did as they pleased. The relationship between vassal and lords was primarily one of equality and was not governed by the hierarchical rules dictated by an absolute center, as in the Roman model. In fact, Occitain society appears to have been clearly a horizontal society, as was the case with primitive Celtic societies.* And although urbanization—a preeminent Mediterranean, rather than Celtic, phenomenon—occurred to a great degree, everyday life had all the marks of a kind of confederation of good intentions with a spirit of democratic tendencies.

The cities of the Midi at that time had large populations and were quite wealthy. Toulouse was the third largest city in Europe after Venice and Rome. These cities had maintained a sense of freedom and independence, and were the first to establish *bastides*,† administered by the inhabitants themselves, which would contribute to a socio-economic upheaval. Consuls, or *capitouls*, elected by the inhabitants, governed democratically and eventually imposed their will on the lords. And while there were social classes—society was founded on this structure—

---

* I have written at length on the structures and characteristics of the typical Celtic society in *King of the Celts: Arthurian Legend and Celtic Tradition* (Rochester, Vt.: Inner Traditions, 1994).

† [*Bastides* are fortified towns. —*Trans.*]

there were no leak-proof partitions between them; the serf could easily be emancipated and become bourgeois, and his son could hope one day to win his knighthood. In this composite milieu, it was customary to rub elbows, know one's neighbors, and display greater understanding regarding those who thought differently. It was certainly not tolerance that led to this so much as it was a considerable effort to find a way to live harmoniously together.

All of these conditions encouraged both commercial and cultural exchange. Occitain literature testifies to this, for it is the result of a synthesis of different traditions. At a time (1229) when the teachers and students of the University of Paris were in revolt because of a blunder committed by Blanche de Castille,* the most brilliant intellectuals were flooding to Toulouse, drawn by the spirit of freedom that reigned over university studies there. All of this could not help but encourage the development of a dualist religion, one of the merits of which was raising fundamental issues, even if it had trouble resolving them. In any event, it explains the Cathar presence.

After 1244—that is, following the capture of Montségur—Catharism became even more secret than before. The Inquisition had certainly delivered a mortal blow to its development. But religions are hardy and cannot be suppressed by new laws or auto-da-fés. A persecuted religion will find clandestine refuge, perpetuate the memory of its martyrs, and maintain its doctrine, sometimes modifying it to new circumstances, before eventually disappearing for lack of recruitment and an actual teaching. This is what happened to druidism throughout the

---

* [Known for her diplomacy, Blanche's delicate touch was noticeably absent when she ignored the prerogatives granted to the University in Paris and disregarded an incident in which police had beaten some students and thrown them into the Seine. Despite the faculty and students' threat to strike if the university's privileges were not respected, Blanche maintained her ill-advised position. The University shut down in protest and the faculty and students left Paris for the provinces and abroad, refusing for four years to return to Paris. Resolution eventually required the intervention of the pope, and when the University did return, it was with new prerogatives granted by Blanche herself. —*Trans.*]

lower Empire; it simply died out on its own or was absorbed by the newly born Christianity. It was also the fate of Catharism, but at least a century would pass before it disappeared.

We know that the besieged Cathars in Montségur were able to evacuate their treasure, and that on the eve of the surrender, four perfecti escaped, carrying "secrets" with them. Elsewhere, in Quéribus as in other safehavens of the dualists, there were survivors, people whose mission was the salvation and maintenance of Catharism. They could well have reformed some kind of Cathar Church. The question lies in knowing where these last Good Men took refuge, and how some of them could have so mocked the Inquisition and overcome the growing indifference toward them of the general Occitain populace.

Between 1150 and 1240, the highpoint of the heresy's development, the Cathars were likely equipped with a solid ecclesiastical organization, which hardly conformed to their traditions and goals, for Catharism excluded any reference to priesthood and hierarchy, but faced with repression, they were obliged to form an anti-Church. This was how they happened to have dioceses, each headed by a bishop. In truth, these dioceses were simply territories and the bishops only perfecti who were chosen for being the most capable of maintaining the doctrine and spreading it.

According to all sources at our disposal, the existence of seven Cathar bishoprics in Italy and another seven in France can be proved. There was a large diocese in northern France, the seat of which was most likely in Champagne, and the other six were located in Occitania, which demonstrates the rather limited presence of Catharism. The six southern dioceses were Albi, Toulouse, Carcassonne, Comminges, Razès, and Agen. As can be seen, they approximately covered the domains of the count of Toulose.

After 1244, however, it became difficult to maintain this organization. Everything disintegrated during the repression, and Catharism, which had become entirely clandestine, had to regroup in remote areas such as the upper Ariège Valley around Tarascon. A large number of perfecti and credenti, fleeing Dominican terror, abandoned Occitania for Lombardy, in hopes of disappearing into the anonymity of its cities and suburbs. Others remained and formed what could be called the last Cathar Church, a kind of diocese of Sabarthes, for that is the name of the land located around the upper Ariège Valley.

Why did they organize in Sabarthes? First, it was off the beaten path, a place sheltered beneath the heights of the Pyrenees—which were not impassable to those who knew their secret paths—as well as protected by the Tabe Massif. Additionally, it was not that far from Montségur, and it is likely that the Montségur treasure, if there was one, was hidden in one of the region's many caves. Whatever the reasons, it is almost certain that during the second half of the thirteenth century the Sabarthes constituted a haven for the last Cathars. It was there that the bishop Pierre Authier, who had come from Lombardy, performed for a dozen years at the end of that century a veritable evangelical mission while escaping every snare set for him by the Inquisition. Its agents tried every means to capture him, even bribing one of the credenti to deliver Pierre Authier into their hands. But the traitor was unmasked in time and summarily thrown over a cliff by other credenti.

Pierre Authier seems to have organized the Sabarthes diocese in a very particular fashion; its doctrine does not seem to be quite what it was at the beginning of the century. Authier had been influenced by Italian Catharism, and dualist thought, which was never set in stone, had evolved over a half century. It was at this time that the famous practice of the *endura* appeared, which has inspired countless studies and an equal number of legends. The practice is a kind of mystical suicide consisting of allowing oneself to die of starvation or exposure. On second thought, in the final analysis, it is simply a religious form of the profane practice performed by the Eskimos.

In 1320, however, Pierre Authier, his relatives, and his friends were imprisoned following a skilled dragnet and were burned alive. Thus ended the last known Cathar bishop. However some credenti escaped under the leadership of the perfecti Guillaume Belibasta and fled into northern Spain. But Guillaume Belibasta was nowhere near as worthy as those burned at Montségur. He called himself a perfecti and he had received the consolamentum that normally would have prohibited him from having any kind of sexual relationship, but this did not prevent him from neglecting his spirituality in favor of his concubine and child. Furthermore, Belibasta's endeavor did not last. In 1321 he was caught in the neighborhood of Toulouse in an ambush set up by agents of the Inquisition. After his capture, he was burned.

In the upper Ariège Valley the Ussel territory has drawn the most attention because it houses numerous caves in which necropolises have been discovered, their walls bearing strange carvings and pictures. It was only a step from making these discoveries to claiming that these Sabarthian caves served as hideouts, even temples, for the last Cathars—a step casually taken in the nineteenth century by certain individuals with an interest in promoting the tourism possibilities of the region. This torch was lit again even more durably in the twentieth century, notably by Antonin Gadal, a retired grammar school teacher who loved his native Sabarthes and—this explains a great deal—who was president of the Ussat-les-Bains Tourist Bureau.

Ussat-les-Bains, a small thermal spa likely known to the Gauls and Romans, was restored to honor in the fifteenth century for the curative virtues attributed to its numerous hot springs, but it quietly fell out of fashion toward the end of the nineteenth century. At that time the spa town was clearly in need of a new youth. Then the Cathars were rediscovered, as was something even stronger—the Holy Grail itself. Why is this so significant? After all, in order to bring attention to Alise-Saintes-Rein (Côte d'Or) a similar association was made, placing there the Alésia of Vercingétorix, *despite all the Latin and Greek texts,* when this Alésia could have been located only in the Jura. But the case of Alise-Sainte-Reine involves official history, Vercingétorix being the ancestor of all the French, as everybody knows, with this certainty based on an imperial decree issued by Napoleon III, supported by the official archaeologists of the Republic, and sponsored by both tourist bureaus and merchant groups. It is thus impossible to uproot. But in the Sabarthes region, Cathar souvenirs do not hold up before official archaeology and are not even taken seriously. This does not imply that we could not discover traces of the Good Men there. But we must take the actual facts into account and avoid indulging delirious interpretations.

Ussat territory is liberally scattered with caves and springs. The evidence of underground volcanic activity there must have inspired among prehistoric peoples both a profane and religious attraction: The hot water that seeped up from the entrails of the earth was necessarily of divine origin, and it is probable that the region was an immense sanctuary dedicated to some nourishing tutelary telluric deity. From the vertical wall housing the Ramploque cave, steam escapes periodically, giving evidence of life within. This "smoking hole" is connected by a gulf to the subterranean lake that is the overflow of the thermal springs. Fifteen or twenty thousand years ago, the water must have drained onto the prairies bordering Ariège today, forming hot streams, swamps, and quagmires. These hot waters must have attracted hunting tribes. Eventually herdsmen settled along the banks of the Niaux, from which it was possible to reach Ussat by way of the famous Lombrives Cavern, one of the largest in all Europe. The hot mud at Ussat healed wounds and gave relief to certain illnesses. It is well known now that river springs and curative waters inspired worship in ancient times, for medicine and religion have always been entwined. In fact, don't people still visit Lourdes today for medical reasons as well as gratuitous religious displays?

Certainly the Lombrives Cavern excites curiosity and admiration. It is immense. The various rocky chambers, one leading to another, reveal a rare combination of limestone formations, stalagmites, and stalactites. In addition, a host of enigmatic drawings have been discovered that can induce even the most rational visitors to give free rein to their imaginations, and they are an important harvest of archeological "material." Throughout the nineteenth century, both open-minded researchers and those with ulterior motives made full use of the cavern.

In 1877, the archeologist Gustave Marty described his exploration of the Lombrives Cavern as follows:

When the stairways to the bottom of the "Great Hall" were built, pieces of stalagmite were pulled from the cavern floor, a kind of voluminous paving stone used to construct the stairs; there were then found large quantities of human remains. I obtained some. . . . The cemetery was at the end of a narrow passageway. One enters this lugubrious chamber where more than five hundred people were interred, but covered over again by layers of stalagmites. This room is eighty-six yards long and its average width is nineteen yards, including the large recess located on the right. Its height varies from nine to sixteen yards. This chamber is plenary. In this place a large quantity of human bones were discovered; this is the origin of the name bestowed upon it by the guides. A quantity of highly remarkable Bronze Age artifacts have been unearthed: polished stone axes; bronze fish hooks; pierced wolf, dog, and fox teeth. Some of these pieces are on display in the natural history museums of Toulouse and Bourdeaux.

At the far end of the cemetery, the passage called the Sahara Desert, as named by the guides, is located. . . . A little farther, the passageway makes a barely noticeable curve, and at the center of this curve there is a recess that is also well provided with sand. Poking around in this I discovered human bones and the pierced teeth of wolves and foxes. In this room I found human bones, hearths with charcoal, four molds of schistic stone, one for hairpins, another for laces, the third forming a large needle or etui, the fourth for molding the point of a spear of very pretty workmanship and perfectly preserved. The interior of this mold formed of two pieces contained the bronze core intended to form the passage of the haft. I also discovered some pottery remanants.*

---

* Gustave Marty, *Les grottes de l'Ariège et en particulier celle de Lombrives* (Toulouse, n.p., 1877).

It seems accepted that the sepulchres and workshops discovered in Lombrives Cavern are of protohistoric, not to mention prehistoric, origin. The journalist Jules Metman, who never claimed to be an archaeologist and never concerned himself with scientific history, laid claim to using the natural decor of the cavern only to imagine beautiful stories meant to tweak the heartstrings of the average reader. He wrote the following in 1892 in the newspaper *La Mosaïque du Midi:*

> The Lombrives Cavern opens in the side of the mountain, almost directly facing the thermal spa. It was my great delight to visit it last year, [and] never have I seen a cathedral whose vaults were sturdier or a more spacious nave; I know of no palace with galleries that are larger, more sonorous, and more evenly extended. I still recall with great emotion the moment when, as the four of us had reached the largest room of this marvelous cavern, each holding a weak source of light whose pale reflections half illuminated the white stalactites hanging down from the vault or rearing up from the ground in fantastic shapes, in hollow and lugubrious tones we began singing the opening verses of *Dies irae*, then sang at full volume the admirable chorus from the third act of *Robert the Devil.**

The tone was set. Jules Metman took advantage of it to recount an event that was to have taken place in 1802 in the Ussat region and the Lombrives Cavern: Because hardened smugglers-turned-brigands were then making use of this cave as their den, and their atrocities had become intolerable, an appeal to the army was necessary. The soldiers then engaged the brigands in a terrible battle, which unleashed, at the very heart of the cave, a horrible massacre of both soldiers and brigands. After he told his tale briskly and—here is a case that deserves this description—with a certain sense of the time and with authentic literary talent, Jules Metman concluded:

---

* Quoted by Christian Bernadac, *Le mystère Otto Rahn* (Paris: France-Empire, 1978).

The cave still bears, in many places, remnants from the scene of
carnage . . . and the quantity of skulls and human bones with
which the ground, in certain spots, is seemingly petrified proves
that, despite the care taken to gather and carry outside the remains
of the victims of this bloody expedition, their number was so considerable that many escaped all search and will keep for a tomb the
very spot where they lost their lives.

It is quite possible that the brigands used the Ussat caves as their
lairs or for storage, especially during an era when popular imagination
still viewed the depths of the earth as the location of disturbing worlds
that were only frequented by diabolical beings. Inhabited during the
great Ice Age of prehistory because they formed the sole possible refuge,
caves, especially those that are deep and dark, have inspired the worst
terrors and diverse fantasies during those periods when life on the
earth's surface was good. It was only in the case of absolute necessity
that anyone would enter these devil's caverns, save for a few audacious
souls who either claimed the treasures of the Other World were there to
be discovered or devoted themselves to inadmissible liturgies there. The
legends of all lands, particularly those of the Pyrenees, tell of strange
apparitions near caves of this kind. The famous White Lady lives in one
of these, of course, and she drags to it the children she has kidnapped
from the villages. There are also ogres who meet there and feast happily
on human flesh; and there are devils that hold their Sabbaths there in
the company of witches. These are the only beings who have no fear of
entering such places. Caves represent the forbidden world.

And consequently it is also an alluring world.

Toward the end of the nineteenth century, while the scholars of the
canton seat, as they were so prettily referred to, gathered all they could
discover of oral folk traditions as filler for the bulletins published by
learned societies, an Occitain writer, Napoleon Peyrat, deeply enam-
ored of his native land, published a three-volume *History of the
Albigensians.* These lines concerning the Lombrives Cavern are included

in the third volume: "How to bring into light this obscure drama, lost 2,200 yards in the depths of the earth for more than five hundred years, and of which there remains no testimony other than the mute piles of semi-petrified bones?"

He then drops us rudely right into the Cathar world of 1244:

> From the day the pious Loup de Foix came to pray in the cave of Ornolac, five or six hundred *montagnards*, fugitives from their hamlets, had settled there, men, women, and children in these dark depths, forming around the Cathar pastor a mélange of mystic colony and hunting camp. A new Montségur was organized, no longer chivalrous and perched among the clouds like the other, but to the contrary, rustic and lost in a mountain cave, a gulf perforated by a diluvian torrent.

This was believed to be true. But that is not all: Taken note of by the Inquisition, the Lombrives Cavern was invested with royal troops accompanied by the blessing of the Lord of Castelverdun, owner of the Ornolac territory (where this cave was located), a lord who himself had recently converted to authentic Catholicism.

> The seneschal entered beneath the vast porch, forced a way through the bottleneck, and thought to catch them all at once in a net, like a nest of wild beasts in the back of a hidden den that had no exit, beneath the dome of Loup de Foix. But the cave was double in size, or rather, the eastern corridor through which he had just passed and which was about a quarter of a mile long, was merely the vestibule of a higher gallery that was three times deeper and formed the mother cavern.
>
> Its height could be scaled via a vertical cliff of about eighty feet in height, divided by five or six shelves whose entablatures supported the wooden ladders that had been raised against the rock. Pulling up the ladders behind them, the Cathars were in an instant

impregnable in the obscurity of their subterranean aerie. The Catholic host, who believed they could corner the Cathars in the impasse of the dome, were themselves spat at, crushed, and wiped out by a flood of whistling arrows, bounding rocks, and savage shouts rolling from that somber mouth, which, according to geologists, vomits the oceanic torrent.

The epic style of this description is undeniable. It is unfortunate that Napoleon Peyrat claimed to be not a writer but a historian. He went on to say:

The seneschal retreated, gathered up his dead, and walled up the narrow eastern bottleneck, sealing the victorious Cathars in their fortress that had become their tomb. He camped for several more days at the cavern's mouth above the Ariège. Then, when he could no longer hear any stirrings within the bowels of the rock, and thinking it was all over, he quietly made his way back down the mountain and returned to Toulouse.

All of this seems implacably logical. In any case, it is an event recounted in the tone of the undying struggles of the era. The problem is that Napoleon Peyrat was the only person to relate this story, and he never cited any source. He even indulged in a description of the death agonies of the entombed Cathars:

They submitted quietly to their fate and smiled sadly at their tomb. Fruit eaters and lengthy fasters who willingly imposed upon themselves the *endura* that they held for their final sufferings, they tranquilly accepted this torture by starvation, their customary religious suicide. They survived for some time; they had piles of vegetables and clay pots full of them stored in the hollows of the rock. Not far from where they were there was a small lake of pure water. But a day came when there was nothing left. They then gathered together with their families. For several moments, the voice of the Cathar minister could still be heard above the pious murmur of prayer, confessing the Word that was in God and that was God. The faithful deacon gave the kiss of peace to the dying and went to sleep in his turn. All now rest in eternal sleep and only the drops of water from the vaulted ceiling have troubled the sepulchral silence of the centuries.

This is what makes an excellent news story. But Napoleon Peyrat no doubt feared that no one would have faith in his tale. And because he cited no contemporary source as the basis for what he was saying, he immediately moved on to the time of the Hugenots:

Jacques de Castelverdun was lord of Ornolac and its sinister cavern, which had been sealed for some two and a half centuries. The work of time had recently reopened that Albigensian ossuary. Protestants who were perhaps searching for ancestors in the mountain caves, guided by vague and tragic recollections, entered these funeral crypts. On entering, they made their way to the oratory of Loup de Foix by climbing to the upper cave on the ladders that were still standing. Here they discovered a terrible marvel: an entire people lying in eternal slumber as if almost turned to stone themselves in the rock coffins.

It will be noted that Napoleon Peyrat no longer clearly recalled the details he had described so well earlier. The ladders that the Cathars had pulled up behind them before being walled up in their cave were now *still standing*, a surprise, to say the least. It is quite possible that Protestants did enter the Lombrives Cavern during the Wars of Religion, not to find some hypothetical ancestors but simply to hide. And if they forced their way in through the entrance of the central cavern, they inevitably would have found human bones, for these had been in evidence there since prehistoric times. But we possess no document of any such discovery in the sixteenth century, and again, Napoleon Peyrat never cited his sources.

But the story gets even better. This discovery of Cathar skeletons by Protestants concludes with a fantastic vision:

> The mountain, which had mourned its children for more than three centuries, had built them tombs of stalagmites out of its congealed tears. What's more, it had raised them up like a triumphal monument, transforming the appalling cave into a basilica wonderfully decorated with moldings and symbolic sculptures. There could be seen a rostrum, candelabras, urns, and sacerdotal ornaments such as a pallium and tiaras, and even fruits spread about the dead—melons and mushrooms, emblems of life. Finally there was a bronze bell whose enormous top, as if fallen from its vault, lay on the ground, a symbol of both eternal silence and the victory won by these martyrs over the Prince of Air, whose mute bugle adorned their sepulchral cavern.

Although it is hard to understand what tiaras and rich sacerdotal adornments were doing there—even if the result was due to an optical illusion—with the Perfects who renounced the world and the vanity of Satan's wealth, there is something moving about this delirious evocation.

It so happens that in a small, anonymous brochure published in Ussat-les-Bains in 1963, but simply a reprint of the fragmentary texts of Antonin Gadal, who was president of the Ussat Tourist Bureau, the following lines can be read:

> After the year 1000, the Cathars lived in caves, immense dwellings that were both safe and pleasant; they fortified some of these, turning them into veritable castles. These latter are known as *spoulgas*, or fortified caves. This is how the Bouan *spoulga*, site of a bishop's sojourn, became the Bouan church.

Then further along there is this concerning the rooms in the Lombrives Cavern:

> Mysterious symbols and inscriptions from down the centuries cover their walls. In the cavern's immense heart, we find the Cathedral of the Cathars (in 1244, following the fall of Montségur, the cave became the seat of the Cathar bishop Amiel Aicard). For a long time it was easy to make one's way between the Ariège and Sos Valleys through tunnels connecting the Lombrives and Niaux Caverns. Thus in complete security and secrecy, the members of the temple of the spirit had created a way to cross between them.

And in another small booklet published in Ussat-les-Bains, but this time under the name of Antonin Gadal, a condensed version of the walling up of the Cathars can be read that is clearly based on the account of Napoleon Peyrat. Also to be found here is all the information anyone could want on the "troglodyte republic of Sabarthes," accompanied by a ringing homage to Napoleon Peyrat, who is dubbed here the "Aquitaine bugle," and to a certain Father Vidal, who allegedly purloined from the Vatican Library a document "of the highest importance" that had been leafed through by only a few untrained hands. We are still awaiting the publication of this document.

Antonin Gadal, president of the Ussat Tourist Bureau, was friend, mentor, and initiator to the mysterious Otto Rahn. Gadal revealed to Rahn not only the refuges and cathedrals of the Sabarthes Cathars, but also the symbolic signs that could be found in the caves, particularly in Lombrives. This earned this magnificent page in Otto Rahn's *Lucifer's Court*:

> Naturally I was most moved by the evidences from the Albigensian era. There are quite a few, but they are hard to find. I spent an entire year not seeing one that was right before my eyes, one that a Cathar hand had drawn upon the marble wall in charcoal and in the cavern's eternal night some seven centuries earlier. It depicts a

boat of the dead with the sun as its sail, the sun, giver of life that is reborn each winter! I saw a tree as well—the tree of life—also drawn in charcoal, and last, within a very mysterious crevice, the outline of a dove carved into the stone, which was claimed to have been the symbol of the Holy Ghost and which figured on the coat of arms of the knights of the Grail.

So the Grail is in the Sabarthes, although others claim it is to be found in Montségur. These assertions are all the more annoying because in the parallel valley of Vicdessos, the castle of Montreal-sur-Sos contains an enigmatic drawing in which even scientists have claimed to spot a depiction of the Grail. This drawing, however, dates from the end of the Middle Ages, perhaps even the seventeenth or eighteenth century, and has nothing to do with the Cathars. As for the dove, the tree of life, and the boat of the dead, Antonin Gadal and Otto Rahn are probably the only ones to have seen them. But this is how Gadal—for he is the inventor of these three—connected the Cathars to solar worship and the German version of the Grail legend.

Naturally there is a great deal of graffiti from all eras in the caves of Sabarthes, including countless perfectly authentic drawings and carvings that go back to the high Paleolithic Age. The Niaux Caverns are particularly rich and interesting in this regard. But what connections do these have with the Cathars? The fantasized declarations of Antonin Gadal have evolved into veritable novels: the Ussat caves have been turned into initiatory sanctuaries for the Cathars—as well as for the knights of the Grail. And because the graffiti are worn and not definite enough, new ones were made or the tracings made of the graffiti were doctored.*

---

* I have personally witnessed this kind of manipulation of the carved supports of the Morbihan dolmens. Because the carvings are hard to photograph due to the deterioration they have suffered from the effects of time and bad weather, the lines have been emphasized by tracing over them with chalk. But in doing so it is very easy to complete or "arrange" a depiction according to what a person wishes it to mean. This deception is not discernable in the final photo, which thus allows certain "inspired" individuals to indulge themselves in analyses that defy not only good sense, but also the most elementary concepts of honesty. Christian Bernadec witnessed similar procedures in the Ussat caves.

Christian Bernadec, a native of Ussat who knew Antonin Gadal well, refuted all of these allegations in the concise inquiry he made in *Le mystère Otto Rahn*. He recalls that the historians who specialize in prehistory and who took an interest in the wall art in the Sabarthes caves long ago shed light on the various origins of these pictures, none of which dates from the Cathar era.

It is obvious that Cathars did live in the Sabarthes region at one time. In fact, for a time the upper Ariège Valley offered them a fairly safe refuge from the Inquisition. But we do not have the proof, nor any proof whatsoever of their settlement in the famous so-called initiatory caves or alleged secret sanctuaries. Christian Bernadec is quite clear on this point:

The Cathars never lived in the caves. The Cathars were never initiated in the caves. The Cathars never drew the slightest symbol on the walls of Lombrives, Bethléem, or the Hermit (two other caves in Ussat). The Cathars never fortified the porch of any cave. The Cathars were never pursued through the caves' "dark corridors." The Cathars never celebrated any kind of worship in the stone cathedral in the deepest depths of Lombrives. Only once in the files kept by the Inquisition does an accused confess that he hid in the entrance of the Bédeihac Cave for several hours to escape his pursuers. Today we know perfectly the location of "safe houses," "seminaries," "cabins," and "forest clearings" where the hunted could find shelter. Every testimony before the Inquisition includes explicit mention of itineraries and welcome centers.

In a word, provided we wish to remain objective, it is impossible to consider the caves in the upper Ariège Valley as having served the Cathars as refuges or sanctuaries. This may be cause for regret to the fans of mysterious or colorful esotericism, but that's the way it is. In any event, there is no need to regret this reality, for the mystery simply lies elsewhere.

5

The Earldom of Razès

The Razès is certainly one of the strangest locales on the planet, both for the beauty of its rugged countryside, which brings to mind the wasteland surrounding the Grail Castle, and for its vast horizons that look out upon the sea, the peaks of the Pyrenees, and the vague swellings of the Central Massif. When in this area, the visitor has the impression of being somewhere else, a feeling similar to that inspired by the moors surrounding the Brocéliande Forest in Brittany. This is not, however, the only subtle link that ties the Razès to Amoricain Brittany.

To start, there is the very name Razès, which stems from the evolution of the ancient Rhedae, confirmed by numerous documents. Because the Visigoth presence was quite significant in this region, the word has been presumed to be of Germanic origin. It was the Visigoths who founded the fortress of Rennes-le-Château at the very heart of Rhedesium, or the pagan Reddensis. It is from this latter name that the current names Rennes-le-Château and Rennes-les-Bains derive. It will be noted that this is the exact same name as the Breton capital, which, after being first called Condate (confluence), took on the name of its Gallic inhabitants, the Rhedones.

The root of Rhedae and Rhedones is strictly the same but has nothing to do with the Visigoths. It was mentioned by Caesar (*Rhedis equitibus comprehensis,* in *De Bellum Gallico* VI, 30) and other Latin authors in reference to extremely fast war chariots. The original etymological meaning seems to have been "to run fast," and its derivatives are also the names Rhine and the Rhone, which are swiftly flowing rivers, as well as the modern Breton verb *redek* (to run).

There can be no doubt about all of this, despite the delirious interpretive fantasies of some who see in the original word "Red, god of thunder and storms, whose temples were underground," probably because they recognize its similarity to the English word *red*. But what would the English language have to do with this area? The height of the ridiculous, however, is attained by those individuals claiming to be writers and, more important, "initiates" (of what?), whose output is mainly diffused by the local tourist information bureaus. These people integrate in their ravings a hodgepodge of tongues that are as disparate as they are astonishing, making the provenance of the name Razès "Aer-Rod, the racing snake or the mystical Wouivre." This etymology is certainly Celtic, as is the legend of the Wouivre—who becomes Melusine in the Poitou region, and *aer* actually does mean "snake" in modern Breton. But what is the Breton language, moreover modern Breton, doing in the Razès? Some will raise the point that relations between the Razès and Armorica are a certainty. Yes, but with the subtle distinction that the Rhedones people never spoke Breton. Their language was Gallic, a lost language because the druids forbade the use of writing, and because linguists such as Georges Dottin, during the time between the two world wars, had a great deal of difficulty reconstructing its basic vocabulary. It could also be pointed out that a small town of Razès is named "La Serpent." But what does that prove? There were snakes in the Razès as elsewhere, and the term was once a feminine noun. Why see in it only the memorialized image of an ancient ophidian deity? Furthermore, it is quite difficult to integrate *aer* into the word Rhedae. This kind of delusional interpretation, while claiming to provide answers to lingering questions, only thickens even more the shadows surrounding them and in no way eliminates the questions. On the contrary, it simply raises them again, for there exist no legends—and thus the relentless need to make bizarre interpretations of them—unless there is a profound reality concealed behind them. It is this reality that we must hunt down.

One thing is sure about the Razès: The people who gave the land its name were a Gallic people, the Rhedones, whom we also find in Armorica, in the Vilaine basin. It may appear odd, at first glance, that the same people would have settled in two spots so far apart from each other. But it is not exceptional—far from it—and migrations have always taken place. Regarding the Gauls alone we find the Artebrates in Arras—where they left their name—and in Great Britain; the Boiens in Bohemia (the name of these people can be recognized here) and in La Teste de Buch near Arcachon, (where they also left their name); the Vivisci Bituriges on the shores of Lake Lausanne in Vevey, which gained its name from them, and in the Médoc region of France; and the Osismes in northern Finistère and in Exmes of the Orne region, which also bears their name. There are also the Gabales, established in the Cevennes region, where they founded a settlement in Gavaudan (Gabaloduno) in the middle of Lot et Garonne, a land occupied by the Nitobroges and bordered by that of the Petrocores (Périgueux).

The process of Gallic settlement is well known. All of the Gauls originated in Harz. During the second Iron Age, the era known as the Tène, around 400 B.C., they all crossed the Rhine. Among them were the Rhedones people, who split into two groups. One went west to Armorica, the other south toward the Corbières. There might also have been a later emigration in 56 B.C. from the Vilaine Basin, following Caesar's defeat of the Armoricain confederation headed by the Venetes of Vannes, in which the Rhedones took part. The Rhedones thus settled in one of the most underprivileged regions in a vast territory occupied by the Volques Tectosages, a land that was already subjected to heavy Roman influence.

In addition, the toponymy of Razès bears the strong imprint of Celtic elements, especially in the neighborhood of Rennes le Château. There we may note the word *bec,* meaning "point," found in Saint Julia de Bec and Coume de Bec. The word *coume* is Gallic and means "hollow" (the coomb) and can also be seen in Comme de Hadras. Bézu, meaning either "birch" or "tomb," can be found here and there all over. As if by chance, the name Alet appears to be the same as that of the ancient appellation of Saint Servan (Ille et Vilaine) in the land of the Rhedones in Armorica. Artiques is derived from the root *arto,* meaning "bear." The name of Chalabre Peak comes from the root *calo* meaning "hard." The Verdouble River gets its name from the ancient *vern-odubrum,* meaning "water course through the alders." Cassaignes is derived from the Gallic word *cassano,* meaning "oak." Belvianes and Belesta, as well as other composites of "bel," most likely stem from the name of the Gallic solar god, Belenos, "shining one," rather than the adjective describing beauty, although the ancient French *bel,* which has nothing to do with the Latin *bellum,* may or may not have come from the same root word expressing "luminous beauty." Specifically regarding the solar god, we find the nickname of the Gallic Apollo—Grannus—in the village of Granès, but the Gallic Apollo (who is the Irish god Dianecht) is much more a healer god than a solar deity. As for Limoux, the most renowned town in the Razès because of its famous *blanquette** and its carnival, its name, which is the same as Limours in the Ile de France region, is constructed atop the Gallic name for "elm" that can also be seen in Lake Leman (also known as Lake Lausanne or Lake Geneva) and Limoges, the city of the Lemovices. Numerous additional examples could be cited, all of which reveal a strong Celtic presence in this land whose southern character, at least on the surface, cannot be doubted.

So it was not without reason that Father Henri Boudet, who was the priest for Rennes-les-Bains around 1900, wrote and published in 1886 a work entitled *La vraie langue celtique et le cromlech de Rennes-le-Bains.*[†] This ecclesiastical worthy who led a retiring and sensible life

---

* [*Blanquette* is a traditional French dish usually consisting of white meat and vegetables in a sauce with a cream and egg base. —*Trans.*]
[†] [The True Celtic Language and the Cromlech of Rennes-le-Bains. —*Trans.*]

claimed to have rediscovered the lost Gallic language through the stones of his region. In support of his claim he made bold use of numerous languages, particularly English (one still wonders why), and authors such as Châteaubriand, who knew absolutely nothing about linguistics.

This was how Father Boudet came to interpret the names of Rennes and Rhedae in rather original fashion: The people of the Rhedones—those of Armorica and those of the Corbières—would have been "the tribe of the teaching stones (*read, red* = teaching, *hone* = carved stone). Study and science were indispensable for understanding the purpose behind the construction of the megaliths. Only those who learned it directly from the mouths of the druids had the intelligence and sense to do so."

This acknowledges the fact that the druids possessed a great science, something all the Greek and Roman authors confirm unanimously. The problem is that the megalithic monuments belonged to a completely different civilization than that of the Celts and were built at least two thousand years before the arrival of the druids, which is rather unfortunate for Father Boudet's theory. And why is there a need for the basis of hazy English in his explanation? It is likely that the author absolutely required these teaching stones to justify his thesis. And because misfortune comes in pairs, we must also note that there is not, nor has there ever been, a single cromlech in the vicinity of Rennes-les-Bains.

But Father Boudet, who was not short of arguments, would not be held back by this:

It may certainly be asked why the name of Rennes has been applied to our thermal spa. The reason is easily discovered when one closely studies this strange land: Its rock-crowned mountains form an immense cromlech of ten to twelve miles in diameter.

Once someone has come up with an idea, all the rest becomes so clear. Thus it is not at all unlikely that through close examination an even more impressive cromlech could be found in the mountain chain of Puys d'Auvergne, probably in honor of the god Lugh/Mercury. I predict that a researcher who is just as skilled as Father Boudet—perhaps one of his many imitators, for he does have them!—will certainly seek to examine the situation closely. However, this obsession over carved stones and their attribution to a people who never used writing is quite amazing. When examined closely, "a group of large boulders bearing the name of Cugulhou," is given an interesting interpretation by Father Boudet: "This mass is not entirely the work of nature; the work of the Celts is clearly evident in the eight or ten large, round stones that were carried and placed on the summit of the megalith."

After all, the word *megalith* does mean "big stone" and therefore can be applied to a mountain, but in passing we have to wonder at the imprecision of an observer who doesn't even know if there are eight or ten large round stones on a site that is one of the keys to his argument:

> Fortunately, the very name Cugulhou sheds light on this subject. These rocks are authentic menhirs [let's leave it at that], but they have degraded and do not display the ordinary shape of other raised stones: *Cock* means "to lift up"; ugly *(eugly)* is "deformed, degraded"; and *hew (hiou)* is "to carve."

Here is a rather acrobatic—and, of course, entirely English—kind of etymology, with the additional bonus of a play on words that the worthy ecclesiastic neither understood nor intended: In older, common English to *cock* also meant "to obtain an erection."

From the linguistic or toponymic and historical perspectives, Father Boudet's work is not even amusing. It is an unlikely collection of almost aberrant falsehoods, inanities, and naïveté lacking all justification, even if we are inclined to show the most extreme indulgence. Furthermore, certain "hermeticists" and journalists who had been drawn to Boudet's work by the mysteries of Rennes-le-Château and its surroundings, having been thoroughly embarrassed by a text they had formerly lauded, eventually came to view it as an ingenious and subtle cryptogram. With that, Father Boudet's work was transformed into a precursor of Jacques Lacan's book—a code for rediscovering the "treasure" hidden in the Razès. So why should this not be the treasure of the Cathars? I heartily wish great enjoyment to its fans, who are quite numerous, it appears.

Though Father Boudet's book constitutes such an atrocity, we are obliged to raise this essential question: *Are we sure that this was not his express intention?* We know full well that the great works of the Middle Ages, namely those of Chrétien de Troyes and those concerning the Grail Quest, are peppered with snares, inconsistencies, paradoxes, dead ends, false testimonies, and obvious exaggerations, all fully intended by their authors. These texts are actually coded, and it takes patience to untangle the web they form together. It seems that Father Boudet's book may be of the same nature and may form part of a larger whole. Therefore it is not appropriate to examine it at the linguistic or historical level, or even as word play, but as part of a larger unit.

For the Razès, while it is a specific place and its own entity, cannot be separated from the Cathar domain, including the Sabarthes and the Montségur region, of which it is the incontestable center. It is all well and good to hunt down the Celtic components of Razès, but they are a kind of mirror by which other images add their interference. When we stubbornly confine consideration only to the exposed portion of the iceberg, we run the risk of colliding into the submerged part, which is considerably different, and thus sinking. It so happens that the Razès has a history.

This history began very early. Excavations undertaken in 1930 beneath the promontory of Rennes-le-Château have brought to light Solutrean sepulchres dating from the high Paleolithic Age, around 30,000 B.C. Human occupation of the area was uninterrupted; some traces remain of the Magdalenian era at the end of the Paleolithic Age, as do a few examples of the megaliths from the time around 4000 B.C., when the ground of Razès was studded with such monuments as the Peyrolles menhir, known as Peiro Dreito, the "straight stone."

The Iron Age brought with it the Celtic occupation by the Volques

Tectosages and the Rhedones. The worship of water, confirmed at Rennes-les-Bains and Alet, gives reason to believe that the Razès region, which was fairly isolated and forest-covered, must have contained numerous worship sites, the famous *nemetons* that are sanctuaries or clearings consecrated to healing or tutelary deities such as Grannus.

In 121 B.C. the Romans occupied what would become Gallia Togata, or the Narbonnaise. Traces of the Romans are still visible in Alet and Rennes-les-Bains, whose springs they used and converted just as they did almost everywhere such springs were discovered in Gaul. Remnants of a Roman way have also been found between Alet and Rennes-les-Bains, a fragment of a larger road that must have connected to Carcassonne on the Catalan side after passing through what today is called the Col of Saint Louis. But there is no trace of any Roman occupation in Rennes-le-Château, which is explained perfectly by the Roman custom of settling in valleys to better watch over and maintain the major roads, which constituted a vital system to an administration responsible for a vast region of scattered settlement.

It was under the domination of the Visigoths that Razès took on particular importance. There was a significant fortress there known as Rhedae, which people persist in perceiving, without any proof, as Rennes-le-Château. In 507 A.D., following the battle of Vouillé, which was won by Clovis and the Franks, who advanced all the way to the Pyrenees, the stronghold of Rhedae seemed to remain in Visigoth hands. It also seems that at that time the area benefited from settlement by people of Jewish origin, probably Jews of the Diaspora fleeing from regions threatened by war or those who wished to escape possible persecution.

At the time the Carolingians seized power, the earldom of Razès was no doubt the home in exile of the Merovingian prince Sigisbert IV (676–758), most likely the son of Dagobert II, who was assassinated on orders of Pippin of Heristal. It is believed that the descendents of Sigisbert IV were forced to hide in the Razès mountains to escape the threat of the Carolingians before emigrating to Armoricain Brittany, where they set down roots. In the thirteenth century, figuring among their possible descendents was one Hughes de Lusignan, count of the March, and Alix, titular duchess of Brittany.

This was not only the most contested period in the history of Razès but also the richest in events of all sorts. Charlemagne took a great interest in the region, and to keep apprised of what took place there, he sent the bishop of Orleans, Theodulfus, who composed a poem on his travels that notes a Rhedae not far from Carcassonne. This is no doubt the first official mention we have of this name, and the text lets it be understood that at this time Rhedae was just as important as Carcassonne. Southern tradition maintains that the city of Rhedae consisted of thirty thousand inhabitants and seven slaughterhouses, as well as a monastery of monks equipped with the means to defend themselves. All of this appears suspect. Though southern tradition exaggerates, Rhedae's importance is confirmed by subsequent documents. It is impossible, however that such an agglomeration might have occupied the site of Rennes-le-Château, which is much too confined and narrow on its promontory to give the impression of a large city. And nothing in the substructures there can confirm such an identification. At most, Rennes-le-Château was an observation post with a small garrison, and it is more likely that the original Rhedae was to be found on the current site of Limoux.

To defend this region of Septimania, constantly exposed to Saracen raids, Charlemagne named Guilhem de Gellone as responsible for the Marches. After an eventful life, Guilhem de Gellone would spend his final days in the monastery of Saint Guilhem of the Desert, which he founded. He is known to have been a Merovingian and a descendent of Sigisbert IV. He has also become consecrated by legend: He became William of Orange, valorous destroyer of the Saracens and protector of Louis the Pious—the hero of the *Chansons de Geste* cycle of Garin de Montglane.

In 813, the count of Rhedae, Béra IV, founded the Alet Abbey, at least if we are to believe a donation record that may well be a forgery. All we can know for certain is that at the end of the tenth century, the solidly established Alet Abbey formed part of a congregation led by the abbot of Saint Michael of Cuxa. A century later, in 1096, Pope Urban II stayed at Alet, which testifies to the importance the abbey had assumed. A period of decline began at the end of the twelfth century, a time when the Cathars were growing in numbers in Razès. In 1317 Pope John XXII created the diocese of Limoux, but following quarrels about the revenues on Limoux—revenues held by men of the church there—the bishopric was transferred to Alet in 1318, whereupon its abbey church became a cathedral.

Long before this, however, in 870, the earldom of Razès was transferred to the House of Carcassonne, and subsequently the city of Rhedae, whether it was Limoux or Rennes-Le-Château, became the object of lordly disputes between the counts of Carcassonne and the counts of Barcelona. It was sometimes part of one domain and sometimes part of the other until 1067, when Countess Ermengarde sold her sovereignty over Carcassonne and the Razès to a relative, Raymond Béranger, count of Barcelona, for a sum of one thousand gold ounces.

This was the time of the Cathars, and the Razès found itself under the banner of Raymond-Roger Trencavel, viscount of Carcassonne and Béziers and acknowledged protector of heretics and Occitain independence. During the crusade in 1209, Raymond-Roger was taken prisoner by Simon de Montfort and died in the dungeons of Carcassonne. His son was entrusted to the care of the count de Foix and raised at his court, which—and this was no secret to anyone—teemed with heretics of all kinds who shared one thing in common: hatred of the French. The young Trencavel made clear that his life's purpose was the conquest of the heritage that had been stolen from him: the earldoms of Carcassone, Albi, and Razès.

Trencavel was a curious figure. He was the heart and soul of the revolt of the faidits (the dispossessed lords) in 1239 and 1240, along with Olivier de Termes, one of his vassals who still held control of the Corbières, the Teremènes, and the fortresses of Quéribus and Peyrepertuse. In the revolt Trencavel achieved some stunning successes that he failed to capitalize upon, and it appears that at about this same time, following a long delay, Raymond VII of Toulouse did not come through with any aid. Olivier de Termes submitted formally to the king following a vigorous French counteroffensive, and no doubt after having been bought by the Capets, he eventually betrayed the Trencavel cause. The revolt ended in failure and the Razès was occupied by French troops who hunted down the heretics. Because there were large numbers of them, as is attested to by the creation, in 1225, of a Cathar diocese within the earldom, many were forced to seek refuge in the more inaccessible areas. There was no lack of these in the Razès region. Trencavel formally surrendered to the king, but his domains were not restored to him and he was forced to sojourn in Aragon.

One certainty is that Trencavel made a desperate attempt to win back the Razès, which seemed to hold an exceptional importance for him. Likewise, Louis IX and Blanche de Castille pulled out all the stops to maintain their domination over the Razès, and to eliminate Trencavel. It was this intense determination displayed by both parties that has brought Trencavel to the attention of historians as well as observers. Did he know some secret connected to the Razès, or was he aware of an enormous treasure in the area? The result has been a horde of interpretations that are as varied as they are astonishing. It has even been declared that Trencavel served as the model for Perceval/Parzival (Antonin Gadal again!) based on the onomastic argument that Trencavel means "slice well" and Perceval means "stab well." However, there is no relationship between these two names, and Perceval can also mean "pierce valley" or "lost the vale," which seems to fit best. As for Trencavel's identification as the model for Perceval, inspired in large part by his life, it is a flagrant absurdity. The young Trencavel was not yet born when Chrétien de Troyes wrote his story of the Grail, in which he placed on stage for the first time in literary history the figure of Perceval. Could the model, then, have been his father, Raymond-Roger? Simon de Montfort's victim died in 1209; this identification holds no more water than the first.

It should also be noted that the Razès was often frequented by the

Knights Templar, who had established a commandery in Bézu. It certainly seems that these Templars played a fairly ambiguous role at the time of the Albigensian crusade. In truth, they did not take part in it at all, apparently remaining on the sidelines for the entire affair. They did sign a treaty in 1209 with the Aniort family, owners of the Rennes-le-Château region, which consisted of a fictive transfer to the Templars of property belonging to the Aniort family and subject to royal seizure, in particular Lavaldieu and Coume Sourde, implying that the Templars had accepted the mission of aiding the Razès Cathars. They had performed a similar operation a century earlier with property owned by the Jews of Razès, for a document specifies that in 1142 the Jews had given their land to the Templars to be held as tenant farms.

In 1156 Bertrand de Blanchefort had been elected Grand Master of the Templar Order.* It was then that the Templars living in Bézu established a veritable colony of German laborers—casters, to be exact—to work in the local mines. These lead, silver, copper, and gold mines were, in truth, not very important and had already been exploited during the time of the Romans. What is surprising here, however, is that the Templars invited not miners, which would appear logical, but casters. Exactly what kind of work was this? Intriguing, too is the fact that it was not local labor, or even French labor, that was recruited. It seems as though the intent was to use workers who spoke a foreign tongue that the local populace could not comprehend. It is easy to understand, then, why there are so many local traditions concerning a treasure hidden in the Rennes-le-Château area. Sometimes the legends tell of magic gold guarded by the devil in a cave beneath Blanchefort Castle. Sometimes they involve the cursed gold of Toulouse, and sometimes the treasure from the Temple of Jerusalem. Sometimes it is the Templar's lost treasure. It is even, sometimes, the Grail. But most frequently the tales refer to the Cathar treasure.

---

* It has been thought that he was a member of a Razès family, but in reality he belonged to the family of Blanchefort de Guyenne.

All of this is obviously connected to Montségur. It is now established that the bargaining sessions between the Inquisitors and the defenders of Montségur, Pierre-Roger de Mirepoix and Ramon de Perella, were conducted under the safeguard of Ramon d'Aniort, lord of Rennes-le-Château and Rennes-les-Bains. We also know that after the escape of the four perfecti charged with transporting the "treasure" (whatever it was), a fire was lit upon the summit of Bidorta by a man named Escot de Belcaire, special envoy of Ramon d'Aniort, to alert the besieged inhabitants of Montségur that the operation had been a success. It is quite likely that the four escapees were met and hidden in the Razès.

The Aniort family as a whole appears to have played a discreet but effective and singularly disturbing role in Albigensian affairs. By all evidence, they took the side of the Cathars during the crusade: The four Aniort brothers, Géraud, Othon, Bertrand, and Ramon, along with two of their cousins, violently opposed Simon de Montfort and were of course excommunicated. Their castles were confiscated, but curiously, a short time later, their excommunication was lifted and a portion of their domains was restored to them. The castle of Aniort was scheduled to be razed, but at the last moment Louis IX sent a messenger to halt the operation. Furthermore, we know that Ramon d'Aniort was received at court by Louis IX, who showed him surprising deference considering he was a rebel and was allied with heretics. While questions arise that greatly risk remaining forever unanswered, they do permit conjecture that corroborates a theory regarding Blanche de Castille's indulgent attitude toward Raymond VII of Toulouse: It is possible that Ramon d'Aniort had in his possession, or at least knew the location of, a "treasure"—in this instance, documents proving the existence and survival of a Merovingian line, the legitimate dynasty that had been concealed until it was chased out by the usurping Carolingians and their successors, the Capets. *This is only a hypothesis, nothing more.* But it appears logical and would explain the ambiguous attitude displayed by Louis IX and Blanche de Castille toward certain Cathar leaders and some of their allies, as well as their determination to occupy Occitain territories.

This theory would also explain the case of the mysterious abbot Béranger Saunière, priest of Rennes-le-Château from 1885 to 1917. Wishing to restore his church, the parish being very poor and he himself without means, he was said to have discovered within a pillar a "treasure" that allowed him to complete this restoration and even to undertake a very strange embellishment of the sanctuary and its immediate surroundings. Whatever the truth may be concerning the reality of this "treasure," Father Saunière suddenly became very wealthy but never revealed where he had gained his fortune.* Could he have sold certain documents or at least promised, in return for money, to keep them secret? Though this theory may hold up, it is still only a theory, mind you, for the sole certainties in the story are Father Saunière's fortune and the works he undertook.

We are certain, however, that the Aniort family provided protection to the Cathars and Templars in the Razès. The Voisins family, established by the king as "guardian" of the Razès, was also on good terms with the Templars, and following the order's condemnation by Philip the Fair, a family member rescued some of the Templars, who then found refuge in Spain.

Philip the Fair is exactly whom we find in the Razès in 1283. He was accompanying his father, King Philip the Bold, son of Saint Louis, on a journey through the Languedoc. The king made a stop at the home of Pierre de Voisins, lord of Rennes, who held sway over all of the Razès in the king's name. In making his visit to Pierre de Voisins, Philip the Bold's intention was to obtain the neutrality of the local lords, some of whom were vassals of the king of Aragon, in the war he was preparing against Aragon. But the king also visited Ramon d'Aniort's home, where he was warmly received by Aniort as well as by his wife, Alix de

---

* For more on this, see M. Baigent, R. Leigh, and H. Lincoln, *Holy Blood, Holy Grail* (New York: Delacorte, 1982).

Blanchefort, and his younger brother, Udaut d'Aniort, whom Philip the Fair would have loved to make his companion in arms but who preferred to become a Templar.

But why this visit to a family that was more than suspect? Two of Ramon's uncles were acknowledged Cathars and Alix de Blanchefort was the daughter of a heretical faidit lord and sworn enemy of Simon de Montfort. It may have been to conclude a marriage alliance. In fact, sometime thereafter Pierre III de Voisins, a widower, wed Jordane d'Aniort, Ramon's cousin. Thus the two families were joined. But what was the motive for this marriage, which was undoubtedly arranged by the king and which, to a certain extent, rehabilitated the Aniorts?

Later, in 1422, the heir of the Voisins, Marcafava, wed Pierre-Raymond d'Hautpoul, heiress to one of the oldest and most illustrious families of Occitania. The founders of this lineage were known as the kings of the Black Mountain. At the time of the Abigensian crusade, they had been stripped of their lands and castles for having protected the heretics. And in 1732, François d'Hautpoul wed Marie de Negri d'Ables, who was the sole heir to the property of the Aniort family. They had three daughters, Élisabeth, who lived and died a spinster in Rennes-les-Bains; Marie, who wed her cousin d'Hautpoul-Felines; and Gabrielle, who married the Marquis de Fleury.

It so happens that Élisabeth d'Hautpoul had some differences with her sisters over the division of their inheritance. At this time she refused to communicate the papers and deeds of the family under the pretext that it was dangerous to examine these documents and that it would be more suitable to "have them decoded and determine which were family records and which were not." This seems to imply that the Hautpoul family, heirs of the Aniorts, possessed in their archives papers *that were not family papers,* and that it was better not to look at these. But what were these mysterious papers? We will probably never know. It is said that in 1870, the notary entrusted with the keeping of the family papers refused to turn them over to Pierre d'Hautpoul under the pretext that he could not release such important documents without committing a serious act of folly. It is added that among these documents were genealogies bearing the seal of Blanche de Castille that proved the permanence of the Merovingian line. How was anybody to know? For the notary refused to turn them over. In truth, the entire matter is quite vexing, as one coincidence to the next buries us deeper and deeper in mystery.

When Father Saunière made his discovery in the church of Rennes-le-Château—for he certainly did discover *something*—it was claimed to be the treasure of Blanche de Castille, which indicates that throughout this entire affair an active complicity between the Cathars and the Templars had been operating. Hasn't the suggestion been made, with some good reason, it seems, that the Templars were the secular arm of the Cathars, who themselves were prohibited from bearing weapons? It has been shown that in the Razès, in any case, their collusion was fully operational.

They had built a formidable fortress in Bézu, the ruins of which can still be seen today:

On the Lauzet plateau, to the southeast of Rennes-le-Château and northeast of Bézu, there is a site known as the Castle of the Templars. This is a recent appellation, for the 1830 administrative map still has it as the Ruins of Albedun. This name is Celtic, *albo-duno,* and oddly enough its translation in Franco-Occitain— Blanchefort Castle, natal home of the Blanchefort line—is just a few miles from Rennes-le-Chatteau and Rennes-les-Bains and is, in fact, a *blanque fort,* a "white fortress."* It should be noted that almost everywhere in the territory of the ancient Gauls, the sites of fortresses, camps, and even cities were designated by a frequently occurring name: the white city. This is also the meaning of Vienne in the Isère region, the former Vindobona, "the white enceinte," a

---

* Some declare that Bézu derives from Albedum, which is phonetically impossible. Furthermore, the name Bézu ("birch" or "tomb," as in the Grand-Bé at Saint Malo) is very widespread, including places where fortresses never existed.

compound of two other Gallic words, *vindo,* "white," and *bona,* "fortified enceinte."

Now, on the Lauzet plateau I picked up the traces of three large, concentric enceinte walls of which I took some gripping photos. They carried an imprint that was without a doubt Visigothic for several reasons: First, these were so-called cyclopean blocks, each weighing from three to four tons, that cannot therefore be confused with low walls; next, the remnants of the walls were manufactured in the style known as "fish bone," which was characteristic of the Visigothic era and was never used afterward. This site, therefore, seems a more appropriate location than Rennes-le-Château for the former Rhedae.*

In fact, it is possible that the site of Albedun may be the site of ancient Rhedae. But it could also have been simply one fortress among many others in this land that lends itself so well to fortresses situated on heights, the better to keep watch over the surrounding countryside. In any case, the Razès is an ideal spot for hiding fugitives and secrets; surely they would be well guarded.

But why couldn't the Cathar "treasure" have been hidden in the church of Rennes-le-Château? After all, anything is possible . . . There is no proof to support this argument, but neither is there proof to rebut it. It would be beneficial to look closely at the conversions Father

---

* Jean-Luc Chaumeil, *La trésor du triangle d'or* (Paris: A. Lefeuvre, 1979), 114. The author categorically rejects the theory stating that Limoux is the ancient Rhedae, which is what I personally believe. In fact, despite the claims of Jean-Luc Chaumeil and many others in defiance of the most elementary laws of phonetics, the name Rennes cannot derive from the name Rhedae. Where does the double *n* come from? Rennes is an ancient form in French, flowing logically from Redones (as in Ille et Vilaine), unless it is from the second part of Pagus Reddensis, which designates the entire country, and not simply a fortified site. The Occitain evolved form is Razès, and just as in modern Breton, Rennes is pronounced as Roazhon. In the Razès, Rennes is a generic name used in this form for two locales, but Razès originally means the same as *pagus.* Rhedae, however, designates "a fortified place," but there is nothing connecting it to Rennes-le-Château specifically.

Saunière made to his church and its immediate surroundings following his famous discovery. In fact, this investigation should be carried out regardless of his true motives and especially without taking issue with any of the interpretations of this strange case—as varied as they are delusional—that have appeared since the end of World War II.

The church of Rennes-le-Château has undergone many renovations, but the twelfth-century apse is the oldest part of the structure, which is not to say that there was not another, earlier sanctuary. It has been named after Mary Magdalene, which immediately lends it an Eastern connotation. According to tradition, Mary Magdalene landed in Provence, charged with the task of giving a message to the Western World. But:

[t]hrough the unfortunate circumstance of a flamboyant ugliness, unjustly labeled as Sulpician by some, numerous visitors to this small, over-stuccoed sanctuary have felt a sense of uneasiness that is unexpected in a consecrated place. But it is the means of collecting one's thoughts and meditating and praying before these almost vulgarly overdone paintings and statues that would have earned the imprecations of Huysmans in his book on the cathedral.*

And this feeling of uneasiness begins outside, when we first see the inscription above the porch: *terribilis est locus iste,* "this place is terrible." Of note is the use of the Latin *iste,* which has a pejorative nuance or could indicate possession by a second person. Should this be translated as meaning "this ignoble place is terrible," or perhaps "your place is terrible"? Fans of mysteries and those who decode the phonetic kabbalah will appreciate this conundrum and choose their preference according to their own convictions.

I can well remember the sunny, almost torrid September day when I visited Rennes-le-Château. Coming from Couiza, my companion Marie

---

* Jean Robin, *Rennes-le-Château, la colline envoûtée* (Paris: G. Trédaniel, 1982), 28.

Môn and I followed the road that climbed a mountain before crossing onto the other side to face a new horizon. I had the vivid impression of crossing a frontier, one of those passes in which, according to ancient legend, mysterious beings wait to lead to safety or destruction (depending on their mood) any traveler who ventures there. From here we entered the sun-drenched, closed village that seemed almost dead, as if weighed down by a torpor emerging from the very depths of the earth. Sitting at the end of a promontory, the Magdala Tower assaulted the sky at the edge of an abyss over a desolate, stony landscape crowned on the west by blue mountains. It was a grandiose landscape if ever there was one, but somewhat disturbing nonetheless. What could be hiding in the valley or behind those erratically shaped blocks so easily confused with warriors turned to stone, like those Saint Kornely changed at Carnac in my native land? And behind us, hidden behind a screen of greenery, was the church, hardly any taller than the surrounding houses and no easier to distinguish in that slumbering mass.

In Montségur I had been attacked by dizziness, a panicked fear of the void. Here the void was absent. But I did feel as if the place were inhabited—no doubt by ghosts of all the mysterious figures who had strayed onto this land over the course of the centuries. They had inevitably left traces of their presence, which was what I was trying to discern without having much confidence that I would succeed. These phantoms kept watch on me, no doubt in expectation of the signal I would give them. But I did not wish to make any signal, for I knew nothing of the true nature of these beings. This was surely excessive caution on my part, but it could be explained by the feeling I had of being watched by perfectly real beings who knew who I was and wondered why I had abandoned the thickets of Brocéliande to stray into a labyrinth to which I never should have been given access.*

But the weather was so nice that day in Rennes-le-Château that I

---

* This feeling had a foundation in reality. Three months later, someone who was not present that day gave me a detailed account of my visit to Rennes-le-Chateau.

totally neglected to recite the litanies of the fog. We wished to see the church, but it was closed and we had to wait until the afternoon to visit it. We ate lunch beneath the trees in a spirit of peace and tranquility with the knowledge that we were living a privileged moment. A sassy young girl flitted among the tables and the trees just as she flitted through the streets of the village—a strange girl named Morgane. These details are not invented; I must admit that since childhood I have lived in the company of Merlin and the fairies of Brocéliande, and they never miss an opportunity to remind me that they are my guides in the world of obscure realities.

We then went toward the church. The structure itself, the small park to the south of the chevet, and the cemetery form a strange unit that is not dissimilar to the famous parish enclosure of Leon in north Finistère, though less beautiful and majestic. In fact, what is truly striking at Rennes-le-Château is the mediocrity of everything the eye can see. The gate that leads into the cemetery, with a skull whose laugh reveals its twenty-two teeth, is somewhat sordid. Where was the sober and somber majesty of the triumphal porches of Brittany? For this was such a vulgar imitation of them.

There are, of course, odd objects: a pool; a Calvary scene in which the cross is centered within a circle, as was depicted by the ancient Egyptians; a false cave; an altar to the dead that is another imitation of Breton funerary art (the famous ossuary); and, most prominent, a statue of the Virgin on a Carolingian pedestal that has been recut and carved and presented *upside down*. We have good reason to ask why. We are told it is symbolic. Of course, it is all symbolic, insofar as we can observe the use of symbols belonging to different traditions. But a heteroclite mélange of symbols doesn't necessarily mean anything. Syncretism is always a degeneration that results when nobody knows anymore the exact meaning of the symbols they observe in order to fabricate a mystery. And so what if there is a Masonic tomb in the cemetery? After all, he who is laid to rest there had a perfect right to make a tomb according to his personal convictions. There is nothing so surprising about that.

The moment I entered the church, I was gripped by a feeling of unease. At first glance everything seemed unhealthy, beginning with the hideous statue of the devil Asmodeus next to the door. His eyes starting out of his head are staring fixedly at the black and white tiled floor. He knee is bent—the left one, of course—and he is holding a heavy font. His right hand forms a circle and once held a trident. Altogether he is a completely conventional image of the devil. Above him, each of four angels is making a part of the sign of the cross, and on the statue's pedestal, along with the initials B. S. (for Father Béranger Saunière) in a little circle are these words: By this sign you will vanquish him.

Toward the top of the wall in the back of the church is a fresco depicting Christ surrounded by a crowd of people on a flower-covered mountain. At the foot of the mountain there is a kind of burst sack from which grains of wheat seem to be escaping. In the background is a landscape in which we can make out several villages. It has been surmised that this represents the surrounding area of Rennes-le-Château and that the grains of wheat are symbolic of the fabulous "treasure" hidden there.

On either side of the choir are plaster statues, created in the purest pre-war Sulpician style, representing Joseph and Mary, each of whom is carrying an infant Jesus, which seems bizarre. There are also a statue and a painting whose subjects are Mary Magdalene, patroness of the church, with a human skull atop an open book sitting at her feet. It is easily and immediately seen that the Way of the Cross is anomalous here: It is in fact arranged in the exact reverse of how it is customarily set up in churches. Among the other statues—all ugly and of little interest—there are two Saint Anthonys, Anthony of Padua and Anthony the Hermit, who is holding a closed book.

What is Cathar or of the Cathar spirit in all this? Little, in fact. The devil's choice position perhaps recalls that the Cathars believed in a principle of evil embodied by Satan, almost a god of evil in opposition to the god of good. This dualistic concept is also illustrated by the two saint Anthonys and especially by the two statues of the infant Jesus. It has been said that the child held by Joseph represents the masculine element, in other words, *that which is apparent,* and that the infant held by Mary represents the subtle feminine element, *that which is hidden.* Why not? They could also illustrate a belief that appears in two Cathar texts: Jesus and Satan are the two sons of God the Father, the two manifestations of a divinity that is both good and evil. This aspect of the Cathar doctrine, which is generally neglected by the experts and shows that Catharism was in reality a false dualism and an authentic monism, seems to have been consciously emphasized in this church by this unusual duo.

But what deforms everything is the bias of reversal, which can first be seen outside the church in the Carolingian pedestal that is placed upside down. Joseph is on the left—the *sinister* side—when looking at the altar, though usually this sinister position was the woman's place during ceremonies, and it is on the north facade that devils and scenes of "deviltry" are depicted,* those motifs that were so frequently included in medieval cathedral sculpture. Here in this Saint Mary Magdalene Church, Joseph the man, *the appearance,* is on the left. Would the child he is holding thereby be Satan? Would therefore the child held by Mary, *the hidden reality,* on the right be Jesus of the Gospels? But then why is the grotesque statue of Satan located on the right, and why is the Way of the Cross reversed? A visit to this church leaves a strange and unwholesome impression. This sanctuary appears more auspicious for a Black Mass than a conventional one.

There is only one church of the same size that can be compared to Saint Mary Magdalene of Rennes-le-Château: the Sainte-Oenne de Tréhorenteuc Church (Morbihan) in the Brocéliande Forest. I am very familiar with it from having participated to a certain extent in its fairly recent restoration and decoration, which, while not taking place under exactly the same circumstances as those in Rennes-le-Château, went

---

* [North is synonomous with left. This classic orientation is derived by facing the rising sun. —*Trans.*]

through a fairly similar process. But at Tréhorenteuc, although the artistic quality remains subject to debate, everything is clear cut. There is no question of dualism, much less a "treasure," and there is not the slightest ambiguity in the symbolic adornments.

What is so striking in the church at Rennes-le-Château is the accumulation of details that are seem logically connected but that under examination reveal themselves to be divergent, if not downright contradictory. Borrowings from Masonic and Rosicrucian symbology can be found there: By all evidence the floor, which resembles a chess board with its black and white squares oriented to the four cardinal points, is reminiscent of the Freemasons' "mosaic pavement." In this chessboard floor another allusion to dualism can be found: The game of chess is a confrontation between the children of light and the children of darkness. Why not? In any event, Manicheaism is inscribed within the toponymy of the area: Facing the citadel of Blanchefort (white stronghold) rears up the jagged ridge of Roco Negro (black rock).

But there are other Masonic allusions. The eighth station on the Way of the Cross shows a woman in a widow's veil holding by the hand a child wearing a Scotch plaid, and the ninth depicts a knight who has no relevance to this station but brings to mind the grade of the Benevolent Knight of the Holy City from the Reformed Scottish Rite. Likewise, it is not by chance that roses and crosses adorn all the stations of the Way of the Cross. It should also be pointed out that during the nineteenth century one of the best known members of the Hautpol family, François, was grand master of the Carbonari Lodge in Limoux. It is, however, worth noting that following Antonin Gadal's fantasies about the Sabarthes Grail, a Rosicrucian sect founded a center in Ussat-les-Bains and even erected a monument there to Galahad, son of Lancelot of the Lake and discoverer of the Cistercian Grail. In Montségur we find the Cathars, the Grail legend, and the Nordics,* not

---

* [A catch-all term for those who find their spiritual roots and/or inspiration in Norse myth and tradition. —Trans.]

to mention the Nazis. In the Sabarthes, we find the Cathars, the Grail Legend, and the Rosy Cross. In the Razès, we find everything: the Templars, the Freemasons, the Cathars, the Rosicrucians, the Grail legend, the Merovingians, and of course, the Nordics, but the last have a much more British allure, no doubt because of the Scottish origin of Freemasonry. I almost forgot to add the druids to this list—but yes, we find them too, those whom I thought had definitively disappeared at least fifteen hundred years ago:

> The Aude region has always provided a welcome to wizards and sorcerers, and it is not the bishop of Carcassonne who will prove us wrong if we declare that forbidden practices (at least this was the case when the Inquisition was raging) have undoubtedly more right to be cited here than elsewhere. Father Saunière, a native of this region who was, we are told, very close to the local people to boot, could not have been unaware that the majority of sorcery rituals are simply religious rites performed backward, and all folklore experts, for want of exorcists, have an abundance of backward prayers in their files, as well as old wives' tales of walking the Way of the Cross backward while muttering inaudible threats.*

Furthermore, we know that Father Saunière supposedly went to Paris to have examined the documents he discovered in his church. There, according to Father Bieil, director of Saint-Sulpice, he met Emile Hoffet, who was well versed in esoteric studies and would one day become a priest. Hoffet was a frequent visitor of the singer Emma Calvé and eventually became her lover and an intimate in a coterie of crackpots and hermeticists drawn to authentic artists such as Claude Debussy, Stéphane Mallarmé, and Maurice Maeterlinck (in other words the symbolist and decadent milieu), with well-known connections to members of the Theosophical Society, the Freemasons (Scottish Rite),

---

* Jean Robin, *Rennes-le-Château,* (Paris: G. Trédaniel, 1982), 144.

and the Rosicrusians. This very Parisian milieu had just recently dis-covered Wagner, notably his *Parzival,* in the era when medieval texts such as *The Quest for the Holy Grail* and *Tristan and Iseult,* as well as previously forgotten texts from ancient Celtic, Welsh, and Irish litera-ture were being translated and published. It was no secret to anybody that Maeterlinck's and Debussy's *Pelléas* (the name of the Fisher King) was an initiatory lyrical drama based on Germano-Celtic cultural lodes. Was, then, Father Saunière the bridge connecting the worldly and intel-lectual occultism of Paris with the operative sorcery of Razès? Was he capable of this?

Based on a close examination of what he did to the church of Rennes-le-Château, the answer could only be no. Unless the church is simply a smokescreen, Father Saunière merely made—in truly excep-tional bad taste—a superficial reproduction of the teachings he had been given. For such an accumulation of hideous, heterogenous sym-bols and pureile reversals is too remarkable to be the work of chance. Saint Mary Magdalene Church is only a vulgar snare or delusion intended to divert our attention. The Cathar "treasure" is necessarily somewhere else, and it is a waste of time to search for the map leading to this church, which truly is a "synagogue of Satan."

But Rennes-le-Château is not the entire Razès. It is not even ancient Rhedae. There are other locations in this strange and magnif-icent land. This is not the only Rennes; there are two. Why overlook Rennes-les-Bains, which, by all evidence, was a place of worship in the time of the Gauls, and which reveals many mysteries, though they possess that quality of silence specific to such phenomena? It is true that the public notoriety of Father Saunière has completely eclipsed Father Boudet, priest of Rennes-les-Bains, Saunière's colleague and friend who made the mistake of living a simple life devoid of any scandal.

It is a mistake to overlook Rennes-les-Bains. It is an astonishing thermal spa that has been worn away by time and that continues to dis-integrate slowly amid the indifference of the few hydrotherapy fanciers who still come "to take the waters."* This small village, nestled in its valley, within a green hollow that stands out in stark contrast to the aridity of the neighboring plateau, holds a strange charm, perfectly old-fashioned and in keeping with the tastes of days gone by, and there we can feel a nostalgia not yet stripped of pleasure. There, in the comfortable stillness disturbed only by the noise of the waterfalls of the Sals River flowing through the entire length of the village and opportunely reminding us of the existence of numerous saltwater springs nearby, a visitor feels as if he is in another world and another century.

There is in fact a hot spring in Rennes-les-Bains, known as the Bath of the Queen, that has traditionally claimed to have earned its name from Queen Blanche de Castille, who came here for treatment. The water here, which exits the ground at 106 degrees Fahrenheit (41 degrees Celsius), has a decidedly salty taste, and analysis has shown it to be high in sodium chloride. Farther on is the Spring of Madeleine or the Gode, where a sulfurous component joins the salt. We know that there were important worship sites near saltwater springs during Gallic times, as is demonstrated by the salty fountains at Saint-Pierre-sous-Vézelay in Burgundy and at Salines in the Jura, not far from the true Alésia, which was a fortress sanctuary. This confirms the role of Rennes-les-Bains as the veritable religious center of the entire Razès.

Strange memories can be found here: of Blanche de Castille; of the White Lady, otherwise known as the Fairy of the Waters, the folklore image of an ancient goddess of the druids who dwells in a cave; of Mary

---

* Here is a fairly colorful detail: On the facade of a spa hotel that is currently closed a visitor can read a list of the illnesses treated there, among which is catarrh. No, this is no lie—especially in a land where people push word games too far, not to mention the Language of the Birds.†

† [The Language of the Birds is a mystical term for the Magical Language that is well known to devotees. For example, the Church never would have sponsored many of the designs on Europe's great cathedrals, and so the masters who created them used the Magical Language (also called the Language of the Birds, or the Green Language) to conceal their designs. Only a mind that was ready for Truth would be able to decode the symbols, letters, and numbers of the structure. —*Trans.*]

Magdalene, a perfectly obscure figure whose legend lends itself to far-ranging commentaries; and finally of a divine entity we know thanks to Caesar, who called him Apollo. Rather than a solar deity, this is Apollo Grannuus (his name can be seen in Granès), the equivalent of the Irish god Dianecht, who, according to Gaelic epic, formed a Fountain of Health to heal the wounded and resuscitate the dead.*

Here the church itself merits a visit. We enter beneath a vault and, once inside, truly feel ourselves to be in a place of self-reflection and prayer, and not, as at Rennes-le-Château, in a bazaar. This church is rendered in the simplicity restricted to Jansenist austerity. Its essential features have been restored and kept in good repair, and have not been burdened with the wild imaginings of various occult detectives. The church speaks to those who know how to listen, and also to those who know how to look. For there is a fairly strange, fairly old painting there, *Christ with the Hare,* which, like so many other works given to sanctuaries by benefactors, was donated to the church, in this case by Paul-Urbain de Fleury. But *Christ with the Hare* is not here by chance. We can see that it is a somewhat altered, primarily reversed copy of a canvas painted by Van Dyck in 1636, which is now in the collection of the Fine Arts Museum of Anvers.

The cemetery of the church in Rennes-les-Bains does hold an odd tomb, or rather, double tomb: There are two sepulchers attributed to the same man, the donor of the painting, Paul-Urbain de Fleury. Carved on the tomb are his birth and death dates, which contradict each other, and this inscription, incontestably of Rosicrucian inspiration: *He made his way by doing good.* But why the seemingly intentional errors in birth and death dates? And why two tombs for a single individual? Which of the two is the real one? There are so many questions that all those in quest of the "treasure" should ask themselves.

Farther north, on the Couiza-Arques road in the Peyrolles territory,

---

* Jean Markale, *The Druids* (Rochester, Vt.: Inner Traditions, 2000).

there is another tomb, this one isolated, that has unleashed a storm of controversy. It seems to have served as the model for the sixteenth-century painter Nicolas Poussin's painting *Les Bergers d'Arcadie,* housed in the Louvre in Paris. The same landscape is recognizable, the monument is the same shape, and the painter depicts his shepherds deciphering an identical inscription: *Et in Arcadia ego,* which literally means "I am in Arcadia." The same inscription was said to have once appeared on the tomb of the marquis d'Hautpol in Rennes-le-Château, but Father Saunière allegedly scratched it off the stone. This is all very confusing. The fans of mystery explain that Nicolas Poussin, who was an initiate (of what?), clearly would have used the tomb on the Couiza-Arques road for his model. On closer analysis, however, it seems the contrary is true, for this tomb was manufactured after Poussin created his painting. *It is a copy.* But this solves nothing, for the question can then be asked, what is the reason for this copy? We may wonder all the more because Poussin's painting exists and remains an enigma; its very genesis is cloaked in shadow.

In 1656 Nicolas Fouquet, then the finance minister of Louis XIV, gave his younger brother, Father Louis Fouquet, the charge of contacting Nicolas Poussin—who was then sixty-two years old—in Rome in order to commission a painting. The priest responded to the minister that Poussin had accepted but went on to outline in the letter "certain things" that he could not fully reveal there. The terms of this letter, if it is not a forgery (there are so many fakes in the history of Razès that it is necessary to distrust everything), are quite odd. The priest spoke in fact of "certain things that I shall with ease be able to explain to you in detail—things that will give you, through Monsieur Poussin, advantages which even kings would have great pains to draw from him, and which, according to him, it is possible that nobody else will ever discover in the centuries to come."

Later, in 1661, Nicolas Fouquet was arrested by order of the king and replaced by Colbert for reasons that have never been truly explained. What is all of this about? What are these "certain things" that could give Fouquet advantages over King Louis XIV? Certainly the genealogy embellished on the seal of Blanche de Castille authenticating the Merovingian lineage is not far away. Would this be the "treasure"? We are definitely going in circles here. We know that Colbert ordered the region's archives to be researched and that he also ordered excavations. Given these circumstances it does not matter whether the tomb came before or after Poussin's painting, for the problem remains the same.

We have yet to consider the church of Bézu with regard to the Cathar treasure. Overall, it is of very little interest, but found there is an image that we would unconsciously expect to encounter in the Razès: a depiction of the Grail. The date of the painting is uncertain but cannot be earlier than the sixteenth century, which means it is not Cathar. But this chalice—it may be excessive to label it a grail—is strange in that it is presented in the same way as the beaucéant of the Templars, in black and white. It is true that the Templars had a commandery in the territory of Bézu. And we know that they, or at least their successors, were regarded as the initiators of the Masonic movement. But here again we are going in circles.

Finally, we must consider Bugarach with regard to the Cathars. Located southeast of Rennes-les-bains, Bugarach refers to both a mountain peak some 4,300 feet in altitude and a village from which the mountain received its name, and it is here we reconnect directly to the history of the Cathars.

The village appears to have been named in the ninth century, according to the charter of 889 confirming the possessions of the abbots of Saint Polycarpe (Aude), where the name appears in its Latinized form, Burgaragio. In 1231 we find the form Bugaaragium, which becomes Bigarach in 1500, Bugaraïch in 1594, and Beugarach in 1647 until its current form was fixed in 1781.

This place name is not unique—it can be found south of Toulouse as Bougaroche and near Bordeaux as Bougarach—but what is its meaning? Its root might be the Germanic *burg*, designating a fortress (the equivalent of the Celtic *duno*), but this root was never used before in Occitania. It is more likely that it derives from a native term from which came, during the Middle Ages, the words *bulgari, bugares, burgars,* and *bougres,* as well as the modern French *bulgare.** Eighth-century chronicles mention clashes between the Franks, the Avars, and the Bulgarians. In 1201 an ecclesiastic of the abbey of Saint Marien d'Auxerre noted "a heresy that is called Bulgarian" and "heretics called Bulgarians," and in 1207 the same religious figure wrote that "the heresy of the Bulgarians has expanded." There can be no doubt about these Bulgarian heretics: They are the Cathars who—proof of this is now certain—were the successors of the Bogomil heretics, natives of Bulgaria who passed through Byzantium before spreading across Western Europe.

Accordingly, Bugarach could well bear the memory of an early "Bougres" (a term that still exists, with some pejorative connotation) presence in the Razès. This is a logical explanation that has every chance of being correct. Furthermore, it seems there was a connection between Bugarach and Montségur, from which Fernand Niel has formulated a seductive theory: He suggests that in about 1200 the builders—or rebuilders—of Cathar Montségur would have consciously aligned the fortress to the average position of the sunrise:

This west-east orientation falls on the Pech de Bugarach, apex of the Corbières with both an altitude (4,000 feet) and a latitude (42 degrees by 52 degrees) that are quite close to those of Montségur . . . To the extent that they closely followed this west-east orientation, they saw the summit of Bugarach standing out at the end of their alignment. Solicited in this way, they would have definitively adopted this reference point offered by nature.†

If we accept this theory and also refer to the probable etymology of the name, the *pech* (peak) of Bugarach would be a kind of double of Montségur—unless it was the opposite. In any case there was an obvious

---

* [*Bulgare* = Bulgarian. —*Trans.*]
† Fernand Niel, *Les Cathares de Montségur* (Paris: Seghers, 1976).

and privileged relationship between the Bougres and the Cathars. At this time it is no longer a hypothesis but a certainty: We can very well declare that Bugarach—mountain and village—played a preponderant role in the establishment of the Cathars not only in the Razès region but throughout Occitania. If Bugarach was established earlier than Montségur, perhaps a new hypothesis is in order. It should then be viewed as a central sanctuary, a kind of primitive omphallos around which the heresy evolved. So our search is not for a hiding place for a possible Cathar treasure, but for a sacred mountain akin to the famous Mount Meru, a veritable pole around which the dualist world turned, much like the sacred Hill of Tara was central to the religious options and even the social structure of Gaelic society in Ireland, starting with the druids and remaining so for the Christians. The multiple kingdoms created from the mountain's division reflect their specific features back onto the ideal center.

A strange and little-known work of fiction by a world-renowned author—Jules Verne's *Clovis Dardentor*—can help us understand the omphallos role that Bugarach possibly played. Verne, a Breton native of Nantes, in addition to possessing an unquestionable literary talent and a brilliant imagination, had a passionate interest in parallel or secret sciences, which appears as a constant theme throughout his works, even those that are the "easiest" and most popular. It also adds a dimension of hidden meaning to his more "alembic" novels such as *20,000 Leagues Under the Sea,* which is an initiatory voyage similar to the famous *immrama* of Irish tradition; *The Mysterious Island,* which refers to the myth of the Isle of Avalon; and *The Black Indies,* whose Masonic inspiration speaks for itself. In all likelihood, Jules Verne himself was one of the "Children of the Widow," or a "Son of the Light," if you prefer. And even if he was not an initiate, he spent time with many Freemasons, including his publisher, Hetzel, an extremely peculiar individual named Jean Macé, and his friend Hignard, with whom he traveled in Scotland. Verne was also well informed on the doctrines and practices of the Rosicrucians. His novel *Robur the Conqueror* attests to this, if only by the initials of its hero, R.C.

That said, we find strange adventures in the novel *Clovis Dardentor.* The story involves a treasure hunt undertaken by people whose names are themselves clues.* The quest takes place both on land and on sea in a region called North Africa, which is a transposition of the Razès, specifically the area surrounding Rennes-le-Château. How did Jules Verne know the Razès? Probably through his Masonic and Rosicrucian friends, as well as through Jules Doinel, head curator of the Aude archives, who, under a pseudonym, had published the laying-on-of-hands rite of the Benevolent Knight of the Holy City (the B.K.H.C.), the highest rank in the Scottish Reformed Rite (which also provided significant inspiration to Father Béranger Saunière). Jules Doinel was also the bishop of an agnostic sect that was somewhat suspected of having satanic tendencies. So here we have started anew but with all the same elements. We are still walking in circles around the church of Rennes-le-Château.

But in *Clovis Dardentor* Jules Verne was not simply satisfied with pasting the Razès over the Oran region, spanning the area from Sete through the Baleares. Once his heroes are in Oran, whose name is obviously reminiscent of gold†—which he calls the "Gouharan of the Arabs," bringing to mind the village Gourg d'Auran in the Quillan township— they find themselves at the *Old Castle,* in the *Blanca* Quarter. There is also mention of the Queen's Bat near Mers-el-Kebir, the waters of which have a "clearly saline" aroma with "a slight odor of brimstone." Allusions of this nature are numerous.

What is most important in this novel, however, is the character of the ship captain who transports the heroes of the story. He never leaves

---

* For more on this subject, see Michel Lamy's work, *Jules Verne initié et initiateur* (Paris: Payot, 1984). A profusion of detailed information can be found here, along with very intriguing clues. But the book should be read cautiously, for the author does not appear to differentiate between serious information and the elucubrations of certain zealous fans, which he takes as solid currency without troubling to verify their authenticity. This is really a shame because Michel Lamy deserves all credit for opening broad horizons with regard to an author whose work everyone believes they know so well, but who is revealed to be quite complex in the final analysis.

†[*Or* = "gold." —*Trans.*]

his boat, yet he is the master of the work who appears to direct everything and guide the others. Everyone always strives to find a "good seat at the table"—that is, one near the Captain. And Jules Verne makes explicit that "there is nothing to fear" under his command. "He carries a favorable wind in his hat and he has only to take it off to have a quartering wind." These words are quite clear: It is the captain who knows the way and is master of the winds. So is it any surprise to learn that this strange captain's name is Bugarach?

What conclusion can be drawn from all this? None that is specific, if we are to heed what scant historical veracity there is and resist fabricating at any price things that may not be worth the trouble. But just the same, there are surely too many coincidences for all of them to be mere chance.

The Razès, especially within the quadrilateral formed by Couiza, Arques, Granès, and Bugarach, is a land that breeds mysteries. Everything, or almost everything, is a deceit there, just as in the Brocéliande Forest of Brittany: apocryphal documents; legends imported after the fact; monuments that have been falsified, restored, or fabricated to suit the cause; wild-eyed explanations—all are there. Yes, everything is false in the Brocéliande except for the Fountain of Barenton. It is the only thing that is real without question. But what is its equivalent in the Razès?

In Brocéliande, everything is designed to draw the eye toward the very wide footpaths that eventually disappear completely in the brush. In certain versions of the Grail Quest, the knights searching for the sacred object are sometimes welcomed to castles that have every appearance of the Grail Castle. But they soon see that they are crossing through the enchanted domains of Klingsor—or of Merlin, the master of illusion and, as the representation of the primordial druid, he who knows. If it was necessary to pick one word to describe the Razès, I would say it is a *disorienting* region.

Is this the ultimate snare of the Cathars?

A local legend of Rennes-les-Bains claims that when the rocks of Laval-Dieu turn around, that will be the signal for the end of time. There are many other eschatological traditions like this almost everywhere. But in a land that undoubtedly witnessed the last Cathars of Occitania, the end of time cannot arrive until the final human soul has found salvation. This is when humanity will have regained the angelic purity it lost at the dawn of time, and the stones, having shed the weight of a now-unthinkable Satan, will be able to turn and face the new dawn.

Part 2

WHO WERE
THE CATHARS?

6

Dualism

Catharism is not a religion that suddenly appeared after the preaching of a prophet who, having gathered around him a loyal group of followers, sent them to put his precepts into practice. Catharism is not a "revealed" religion. It is the result of the long ripening of a school of thought that was not specific to Christianity. In fact, while the Cathars were considered to be heretics, meaning deviates from Christian orthodoxy, and were treated as such by the standard bearers of that orthodoxy, it is not at all certain that Catharism can be objectively viewed as a Christian religion. The Cathars contributed numerous elements of their own to Christianity, as well as a certain tradition and texts that must be read anew, but as for being a true deviation from the Christian doctrine, this is still a hard claim to substantiate.

The school of thought for which Catharism was the ultimate expression has existed in every religious system since ancient times. It is dualism: The theory according to which the world and everything related to it in one form or another are the result of a confrontation between two antagonistic principles. This is obviously a simplified definition; in reality things are much more complex, if only in the subtleties contributed by the various concepts of the two principles and in the assessments made regarding the reciprocal action of the two. In this domain, speculations are countless and often contradictory—and according to all the evidence, the Cathars themselves, especially in the thirteenth century, were not immune to these contradictions.

For Catharism does not present itself as a solidly formed religion with a definitive, recognized, official doctrine. Moreover, unlike the Roman Catholic Church, the Cathars had no absolute hierarchy. There were Cathar "churches," but often splinter groups were equal in number to the churches. In the first place, there was a fundamental distinction between those who believed in absolute dualism and those who leaned toward a relative dualism, a distinction that will be clear only when we approach the subject as closely as possible by way of its origins.

It is likely that humanity's perception of the dual nature of life and the world began to be formulated once humans reached a point where they found some freedom from their biological concerns (food, protection, and procreation) and thus had time to reflect on their destiny. This inevitably led to a speculation that could even be classified as metaphysical: The perception of death attested to a necessarily evil principle, from which emerged the idea of a struggle against this principle and an anxious speculation as to what came after. On the surface, death had no justification, and the thought that life and death were two faces of one reality had not yet occurred to humans. They noted only that there was life and there was death, and that these two states were in flagrant opposition, like night and day, hot and cold, pleasure and pain.

All mythologies are more or less echoes of these early metaphysical speculations, and whatever form they take—epic or plastic—they translate the basic assumptions of a tradition into easily perceived images, that is to say into a system of beliefs, memories, observations, and social structures. It is certainly quite hard to disentangle what is ancient from what is more recent in the mythological narratives that have come down to us most often in literary form, which means they have been manufactured, learned, codified, and possibly altered. When speaking of Greek mythology, for example, are we able to determine which narratives come from the Hellenic era and which from the archaic era? Even with regard to Hesiod, who was the first we know of to have displayed the relationship of the gods to each other and to humanity but was also heir to an already long tradition, doubt is permissible concerning the very structure of the myths he presents. In truth, it is the interpretation of the myth that is significant, not the myth itself. Does this imply that the myth is incomprehensible? Absolutely, for it constitutes an abstract entity that, in order to be transmitted, must be materialized in the form of historical events. This is why conflicts, inexpiable wars, crimes, and catastrophes are themes that should not be taken literally but as so many landmarks on an intellectual itinerary.

In Greek mythology, at least in what we know thanks to Hesiod, we can discern the traces of an earlier dualism in the opposition that emerged between Chronos and Zeus. The son, Zeus, rebels against his father, Chronos, then takes his father's place and castrates him, castration being the symbolic equivalent of death. But this conflict existed in a latent state in Chronos himself, for the theme of the father giving life to his children then eating them after they are born is already ambiguous enough on its own. It is Chronos who poses the real problem.

In fact, he holds two contradicting attitudes even if the story maintains that he swallowed his children (meaning he repressed them inside his unconscious) because of a prediction that he would be dethroned by one of them. He is therefore the one who gives both life and gave death, even outside his own conscious intent. It is a much more secret law, the most difficult to express, that gives meaning to this paradoxical attitude, hence the appearance of the notion of Necessity or Fate, to which both gods and men are equally subject. Chronos is thus not all powerful, for conflicting forces are working inside him. Does this imply that the figure of the primordial god (Chronos is not the primordial god in Greek theogony, but this is the role he plays) contains both life and death? We would be tempted to think so.

In any case, it is much more upon this ambivalent attitude of Chronos that the opposition is based than on the War of the Olympians against the rebellious Titans or on the assault upon Olympus led by the giants. This war is only one of the effects of Chronos's duality, which is hereditarily divvied up among his descendants or among those who are consubstantial with him (Chronos is himself a Titan). The same is true in Germanic mythology, according to later but archaistic texts revealed by the Icelanders. The struggle between the Aesir and the Vanir is the result of a conflict emphasizing the inner contradictions of the divinity, contradictions that will be embodied again in the sneaky and almost unconscious rivalry between Odin-Wotan and the enigmatic Loki, which was so magnificently perceived by Wagner in his *Tetralogy*. And although Celtic mythology, properly speaking, does not include a theogony, wars between rival factions of God can also be seen there, if only in those who oppose each other in the Irish epics, the Tuatha de Danann and the Fir Bolg, two successive invaders of the isle of Ireland.

In reality these impressive struggles are only very secondary manifestations. On the one hand, Greek mythology no longer explains the true conflict that sets the two antagonistic forces at odds because the elements have been lost. On the other hand this opposition can be explicitly recognized in the mythological epics of the Germans and Celts, less literary and scholarly than the Greek epics, perhaps, and closer to a tradition that was part and parcel of everyday life.

For the Germans, the world existed only because the gods, having built the fortress of Asgard, kept the giants down. These giants were the forces of darkness who waited for their opportunity to mount an assault against the divine bastion in order to destroy it, and with it, the world. This is why Odin-Wotan sent the Valkyries to human battlefields to gather the souls of the most valiant warriors and bring them to Valhalla (the *Valhöll*). These warriors would form a reserve of soldiers, the necessary rampart to safeguard both the survival of and balance in the world. This balance however is always unstable and subject to challenge.

In Irish tradition, the gods, whoever they were, or the Celts, had to war constantly against the mysterious Fomorians, a very poorly defined people who lived somewhere over the ocean and ceaselessly threatened the equilibrium of the world. Defeated several times in mythological history, the Fomorians reappeared in different eras, a constant presence in the shadows, the unconscious ready to emerge at the slightest display of weakness. Their monstrous appearance made them the equivalent of the giants, but they were something else. They were the power of negation that exists even within the gods, who, without the threat the Fomorians represent, would find it impossible to affirm their own existence.

The difference between the Celtic and Germanic traditions is visible, however, in the hypothetical conclusions of the conflict. In German myth, Odin-Wotan knows in advance that the battle is lost and his actions seek only to stave off the final defeat for as long as possible, to gain time. Germanic eschatology appears rather sinister: The destruction of the world by fire, with the only hope being a later introduction into the tradition, the birth of a new world governed by the mysterious son of Odin-Wotan, the young Baldur, who was murdered through the perfidy of Loki but who will be resurrected. Among the Celts there seems to have been no eschatology: The final battle is avoided thanks to the appearance of a god who stands outside all classes and functions, Lugh, the multiple artisan, who is both Fomorian and Tuatha de Danann, and thus has within himself the two conflicting natures.

But the duplicitous rivalry of Loki and Odin-Wotan, like the double nature of the Celtic Lugh, poses a basic question beneath its anecdotal appearance: How is it that a deity, who by definition can be only perfect, can sometimes be led to commit actions that seem imperfect? In other words, how can a god be both good and evil, even as it is assumed that good, made sacred and placed topmost on the scale of values, is the very essence of this god? All religions, all theological systems have established as a postulate the existence of an infinitely wise, infinitely good god, and it is not comprehensible why all at once this good god may commit evil or at least permit the parallel existence within or by him of an infinitely intelligent, infinitely evil being.

All the theologians and ideologues of every religion, past, present, and future, have collided—or will collide—with this fundamental problem that has haunted humans ever since they became aware of their condition: the problem of the existence of evil. In Genesis the subject is evoked by the Tree of the Knowledge of Good and Evil, and the myth concerning it is quite significant. Before eating the fruit of this tree,

Adam and Eve are happy in the terrestrial paradise. After eating the fruit they realize they are unhappy and are forced to leave Eden.

Translated to the psychological plane, the Fall, whatever its motivations and the reason for the resulting prohibition, consists of a realization. It is understood that humanity lived in a state of perfect innocence *before* the Fall, incapable of distinguishing good from evil. An event then took place: The human being began meditating on his fate and abruptly became aware of a dichotomy; everything changed at that point and it became impossible to remain any longer in the Garden of Paradise. We are told that Adam and Eve were ashamed of their nudity, meaning the reality of their condition. It was an intolerable vision; awakened from their golden slumber they could see that they were imperfect in a perfect universe. Their only remaining choice was exile. The flaming sword of the angel at the gate of Eden is the awareness they then had of their indignity.

But they could grasp this indignity only through its comparison to a higher value, which is the criterion by which an evaluation is always constructed. Adam and Eve, whatever elements these symbolic figures overlaid, *assessed*. And to assess, we must be aware. If they had not assessed anything before, it was because they lacked awareness. Following the abrupt separation from their earlier quietude, they discovered misfortune, suffering, death, and evil. But in discovering evil they also discovered good, which was the souvenir of their earlier condition now projected as an ideal to be attained, a hope for which to live, thus an absolute value with regard to the relative value they attributed to themselves. Taking it further, before the Fall Adam was *one*; after the Fall he discovered he was *two*. It was as if, in the context of a fairly tale, he had uprooted from himself his double, which now took up an independent but parallel antagonistic existence. It is reminiscent of the story of the man who lost his shadow. From the moment his shadow took on an autonomous existence, it no longer had any reason to follow the man who once produced it. But this did not make the shadow entirely independent. Likewise the man had lost an important part of what made him who he was. Things no longer went well for either of them.

The text of Genesis, although it has inspired countless commentaries and interpretation, remains profoundly obscure. It restricts itself to noting that at a moment in human history, men went abruptly from a state of insouciance to a state of anxiety. Men now felt guilty. Guilty of what? We have no idea. But guilt is associated with fault, and fault is indisputable, a violation of something, a violation of a higher reality.

The theme of the Tree of Good and Evil is not the only obscure element in the biblical text concerning the Fall. When we are told that angels, seduced by the beauty of women, came down to Earth to couple with them, thus engendering the giants who inhabited the world before the Deluge, we can wonder, outside of all the rationalist explanations for extraterrestrial intervention, if this story might be a fictional narrative symbolizing the imprisonment of celestial souls in matter, an element that figures prominently in both Plato's and Pythagoras's thought, as well as in the Cathar postulates.

Furthermore, the angels who "knew the daughters of men" were not labeled as such; the text speaks of "the sons of God" in Genesis 6:2, who are absolutely not the cherubim who, in Genesis 3:24, guard the path to the Tree of Life. Angel classification is confusing in the Bible, particularly in Genesis, where the enemy is not even cited. Satan is not the tempting serpent, who is only "the most wily of all the animals of the fields created by Eternal God" (Genesis 3:1). And if we assume the serpent is Satan, we are definitely obliged to recognize him as an animal created by God. But how is it possible that God created an *evil* being?

The official texts remain mute on the revolt of Satan, the greatest and most beautiful of the archangels. And they are equally imprecise on the very existence of these higher beings. The cherubs appear suddenly with no information about what they are. Of course, using the famous Elohim of Genesis 1:2—which many strive to translate as "the spirit of God," despite the fact that its denotative jumping off point is a plural word meaning "the lords"—it is necessary to realize that the Eternal God of the Hebrew Bible is only the first *(primus inter pares)* among a mysterious host of superior beings: archangels, cherubim, and seraphim. After all, didn't the serpent tell Adam and Eve: "If you eat of this fruit, you will be as Gods knowing good and evil" (Genesis 3:5)? And after the transgression, Eternal God utters these ambiguous words: "Man has become one of us by knowledge of good and evil" (Genesis 3:22). Nowhere is Satan designated as the instigator of this fault, and the fault itself seems to be harmless on its own, save for leading to the procurement of the knowledge of good and evil, the prerogative of the Elohim, which they jealously reserved for themselves.

But the Tree of Good and Evil was not the only tree to be forbidden. In the middle of the Garden of Eden there was the Tree of Life, and if we understand this correctly, no one could reach the Tree of Life until he or she had eaten the fruit of the Tree of the Knowledge of Good and Evil. But in his curse, the Eternal God, after deploring the fact that man had "stolen" this knowledge of good and evil, declares: "Stay his hand from the Tree of Life, so that he may not eat of its fruit and thus live eternally" (Genesis 3:22). First, it should be noted for the record that this Eternal God is bad-natured and horrendously jealous, and that he behaves like a rich capitalist who has no intention of sharing his eternity with anyone else. For what pleasure would there be in it if everybody had it?

These verses from Genesis refer back to primitive beliefs held by the Hebrews. For them in fact the human soul was not immortal, and the sole function of religion was to establish privileged relations between humans and God in order to have as long and happy a life as possible. The dogma of immortality and the soul entered the Jewish religion at a fairly late date and is still subject to debate. During the time of Jesus, only the Pharisees and Essenes accepted it. The origin of this belief can obviously be found in Greek philosophy, which itself had been subject to heavy Eastern influence.

All of this boils down to the problem of evil being extremely simplified in the Bible: Jews faithful to the pact sealed with the Eternal God represent good, while other peoples, as well as Jews who are unfaithful to the covenant, represent evil. So discussing who exactly Satan is or what his origin is hardly matters. In fact, whatever name he is recognized by, the figure of Satan is the result of a Persian influence, and the legend of Lucifer the "light bearer," deposed and thrown down into darkness, appears only in the Christian glosses. The metaphysical range of the enemy was, among the Jews, eclipsed in favor of a pragmatic and utilitarian meaning. In an allegorical way, to commit evil was to follow the counsel of the enemy and expose oneself to God's vengeance.

It is true that sociological components were not negligible in the formulation of the concept of Satan, incarnation of absolute evil, because evil is present in everyday life in numerous guises. Poverty, suffering, illness, and death can be only obvious manifestations of this abstract principle that will increasingly tend to take shape—a horrible shape—in the imagination.

But if we accept that the vast majority of people exist in a social framework governed by evil, it is conceivable that the vast majority may have raised certain questions. They were told the gods had created the world and all living things, but in their passivity these people were nonetheless aware of an injustice: Fate does not treat everyone equally, and certain privileged individuals profit tremendously from life while the greatest number work and suffer for the exclusive profit of the former. They grasped that they lived in an evil world, or one dominated by evil masters.

Why did the gods, said to be immortal (the first injustice) and all-powerful, decide that things should be thus? Greek tragedy perfectly illustrates this question: How is it that human beings, even when filled with good intentions, could be crushed so pitilessly by the gods? What's more, these gods seemed to derive pleasure from making men suffer, somewhat like the spectators at the Roman Coliseum, who applauded the condemned forced to fight each other to the death or those who were fed to the lions. This is not so far from Jansenism, which claims that God can refuse his grace even to the just because his designs are beyond human comprehension.

So what is evil and why do the gods tolerate its existence? It is generally accepted that the suggestion of a principle of absolute good immediately leads to the suggestion of its opposite. To our logical thinking, the principle of good cannot be conceived without its counterpart, the principle of evil. The main difficulty is in knowing which one is subordinate to the other, unless they are equals. This is how a doctrine was created that could be described as *dualism*. Over the centuries it would lend its arguments to different mythological traditions and the most varied religious speculations.

Philosophy is obviously inseparable from this. Various contradictory—but often interesting—solutions have been suggested, all of which are completely theoretical. Ordinary religious life, however, requires certitudes rather than hypotheses, no matter how logical and mentally satisfying they may be. In certain cases, evil is accepted as a necessity and it is left to the gods, whose intentions remain incomprehensible, to solve the problem as to why evil exists. This was the traditional system of the Greeks before the arrival of their great philosophers. Earlier, people were content simply to note evil's existence and justify it as the consequence of a misdeed committed at the beginning of time. The audacity of Prometheus, the opening of Pandora's box, the eating of the apple from the Tree of the Knowledge of Good and Evil, the end of the Golden Age, and quite a number of other myths have been the result.

But once philosophical reflection made its appearance, it became difficult to unthinkingly accept the concept of a god dispensing good and evil, even more so because of Aristotle's precise system of logic—to which he gave his name—which postulated the principle of an independent third party thanks to which good is antinomic to evil and vice versa. People refused to believe that evil came out of divine nature, at least directly. It thus became a distinct entity, which led to the opposition of the evil powers that created evil and the powers of good emanating from the true God. Properly speaking, the question is not of two parallel and equally powerful deities, but of two principles the exact origin of which is not defined. This concept of dualism is *false* to the extent that it is presumed these two principles were created by a God, who is unique. But in actual fact, because people eventually came to believe in the personalized existence of these two entities (people made no distinction between an entity and a being; such differences are the fine points of philosophy), it thus became an authentic dualism.

The time came, however, when the dualistic explanation of the world was no longer satisfying and the same problem recurred, namely the impossibility of believing in a perfect God who could tolerate the existence of imperfection. How could a God of good even indirectly inspire evil? To answer that he did so against his will would be acknowledging that God is not omnipotent, as claimed. Thus his responsibility in the matter cannot be avoided. A subtle distinction was then made between *apparent* good and *real* good, which can be best expressed by the old saying, "The road to Hell is paved with good intentions." Reassurance was sought in the determination that God, who is perfect, could create only an imperfect world to avoid humans being gods themselves and thus negating his own uniqueness. This brings us back to the Hegalian idea of an absolute God who is the equivalent of nothingness because he knows he exists only through the presence of others. And in order for him to perceive these as *others*, he and they must be different. Logically their differences cannot make them superior, for then God would no longer be omnipotent, infinite, and perfect. So it is therefore necessary that they be different by virtue of their inferiority—their imperfection or lack of means.

This was how imperfection came to be identified with evil. And because these were abstract, incommunicable notions, they were crystallized into an object: the devil, the demon, Satan, Lucifer. He thus becomes the prism in which all the rays of the black sun converge, and the whole world becomes a battlefield wherein the hordes of Satan and God's angelic legions clash. The human being's only duty in all of this has been to choose which side he will be on. But is this a choice he can truly make?

This is where the question of free will arises. If man is entirely free, he can indeed choose, as Pelagius maintained. But if he is free only in appearance, this choice is imposed upon him by blind fate, as it is in

Greek tragedy. And if man is not truly free, is he truly responsible for his choice? In the case where responsibility is absent, determinism, another form of fatalism, steps into the breach. And this brings us back to the original problem, for the claim could then be made that being forced to commit evil is not the same as doing evil of your own volition. Further, if some people are destined—predestined, perhaps—to commit evil, it is because they belong to a large group of "cursed ones," which must have a leader. Hence the devil appears in his most terrifying guise as the opponent of God's armies.

We are going in circles and find ourselves back at the problematic nature of the Bible in which the "cruel and jealous" God leads his chosen people to conquest of the Holy Land and they massacre everyone they meet en route. Is this evil? Surely not, for from the Hebrew perspective, the chosen people must conform with the Eternal One's master plan. It is *the others* who are the incarnations of evil and a holy war is considered a great good, as has been seen both in the preaching of Mohammed and in history's various crusades, including that against the Albigensians. "Kill them all! God will recognize his own!" This is the Roman Catholic prelate's declaration that human beings are not free and must turn back to God to have a choice.

Yet this is contrary to official Roman Catholic doctrine and, in the final analysis, much closer to Cathar thought. For the Cathars, free will did not in fact exist. But to remedy this, they introduced a new notion, that of necessary reincarnations to purify the self through matter and thus ascend to the Source, next to the Tree of Life, or in the world of essences dear to Plato's heart. This is finally denial of evil as an absolute, for at the end of time, the last soul will have been purified through matter and will have attained the higher world it should never have left. Does this make Catharism a false dualism?

These numerous problems nestled tightly within each other demonstrate the complexity of dualism. In addition, the doctrines colored by dualism contradict themselves in accordance with their own times and according to their adversaries. They have become unrecognizable. In an effort to unravel this tangle, it is preferable to examine certain dualistic concepts that have appeared over the course of the ages in different civilizations. We can note that the so-called polytheistic religions—by the way, there needs to be a re-evaluation of polytheism in light of the social functions embodied by the alleged gods—are much less likely to be at odds with dualism because of the functional distribution of the deity, as opposed to monotheistic religions that are constantly caught up in the contradictions inherent in the unity of divine functions. It is therefore in ancient Persia and within the Judeo-Christian tradition that we need to hunt for the dualists, and consequently the ancestors of the Cathars.

Puivert

Termes

Puylaurens

The Magdala Tower of the church at Rennes-le-Château

The stone column in the church at Rennes-le-Château bearing the date of the church's founding by Father Saunière

Peyrepertuse

Quéribus

Montségur

7

Mazdaism

Mazdaism was the ancient religion of the Indo-European Persians and extended probably from 3000 B.C. until the Hellenic period. This tradition, formed in what is now northern Iran, included both autochthonous beliefs and the numerous traditions from the Indus Valley. The name Mazdaism is recent and was forged from Ahura-Mazda who was god of light in Persian belief. Mazadism has never totally vanished, but rather has melted into other religions and in this way had a healthy influence on early Christianity, especially the heretical sects, along with enduring locally, as can be see among the Parsis of Bombay in India, with their telltale name. As Mazdeans who have undergone a long ripening period, theirs is a doctrine of high spirituality that harmoniously combines archaic rituals specific to primitive Indo-Europeans, a sacerdotal class similar to the Flamines of the Romans and the magi of the druids, and an extremely subtle philosophical system, especially after the reforms undertaken by Zarathustra, otherwise known as Zoroaster.

The sacred book of the Mazdeans, their equivalent of the Bible or the Indian Rig Veda, was the Avesta, a collection of religious and moral precepts, more or less magical spells, mythological tales, and various prophecies. We musn't forget that the only members of a sacerdotal class to have visited the infant Jesus were, according to Christian tradition, the Three Magi, who were guided to Bethlehem by a star. Whether the story is true or false does not matter; this visit of the Magi to the founder of the Christian religion is a symbolic gesture that speaks volumes about the debt owed by the first Christians to Persian religion.

The fundamental precept of Mazdaism appears to be a triumph of dualism. In fact, everything was based on the permanent conflict between two principles: that of good, represented by Ahura-Mazda or Ormuzd, and that of evil, represented by the god Ahriman or Angra Mainyu. These two adversaries were involved in a merciless battle during which each successively gained the upper hand, corresponding to periods in universal history that were controlled either by evil or by good. In short, life was the result of the opposition of these two principles. According to Mazdean belief, however, at the end of time Ahriman would be defeated and sent back to nothingness, leaving the victory to Ahura-Mazda. Thus Mazdean dualism was only a temporary state of affairs that would resolve into a final monism.

This struggle between good and evil is depicted as a struggle between two gods in quite a few religions. The Mazdean concept simplified the problem but did not entirely resolve it, insofar as Ahriman's existence was justified by vague postulates. Furthermore, this god seems to have been the legacy of the ancient religion of the Indo-Europeans before their dispersal, especially before they had settled in the Indus Valley, on the Persian Plateau, and in Northern Europe. Ahriman, in fact, represented the generic god of the Aryans, or that cluster of people we now call Indo-Europeans because of their common linguistic source, their social structures (Dumezil's famous model of a three-class society), and certain technical customs. He can be still seen in some traditions of the Indian subcontinent in the form of Aryaman.

Presented this way, Ahriman was therefore a deity overlying a specific social group, a class of conquerors that tended to maintain its original purity and that was in a position of domination over the other classes, which corresponded to the subject peoples. On further reflection, and stepping beyond a racial context, it can be seen that he was a god of human activity, of manifestation. In comparison to Ahura-Mazda, who represented the absolute, he represented relativity. In short, Mazdean theology was dual. From the public, somewhat exoteric, point of view, it was transmitted as a concrete mythology: the war between two antagonistic deities that justified the turbulent conditions of the world and the instability of all things. But from a more esoteric point of view, it corresponded to a very sophisticated ontology: If Ahura-Mazda were alone, not only would the world not exist, but the god would have no awareness of his own existence. Here was an early representation of the Hegalian concept of the absolute and the relative. Ahriman, who first represented the Aryans, then the whole of creation, was Ahura-Mazda manifested, which is why the world existed.

Of course, given the precarious nature of existence, with its turbulence, injustice, and misfortune, Ahriman took on, over time, more "fire and brimstone" elements and became the one responsible for everything that appeared to be evil, which resulted in Mazdeans responding to life's hardships with a certain lassitude followed by a desire to return to that place from where they had come, the world of essences or ideas. Pushed to the extreme, this becomes the Buddhist concepts of being and nonbeing. We can note this similarity: Being is Ahriman and nonbeing is Ahura-Mazda in his eternal nirvana. This concept is the reverse of the Western conception, and central to it is the question of being: whether we wish to be or not to be. In other words, Mazdaism was much more in tune with the thought of the Far East than the Far West.

We should bear this in mind when trying to understand Catharism, for it is quite obvious that Ahriman served as a basis for the Judeo-Christian Satan. But the Cathars were not content with simply accepting this model; they completely embraced the esoteric meaning of Ahriman and made him the creator of matter, he who dispersed the original energy of the deity throughout an illusory world that needed only to be demystified in order to return to the world of supreme realities, which was that of the spiritual light symbolized by Ahura-Mazda.

Under these conditions, it is not certain that Mazdaism truly qualifies as dualism. Relatively, it was, but the supreme god was still

Ahura-Mazda, whose name means "lord wisdom." This supreme deity, in Mazdean belief, was surrounded by luminous entities, the compassionate immortals, whose depiction exactly matches that of the Judeo-Christian archangels, and who had been given characteristic names: Immortality, Perfect Virtue, and Compassionate Piety, for example. The symbolic element of this supreme god was light; thus all that leads to the light, with fire in first place, was classified in the category of absolute good.

In contrast, Ahriman was depicted as the imperfect reflection of Ahura-Mazda. At one time he took on a caricatured appearance that certainly left traces in Christian folk tradition. The devil in his monstrous, repugnant, and grotesque guise, with his desire to craft a counter world and his reputation in folktales for building bridges from which something is always missing, even if only one stone, is in fact the new image of Ahriman and appears to be in concordance with Cathar thought: The soul is of divine essence and creation, but matter and the body are creations of Satan, imperfect and perishable because the devil does not have the power to create the eternal.

This, therefore, provides a rough but remarkably clear illustration of dualism, which underlies the majority of religions and took on exceptional importance in Western Catharism. The devil was a caricature of God. Ahriman, too, was surrounded by entities who were dark rather than luminous and had names such as Cruelty, Error, and Evil Thought—obviously all the devils that emerged from the medieval unconscious.

This all lead to a normalization of life styles. Morality was necessary because every good action favored the future victory of Ahura-Mazda while every evil action, by increasing the importance of Ahriman, delayed that victory. The choice was clear and it was clearly the reason for the extreme intransigence of the Cathar perfecti.

The duties of the Mazdean believer were threefold: Think good thoughts, speak good words, and perform good deeds. It will be noted that this formulation takes into account three fundamental planes:

thought, which belongs to the domain of the mind, word, which belongs to the domain of the soul, and action, which belongs to the domain of matter and the body. This triad, which early Christians were quite familiar with but which was somewhat forgotten by the official Roman Catholic Church, clearly reappeared in the doctrine of the Cathars.

So there was a precise eschatology in Mazdaism. After Ahriman's definitive fall from power—that is, when he no longer would have any reason to exist (he existed only through the intermediary role of the creatures who followed him, those who do not do good or do it imperfectly)—Ahura-Mazda would proceed to his last judgment and would open the book in which everyone's character had been consigned. Those who had observed the commandments of the Avesta, in other words the whole of humanity finally reconciled with itself, would be welcomed into the paradise of light, the kingdom of Ahura-Mazda. It is impossible to miss the similarities between this and Christian eschatology.

But there are more: The definitive defeat of Ahriman and the forces of evil would be announced by the prophets and especially a messiah, the Saoshyant, or Savior. He would come to proclaim that the time was close at hand and that each individual should make ready for the Judgment Day through prayer and rites of purification. There is nothing of this in Hebrew tradition, and those who continue to be convinced that the New Testament is a sequel to the Old Testament would be well advised to study the Avesta to determine the true origins of Christianity. It was for good reason that Saint Paul of Hellenic Greek culture was considered the founder of the Christian religion rather than Saint Peter the impenitent Jew, who was reduced to a simple symbol of continuity.

As was the case in most ancient religions, Mazdaism at one time included a certain number of sacrificial rites, which lent the faith an aristocratic tendency, for only the rich could afford the luxury of offering animals in sacrifice. But the prophet Zoroaster halted such sacrifice, judging it a cruel custom that only strengthened the forces of evil. This obviously led to a certain democratization of the religion, for henceforth rich and poor were equals in terms of cultural displays. In addition, Zoroaster reduced these displays to their most simplified expressions, and it was this simplification that we find in all religious sects claiming to be dualist, the Cathars in particular.

It is not really known if Mazdeans had temples. The question remains highly debated, but if it did have them, they were located only in the mountains, on the high places where the Persians, according to Herodotus, liked to hold their sacrifices. It seems that the Mazdeans believed, as did the druids, that the deity could not be enclosed in a constructed sanctuary, and that the best means of honoring the sacred and establishing contact with it was to place oneself in the midst of nature, specifically on the peaks, which symbolically connect Earth to Heaven. For the Celts, an ideal location was the *nemeton*, either a clearing in the center of the forest or on the top of a hill—but never inside any permanent construction.

For the Mazadeans who worshiped it, fire was the symbol of both the luminous glory of Ahura-Mazda and the purification through which every created being must pass to rediscover the light of the source. The Greek word for "fire" is oddly connected to the idea of purity. This fire was lit in the open air, on altars—known today as *atech-gah*, meaning "fireplaces," which were most often double, with one slightly higher than the other. Both were cube-shaped, with a cavity constructed on the upper level. In these twin altars it is possible to see an illustration of the primordial Mazdean doctrine of an unending war between two principles. The Greek writer and geographer Strabo declared to have seen similar monuments in Cappodocia, and in them magi who tended a sacred flame.

It is obvious that Zoroaster, who above all else was a philosopher, modified the original Mazdaism to some extent. It is not known exactly when this essential figure of the human intellectual adventure lived. It is likely his reputation was such that he was turned into a legendary hero, but through this we can discern some features of the real man who lived at the end of the seventh century or beginning of the sixth century B.C., at roughly the same time as the historic Buddha lived in India and the beginning of the brilliant Athenian civilization. Herodotus does not appear to have known of Zoroaster, but Plato mentioned him in his *Alcibiades,* and Pythagoras, another semi-legendary figure, was allegedly one of his best disciples, according to Saint Clement of Alexandria. It is thought that he was born in Azerbaijan, in northern Persia, and was killed in the Indo-Greek kingdom of Bactrian during one of the massacres that were unfortunately all too common in ancient history. Legend has it, however, that he was killed by lightning, a death that is obviously more in keeping with the ideal of this inspired prophet. His name, Zarathustra, could mean in the Zend language "gold star," or even "brilliant star," which leads us to believe it may in fact have been a nickname, although modern etymology suggests an actual meaning in the Avestic language closer to "man with the old camels." Zoroaster would have belonged to a noble family by the name of Spitama, which means "whites." This cannot help but bring to mind the generic name of the Venetes of Vannes, a very ancient people of disputed origin who were entirely assimilated by the Celts. Interestingly, the name Celts also means "whites" as well as "of pure race." Whatever the truth may be, this idea of whiteness, light, and purity is in perfect accord with the Mazdean doctrine as well as with Cathar beliefs.

It is generally agreed that Zoroaster contributed to Mazdaism's shedding of its most folkloric elements and that he strove to intellectualize and spiritualize the old myths deservedly honored in the tradition. For example, the sun originally figured among the compassionate immortals or, in other words, was considered to be a completely separate archangel, sort of the direct lieutenant of Ahura-Mazda. But under Zoroaster's influence the sun became a simple symbol, that of the spiritual light and divine purity every human being should attain. Furthermore, Zoroaster codified and organized the ancestral traditions of Mazdaism into a coherent and logical whole. After his death the Avesta, which was placed under Zoroaster's patronage, was rewritten and claimed to provide the words of the prophet, which he declared had been dictated to him by the Great Light. Mazdaism as revised by Zoroaster almost appears as a revealed religion, and in the iconography Ahura-Mazda, who originally was only an incommunicable spiritual entity, became a more comprehensible and anthropomorphic deity depicted as a figure emerging from a winged solar disk.

This depiction seems to have been influenced by the image of Assur, the god of the Chaldeans, and by the worship of the solar disk among the Egyptians. For just as there was contact and intermingling among all the ancient Eastern peoples, there was interaction among their different traditions. This is particularly visible in the contribution made by Mazdaism to Judaism during the time of Jesus. And while Zoroastrian Mazdaism developed primarily in Persia with undeniable success following the prophet's death, it spread far beyond the Persian Plateau. In fact, it existed until the Muslim invasions of the seventh century, meaning it lasted for more than a dozen centuries at least in Persia, a considerable span of time. The famous Magi of the Gospels were priests of Zoroastrian Mazdaism. This tradition has symbolic value due in part to the spreading of its doctrine throughout the East and the valid and enduring influence it left upon every religion that developed in that region afterward.

Because the dramatic concept of this struggle between good and evil was coherent and logical, it could not help but attract adherents, even if the belief were subtlely moderated. Furthermore, just as did the mystery cults that shook up early Greek thought and even penetrated Rome just prior to the advent of Christianity (and whose triumph, incidentally, paved the way for Zoroastrian Mazadism), the final victory of light in Mazadaism emphasizes hope. By separating the evil powers from the good and perfect God, Mazadism provided an explanation of a world that appeared if not inconsistent, at least subject solely to demonic influence. By proposing as the ultimate end the victory of Ahura-Mazda over Ahriman, it also gave meaning to life. The duty of every human being was to work on behalf of the luminous forces to speed the day of triumph and thus benefit from eternal bliss.

During the period several centuries before the beginning of the

Christian era, the East was suffering through a time of complete stagnation as a result of Assyrian expansion. But this stagnation contained a kind of cultural ferment: In a most secret manner, especially in Babylon and Ninevah, the various doctrines were interacting. The Hebrews were held captive in Babylon around 600 B.C., the time when Zoroaster's influence began to spread. We know that this exile marked a point of rupture in Israel's political life, but this rupture was paralleled by a complete religious reformation. New concepts were emerging in the Hebrew tradition. The idea of a messiah whose arrival would announce the end of time had entered Jewish thought, which until that time remained quite vague about any hypothetical savior. The figure of the Hebrew Shatam, very confused in its formulation, began to become more explicit and borrowed the features of the Mazdean Ahriman. Angelogy and demonology made their first appearance in sacred texts, and in what had been an extremely complicated and formal religious ritual a simplification took place, with the ritual taking on more logical meanings. In short, the Jews' captivity in Babylon, thanks to the contacts they had with other traditions, especially the that of the Mazdeans, allowed the refinement of Hebrew thought and the development of a mysticism that appears to have been completely lacking earlier.

But Mazdean influence was just as effective in southeastern Europe, particularly on the Greeks. This was the era when the god Dionysius, who was of Thracian origin but was already half Hellenized, began to penetrate both the religious custom and mind-set in Greece. The adepts of the Dionysion cult, the most important of whom were the priests and wanderers of the Orphic sects, traveled throughout the Greek world asserting that evil was inherent to man's physical body and that this body was a prison for the soul, which was an eternal traveler fallen into a snare in this vale of tears constituting the world of appearances. The only means of escaping this miserable condition and avoiding any future fall into evil's traps was to prepare the deliverance of this soul through asceticism and the celebration of the mysteries. Orphism emerged directly from these preachings as well as from the initiatory legend of Orpheus, who was himself a native of Thrace, the land that later witnessed the emergence of the immediate ancestors of the Cathars, the heretics known as the Bogomils.

It goes without saying that Greek philosophy took into account Mazdean thought. Pythagoras, whether a disciple of Zoroaster or not, expressed the concept of the body as the prison of the soul, and he made numerous speculations that resemble those of the Mazdean magi. Plato, quite aware of what was taking place in Persia and northern India, declared his belief in the lost soul that, having wandered down from the kingdom of the spirit, the mysterious and luminous domain of the higher essences, aspired only to return from whence it came. In the Hellenic world soon dominated by Rome, this became a generalized perception: The world was sick and prey to evil forces. Matter was an inferior creation, but the soul, essentially divine, belonged to another world that was good. In passing from an extremely subtle ontology to a realist philosophy, the primordial conflict between the two constituent principles of the world became an openly expressed dualistic doctrine that allowed men of good faith to find a meaning in life—but not to discover an explanation for it. Intellectual as they were, Mazdean perspectives, through adaptation to the needs of the time and the concerns of men, became a series of practical counsels with an eye to regeneration through liturgy, asceticisim, and renunciation—none of which appeared in Zoroastrian Mazdaism.

This dualism can be seen in a religious system that was in great favor during the High Middle Ages and had spread throughout Western Europe: the cult of Mithra. During the time of the origins of Christianity, Mithra worship was so significant that it would not have required much more for it to have supplanted Christian worship. There was in fact a certain parallel between the Christian doctrine and that of Mithra's zealots, and their basic choices were almost identical.

The name of Mithra was borrowed from primitive Indian (specifically Aryan) theogony. We know for example that the archaic Indo-European society operated around a sacred couple formed by the gods

Mithra and Varuna, the first representing temporal, military, and judicial power and the second representing spiritual and magical power. This corresponds to the ideal image of a social structure depicted in the Celtic world by the druid/king couple and projected upon the divine world as a kind of archetypal model. Janus of the Romans, the god with two faces but also the god of beginnings, offered something similar to this mythological couple.

But the existence of this couple was not the reason that Mithraism contained dualistic elements. There was never any antagonism or struggle between Mithra and Varuna; they were two faces of one reality and the ideas of good and evil played no part with either of them. Mithra and Varuna simply used different means to reach the same goal. In fact, the Mithra of Asia Minor no longer had much in common with the Indian deity; instead he was much closer to Dionysius or Orpheus, to Ahura-Mazda or Jesus Christ.

The cult of Mithra symbolized physical and psychic regeneration through the energy of blood spilled during the ritual sacrifice of the bull; then through solar energy, which was considered the highest form of visible light; and finally through subtle and ineffable divine energy. This regeneration presumed a "fall," a degeneration; living things were considered to be prisoners of an impure and imperfect matter and it was humanity's duty to perfect everything that existed. There was, therefore, a constant struggle between the sons of light against the forces of darkness, a struggle that could rebalance a world that had been thrown into disorder and was prey to physical and moral suffering. The believer was invited to fight with all possible means against the powers of the shadow, meaning evil, in order that truth might triumph and along with it, spiritual purity, the gift of self, and the great universal brotherhood of beings and things.

Mithra appeared as a legendary figure who became the absolute model for human activity. He was the distributor of vital energy, the sovereign of armies, the guarantor of day's purity. He was the *sol invictus,* the "unvanquished sun," he who dies each evening to be reborn each morning. He was the origin of all living things and was also a demiurge. He was depicted as a hero—the one who would soon become the solar, or cultural, hero—who slaughtered a bull, whose blood spilled to give birth to the plants and animals. Sometimes Mithra was seen as a Herculean figure, a human being with a lion's face whose body was coiled within a serpent depicting perpetual rebirth. It was said he was born on a mountain on December 25, several days after the winter solstice, considered to be the rebirth of the sun. It can be seen immediately why the Christians, after some hesitations, fixed the date for Jesus' birth on December 25 and the place of his birth in a cave. Mithra was the son of the Earth Mother, as are all living things. Because he shared the same nature with all living things, he could easily enlist them in his reconquest of light.

But Mithraism remained almost mute on the forces that oppose this reconquest. We gather that it was primarily that which imprisoned the human being within a stubborn egoism, meaning his exile from light. We can note that Mithraism, in contrast to Mazdaism, did not raise the problem of dualism to the ontological plane but only to the physical and psychological planes, which resulted in the creation of a fairly austere morality system. But it did involve a dualism that was also resolved by the victory of light over darkness.

A variant of Mazdaism developed parallel to Mithraism: Zervanism, whose name came from the Persian word for the Greek Chronos, Zervan. It is possible to see in Zervanism the development of an earlier strain of Mazdaism that was not influenced by Zoroaster. In any case, we are attempting to resolve a dualism that was not always very clearcut in Zoroastrian thought due to Ahura-Mazda's essential superiority. In Zervanist conception, Ahura-Mazda and Ahriman were equals, at least at the beginning. One was the principle of goodness and light, the other of evil and darkness. These two figures were in perpetual combat, which explained all the upheaval that took place in the world. But Ahura-Mazda and Ahriman were not the supreme gods; they were emanations of a higher principle, Zervan, which meant "time" in the Zend language—or, more precisely, Zervan Akanara, "infinite time." Some comparisons can be drawn between this Persian Zervan and the Greek Chronos: Both were creator and devouring gods. But Zervan is interesting to the extent that he gave birth to the two principles of good and evil. He therefore contained them both. Thus Zervan was the god of good and/or evil; whether he was one, the other, or both depended on the choice made by those who addressed him. Dualism was resolved in Zervan by the harmonious synthesis of the two antagonistic principles.

In fact, in the absolute meaning, when the supreme god, in this instance Zervan, had not yet created or manifested himself, good and evil coexisted within him in a kind of nirvana where there was no activity but simply passive contemplation. Relatively, however—meaning from the moment the world created by Zervan began to become active—activity was possible only if the two principles were separated from each other so they could collide, somewhat like electricity that does not exist except where there is a confrontation between a positive and a negative current. Prior to this confrontation, electricity exists only as a potentiality.

The absolute Zervan was of course a supreme god before the world's creation because there was nothing opposing him, but primarily he was a *potential* god. And his potentiality served no purpose, according to the Hegelian principle. But when potentiality became *action,* the two components began to move and produced the events of history. These two components, completely antagonistic to each other, were obviously good and evil. According to Zervanism, the world existed thanks only to the perpetual conflict between these two principles. The dualism of Zervanism was resolved by the highest dialectical reasoning. In fact, Zervanism was not dualism at all, for the forces of good and evil were intrinsically nothing but manifestations of a unique totality. Had the proponents of Zervanism given any thought to the ontological conclusions to which their system would naturally lead?

Regardless, Zervanism spread throughout the Greek world. Plutarch, who alluded to Mazdaism, presented it in its Zervanist form.

This doctrine also left a strong imprint on Mithraism and on those other religions that succeeded it, including Christianity. Zervanism is the origin of what would later be called *mitigated dualism,* in which the principles of good and evil essentially do not exist because they are not independent of each other and both derive from a single earlier, sovereign principle. But from the perspective of all those who have professed mitigated dualism, the tangible world, matter, and physical beings are always the work of evil, otherwise known as Satan. This is again what we find in Catharism. But it should be recognized that the Zervanist doctrine was a very skillful compromise between monism and dualism proper, and was, in the final analysis, the recognition of an absolute monism provoking the appearance of a relative dualism.

8

Manicheaism

The early days of Christianity were marked by an astonishing proliferation of sects of all kinds, origins, and opinions. This stems from the fact that this was a time in the Mediterranean region when old values were crumbling and people were beginning to experience deep metaphysical anguish. Rome's official religion was no longer anything but a series of politically motivated rituals, and no one believed anymore in the gods of Olympus, whose foundations had been shaken by Prometheus's excess contribution of rationalism. Greek religion was dissolving into the mystery cults that appeared on both sides of the Aegean Sea. Mithraism had overtaken the banks of the Rhine, transported there in the baggage of Rome's legions. Druidism was seeking refuge in the forests, far away from the great Roman ways in which a policy of persecution was beginning to emerge. And Dionysius invaded the streets of Rome through the introduction of bacchanalias. In this unlikely mix of peoples and ideas, individuals could no longer recognize themselves.

It was at this time that the Christian message began to spread. It had trouble making itself known, and we must note at the very beginning that Christianity was only a tiny sect amid a number of other equally unimportant sects, and that its followers were much less important than those of Isis and Osiris. Furthermore, it would be foolish to present early Christianity as an organized religion that was keeper of a doctrine. Christianity during the first century A.D. was primarily the fairly restrained diffusion of a message. How this message was received depended strongly on social class, place, local custom, and individual need. The dogma was far from fixed, the ritual was quite vague, and the structure was nonexistent. Only local churches that were centered around a missionary—who was not necessarily a disciple of Jesus or an elder (in other words, a priest; the Greek word *presbutos* means "elder" or "old")—were taking hold here and there, especially in Asia Minor. The Jews had been scattered in a diaspora that had ended only recently, and the authorities had a tendency to view Christians as dissident Jews. To complicate matters even further, the distinction between Christians and Jews was not very clear, and apostles such as Saint Paul were vigorously combating the idea of Judaism still promoted by Saint Peter, who claimed that he could not be a Christian who had not first been a Jew. All of this contributed to a confusion the like of which humanity had never previously experienced.

What it amounted to was that the Christian message was interpreted quite differently by different people, and that there was exponential growth, even within what was beginning to be called the Christian people, of a large number of sects, which, once organized, became entirely separate groups that sometimes had no contact with each other. The first consequence of these circumstances was geographical dispersion. The second, which is of no less importance, was that the Christian message was analyzed, manipulated, and finally altered in a number of widely diverging ways. This all took place over the course of several centuries, following Constantine's official recognition of the Christian religion and the Milan Edict, which made it the official religion of the Empire. Subsequently, those not in harmony with Rome began to be treated as deviationists and heretics. Though this was not quite the stage of the Inquisition, the seeds of repression were already planted in the fertile ground in which they would blossom.

Among all the various currents of religious thought at this time, all of which incorporated ancient notions from the so-called pagan religions or even openly borrowed from philosophy, the Gnostics carved out a considerable place for themselves.

What we today call Gnosticism, from the Greek word *gnosis,* meaning "knowledge," was the result of a sometimes tempestuous encounter between three essential traditions: Christianity; Zoroastrian Mazdaism; and Greek philosophy of the Platonic or neo-Platonic schools. While Gnosticism did not in itself constitute a religion, even less a monolithic block, some sixty to eighty schools have been counted that laid claim to this current of thought. There were certainly differences between these schools regarding methods and particular points, but all were connected to a direction of thought that made it a very specific system.

Gnostics refused to attribute to God the creation of the physical world that is the primary cause for the existence of evil. The Gnostics were Christians who remembered the teachings of the Greek philosophers and who, because God could be only perfect, excised evil from divine creation. Besides the immaterial world (the home and kingdom of the good God, which resembles the world of Plato's archetypes) and the tangible physical world (the imperfect work of Satan), they assumed the existence of an additional world inhabited by demigods called *eons,* beings that were half divine and half human. To the Gnostics, Jesus was one of these *eons,* which obviously constituted a heretical declaration, but at that time there was keen debate over whether Jesus was a human elevated to the rank of God or an incarnation of God, and no official position on the matter had yet been established.

The Gnostics' position was above all a position of synthesis: They refused to dig a moat between the evangelical message and the humanist thought of the Greek philosophers and claimed the existence of a continuity in the evolution of the human spirit. They displayed great mistrust for the books of the Old Testament, which they rejected in sum or in part. As far as lived religion is concerned, there was a large variety of Gnostic practices. Some sects recommended the strictest form of asceticism as necessary to achieve total purification, while others based their practice on the assertion that the flesh was a Satanic creation that needed to be burned to total annihilation by experiencing the extremes of physical sensation. This latter concept engendered an entire series of more or less magical sexual practices leading to a kind of debauchery that was vehemently decried by contemporary observers who did not grasp its exact meaning. In fact, this category of Gnostics carried this belief to quite an extreme, but the apparent depravity concealed profound motives that justified their actions.

In any case, Gnosticism was a revolution that allowed historical thought as conceived up to that time to be freed from the Old Testament, which was regarded as the exclusive patrimony of the Jewish people, and as such was suspected of being subject to deviation or alteration, and it allowed freedom from the cold Greek cosmology that claimed to explain the world scientifically. This form of thought, so varied in its manifestations, spread throughout the Middle East and largely dominated Alexandria, which became its veritable capital, as well as Babylon and the majority of the large cities. Gnostic communities gathered together the scholars and sages who represented the intellectual elite of that era—hence the mélange of magic, philosophy, and symbolic mythology that could be found in all the doctrines claiming to be Gnostic.

Gnostic tendencies were soon mirrored in other schools of thought, both neo-Platonic and Pythagorean, which were not part of the Christian world. But Christian churches were not exempt from their influence, and thereby groups evolved that may be classified as heretics, such as the Novatians of North Africa, who required absolute purity of their priests and a complete detachment of any earthly ties that went to the extremes of an impossible disembodiment. The theologians of the time, whom we know now as the "Fathers of the Church," reacted vigorously to divergent or extreme practice, and soon dualism was not only considered one heresy among others but the major and unforgivable heresy.

Manicheaism, a branch of Gnosticism, formed the most perfect example of dualistic heresy while becoming itself a veritable religion with its own rites and specific dogmas. The name has become famous and now designates anything that stems from a fundamental opposition between two principles. For example, it is not rare to hear it said that the themes evoked in a police film or classic Western, although completely removed from religion or metaphysics, are Manichean. The term has come to mean anything that is split or divided, even a very primary manner, into two apparently distinct categories.

The terms Manichean and Manicheaism come from Mani or Manes, a Persian who was born in A.D. 217 in a town in central Babylonia. He was the son of Patek and Maryam, both natives of Persia who in all likelihood belonged to a noble family, the Arsacides, then the reigning dynasty of Persia. We know that his father, who officially professed the Mazdean religion, was a spiritual seeker who had adhered to a Gnostic sect. Mani was thus raised in a milieu whose main concern was spirituality with a particularly Gnostic influence.

What is known of the history of Mani's life is quite confused—the legendary is mixed with the authentic. He is said to have received a divine message at the age of twelve: An angel sent by the King of the Paradise of Light said to him, "Abandon those men (of the Gnostic sect). You are not one of them. You are destined to be a moral example, but you are too young and the time is not right." Twelve years later, the angel delivered a second message: "The time has now come. Make yourself known and proclaim your doctrine to the world." We assume that during those twelve years he had devoted himself to religious or theological study. He then made a voyage to India and on his return made his way to the court of Shappur of the Sassanide Dynasty, which had recently replaced the Arsacides on the throne of Persia. It seems that Mani was well received in this court, which included many well-educated individuals, for he found adepts in the king's entourage and received authorization to preach his doctrine how and where he pleased. It was said that he had even converted King Shappur, and legend adds that Mani pulled the king into Heaven, and that both remained suspended in the air for a certain period of time.

From A.D. 242 to 273 Mani traveled throughout a Persian empire that still bore a strong imprint of the old Mazdean religion. Though his efforts seemed to have gained him an increasing number of adepts, Shappur died in 273, which meant the loss of Mani's primary support. Shappur's son, Ormuzd, certainly continued to assure the prophet of his protection, but his reign lasted only a year and he was replaced by his brother Bahram, who remained entirely faithful to Mazdaism and would not tolerate the preaching of a different religion in his kingdom. The magi, who obviously loathed Mani, took advantage of this to have him condemned. Imprisoned and shackled to the wall of his cell, Mani died in 277. Following his death, his disciples continued preaching his doctrine, carrying it throughout the Middle East and successfully creating a strong church structure that long resisted the attacks of its adversaries, both Mazdean and orthodox Christian.

This church was in no way part of Christianity, however. Mani founded a universal religion by striving to discover the common denominator of all the great religions then in existence. We are well informed on his doctrine thanks to primary documents that have been discovered in Chinese Turkestan and Egypt. Mani declared himself the successor of Buddha, Zoroaster, and Jesus, and while all three of these were prophets who spoke for their respective people, Mani claimed that he spoke for all the people on Earth. He also claimed that Buddha, Zoroaster, and Jesus brought with them only a partial teaching. Each of them held a portion of the truth and knowledge, but integral knowledge was what he, Mani, held, because he was the last link in a long chain, God's final messenger. In contrast to the other prophets who were satisfied speaking their teaching to their disciples, Mani tried to personally write down what God had taught him.

Manicheaism was not only a harmonious synthesis of Mazdaism, Buddhism, and Christianity; it was also a gnosis in that it stressed the importance of knowledge. It is impossible to obtain salvation without knowing; we should avoid "dying as an idiot." This was a key belief in Manicheaism, a doctrine with high intellectual pretensions. The only problematic concept in Manichean belief (also the hardest to resolve) was the contradiction of a divine substance (the soul) existing within a product of the earth (the body) that was considered not only a demonic construction but the initial cause of the existence of evil—a reintroduction of the notion of absolute dualism.

In fact, Mani's doctrine postulated the existence of two eternal and equivalent principles, neither of which was engendered: good and evil, whose simplest representations were light and darkness. But beyond this there was another, more direct assertion: God is good, matter is evil.

This is where the concept became more problematic. It would seem, from this postulate, that everything was straightforward. The view of Saint Augustine, who was a Manichean for a long time before converting to orthodox Christianity and becoming Manicheaism's ardent opponent, is somewhat different. In his *Contra Faustum,* he imagines a dialogue between himself and the Manichean Faustus de Milève. In this dialogue Faustus maintains that there is but one God in Mani's doctrine:

> It is true that we know two principles, but there is only one we call God; we name the other *hylé,* or matter, or, as is said more commonly, the demon. Now, if you claim that this establishes that there are two gods, you would also be claiming that a doctor who treats both health and illness has established the existence of two healths; or that a philosopher discoursing on good and evil, or on abundance and poverty, is maintaining that there are two goods or two abundances.

This discourse is tortuous, but it reasserts that Manicheans, while accepting the existence of two principles, believe in the existence of a unique God. It is all a question of terminology and this terminology has not always enjoyed a welcoming reception by the foes of Manicheaism, as would later be the case with the Inquisitors and the theological adversaries of Catharism.

In fact, the existence of a unique God was not in contradiction with the existence of the two principles of evil and good. They existed within the one God, but were only principles, not deities. Evil—that is, the demon and matter—was in fact an opposition to good, a kind of nonbeing as opposed to being. Evil was only the negation of good, or, as it appeared in Catharism, evil was the absence of good. The difficulty lay in knowing why good was sometimes absent. But there was nothing in this formulation that should have proved shocking to an orthodox Christian, long used to hearing of the tortures of hell, the result of absolute evil, which was the deprivation of God and the opposite of absolute good. The danger in this reasoning is that we can pursue it quite far and claim, correctly to a certain extent, that God may retreat intentionally and, through his absence, call forth evil. This was basically Saint Augustine's position on the issue, which was later further developed by Calvin and Jansenius.

Of course, the Manichean doctrine could not be expressed as we have discussed it here, for only philosophers would have comprehended it. It had to be relayed in the form of picturesque tales that were given substance in such a way that the message could be grasped by the average intelligence. Thus Manicheaism expressed itself through mythological elements. For instance, because good and evil were two opposing principles, they could not dwell together and were thus found in separate regions: Good was located in the north or up high, while evil was in the south or down low. For the sake of tradition, Manicheaism borrowed the conventional images of a celestial paradise and an underground hell.

But this placement, totally symbolic as it was, took on a strange dimension unforeseen by Mani when it was recuperated by ideologues with other goals besides establishing impartial theology. Mani and his disciples did in fact declare that the Father of Greatness, the King of the Paradise of Light, resided in the north on high, while the Prince of Darkness was below in the south. But twentieth-century exegetes, inspired by racist theories and dazzled by Norse mythology, with all its revelations on the subject of whiteness and purity, did not fail to exploit these Manichean themes, most notably with respect to the Cathars and the Grail Quest. Could the Nordics, who rushed—and are in fact still rushing—to the upper Ariège Valley, Montségur, and the Razès, be Manicheans?

Symbols are dangerous to the extent that they are open to questionable and unverifiable interpretations. Strictly on a mythological plane, the Manichean doctrine was simply aiming to use spatial images to make concrete the great separation between opposites. The north is enchanting because it is mysterious, so why not place the supreme kingdom there? Everything is dependent on sociocultural context. Accordingly, the Celts, who oriented themselves by the rising sun, regarded the north as the sinister region, because it was on the left, but this did not prevent them from maintaining that druidism and supreme knowledge came from "the isles north of the world." It is commonplace to fix the throne of higher consciousness in the north. And of course, to the "Nordic" peoples in question, only the south could be the kingdom of Satan—of the semites and the blacks. Up there, in the mysterious kingdom of Thule, God, whatever it is, awaits us surrounded by a host of eons, who revolve under the commands of the *archontes*. We can see here the outline of a militia that has nothing heavenly about it, but which borrows its order from this pure and perfect organization. Below, in the muggy heat of the south, demons bustle around the Prince of Darkness in perpetual disorganization—there can be no order because evil is the negation of everything that takes place on high—during which they massacre each other and are reborn without pause. The myth is entirely consistent on its own.

But all of this leads to a cosmogony. In this chaotic tumult—and at a moment that inaugurates time—the Prince of Darkness abruptly caught sight of the world of light. Could he himself have come from this world of light and have felt some nostalgia for it, as did the Satan described by Victor Hugo, one of the greatest Manicheans ever? This vision of the world high above, a world so wonderful that it could not help but arouse his lust, engendered in him the desire to conquer it. Thus the Prince of Darkness mounted an assault with his demonic troops against the paradise of light.

This attack took the Father of Greatness by surprise. In defense, he created a primal form, the mother of life, who in turn gave existence to the first man, Ahura-Mazda of the Mazdeans. This first man was accompanied by allies who were the five elements: air, fire, light, water, and wind. Ahura-Mazda desperately strove to repel the demons' attack, but he was defeated and swallowed up by the dark shadows below. This was how a piece of divine nature became imprisoned in matter. There is a striking resemblance between this Manichean myth and the Germano-Scandinavian myths concerning both the threat represented by the giants, who were ever ready to mount an assault against the fortress of Asgard, where dwelled the gods, and the great eschatological battle of Ragnarök or the Twilight of the Gods.

However, according to the Manichean myth, all was not lost. First man then addressed God with a prayer he repeated seven times, for seven was the symbolic number for the duration of a cycle. This prayer implored the Supreme Being for deliverance. The King of Paradise then generated several creations, the last of which, the living spirit, came down to the world below, accompanied by the mother of life. Here we can recognize Christianity's influence: the Supreme Being has sent the Holy Ghost down to earth, accompanied by the Virgin Mary. The living spirit then extended his hand to the first man in order to pull him from the world of darkness. This explains and justifies the famous Manichean handshake, which symbolically denoted their elect status.

First man was thus liberated. He ascended back to the heavens above but was forced to abandon the five elements below, meaning, in a sense, that he had left behind his soul. This "soul" that flowed from good and was itself luminous, was soiled by the contact it had with matter. The world was thus organized with an eye to one day purifying this soiled "soul" and reincorporating it by bringing it back up to the paradise of light.

The Supreme Being divvied up the matter that was now mixed with the substance of the divine. The portion that had not been soiled by the darkness produced the sun and the moon, which explains the particular worship the Manicheans rendered to them, for both these astral bodies were considered as sharing divine nature. Another portion that had been soiled, but not entirely, was fashioned into the stars. A third portion that had been entirely contaminated by evil was used in the formation of plants and animals. And finally, as punishment for their unjust attack, the demons' hides, flesh, bones, and excrement became the components of the earth, mountains, and waters.

The demons were thus threatened with forever losing all trace of luminous substance, and not wishing to sink into eternal darkness after their vision of the paradise of light, they concentrated all their remaining luminous energy on the creation of two new beings: Adam and Eve. This explains the birth of humanity: Humans were the remnant of a divine energy that had been collected and concentrated by demons. But the human soul, a divine spark that remained forever, was so enslaved by matter that it lost all awareness of its divine origin. Its natural state was one of eternal ignorance; it had been stripped of knowledge. But the hope of salvation persisted: One possibility of deliverance would be offered humanity. Knowledge was to be granted to it by envoys from the Supreme Being—that is to say, the prophets—the most important of whom were Ahura-Mazda and the transcendent Jesus of the Manicheans, whom they called Jesus the Luminous. The end of time would witness the definitive victory of the King of the paradise of light over the world of matter, which would be annihilated by an enormous firestorm. In this we can note another similarity to Germano-Scandinavian tradition.

This vision of Mani is lacking neither in power nor grandeur. It is a mythology that strove to rationally explain the existence of the visible world and the presence of evil. But Mani had no need to invent it out of whole cloth to achieve this. However real his "vision" may have been, he drew largely from the traditional reserve within his reach, a mythological well to which he added Mazdean structures. He did not go hunting for these myths among the Germans, despite the notably striking similarities. It is more likely that he found what he required in

Persia itself and in its immediate vicinity, the Scythian zone of influence. We know from the works of Georges Dumézil that the mythological narratives of the Scythian people and those of the Germans and Celts are closely related. When Manichean cosomogony is subjected to detailed analysis, curious comparisons are inevitable, especially concerning the Grail legend, and, within this, especially the version that appears in the German Wolfram von Eschenbach's retelling, which is a Persian-German vision of the Grail. In fact it is Manichean, and those Germans who hunted for the Grail in Montségur and elsewhere in Cathar country did so for good reason.

For it is obvious that the Cathars were the heirs of the Manicheans. This also means that Catharism appears more like an *entirely separate* religion than a Christian heresy. What does Christian theology have to do with Catharism's inner purpose? Acknowledging Jesus as one of the Supreme Being's envoys does not exactly conform to the notion of him as the only son of God who came to save humanity through his sacrifice. What is most striking about Manicheaism is its tendency toward an almost complete detachment from the physical—because it was considered evil—that was sometimes pushed to the worst aberrations. Asceticism taken to its extreme ideal means the fastest possible annihilation of our carnal prison—an ideal that leads straight to suicide. Mani did not encourage suicide, nor did the Cathars. However a persistant ambiguity manifested continually over the centuries found its culmination in the famous endura of the Cathars of the end of the thirteenth century.

Far Eastern components were certainly present in Manichean doctrine. If the believer succeeded in detaching himself from the grip of the outside material world and observed the rules of morality, after death his soul would make a triumphant ascent and directly enter the paradise of light—a veritable nirvana. This salvation was principally achieved through a kind of inner illumination that allowed the believer to be convinced of his double nature. Buddhist influence appears tangible here, but in contrast with its doctrine that emphasizes pure illumination of a tangible nature, thus prompting renunciation, the

Manichean doctrine considers illumination from a more intellectual point of view. It is a knowing, a gnosis. Basically, Mani connected to the Gnostic current.

Manichean morality, which advocated aiding individuals to rediscover their original purity, became by virtue of this a morality of inaction, which is ambiguous. The outside world was the work of the devil, and all actions to shape this world, no matter their form, were an encouragement to the god of evil. Further, any material improvement, all civilized progress, any scientific discovery, any new technique all contributed to expanding the power of the god of evil and perpetuating his work. Under these conditions, strict application of Manichean morality would lead to a refusal to live and extinction of the species. Yet it does not seem that the Manicheans went so far as to advocate these extreme solutions.

Furthermore, they made distinctions among their adepts. There were the Pure, or the Elect, and there were the Auditors, or simple believers. The former were constrained to follow a rigid and intransigent asceticism; but the latter lived in the world just as everybody else did. They married, worked, and took part in the social life of their class. Their particular duty was to support the survival of the Elect with whatever this group needed. In this way the Elect were never given any opportunity to sin. This may appear shocking, and it does reveal certain possibilities for exploitation. But every religion has practiced this system to a certain extent. "Work, suffer, and feed us, for we will then pray for you." The Buddhist bonzes and the mendicant orders did exactly the same. Furthermore, the simple Manichean believers seem to have fully accepted this hierarchical system. We find it integrally recreated in Catharism: Only the perfecti were constrained to practice a rigid asceticism, while the credenti, who were able to live in the normal world, supplied them with sustenance.

Of course, only the Pure or Elect could lay claim to entry into the paradise of light after death. But others could cling to hope because, according to Mani's doctrine, all believers reincarnated after death and would do so until they too became Pure in a later life. If, however, they lived a life entirely devoted to the physical, they could be reborn as animals. All of these beliefs can be found in Catharism.

Manichean worship, like the Mazdean worship that preceded it, was reduced to its most simple expression. The Manichean religion seems to have had no recourse to sacraments in the sense that Christianity understands them. The sole rite comparable to a sacrament was that of the imposition of hands, performed when a believer entered the level of the Elect. Through this gesture, analogous to that of Christian confirmation, the believer received the spirit. In this, of course, we see the consolamentum of the Cathars.

Beyond this rite, worship consisted primarily of songs, prayers, and sermons to strengthen the faith of believers and convert unbelievers, and sometimes of very strict fasting that might last as much as a month. There were also public confessions of believers to the Elect and of the Elect to the Elect, and a general confession of the community when the Bêma Feast was celebrated. *Bêma* means "rostrum" and is an allusion to the symbolic rostrum from which Mani had spread his teachings. The ceremony, at which the prophet was assumed to be present, therefore took place before a high dais. In another ceremony, accompanied by song and prayer, Mani's passion and ascension to the paradise of light were commemorated.

The question of whether or not Manichean temples existed remains a subject of controversy. No authentic temples of the Manichean religion have been discovered. But according to Saint Augustine's testimony—no one was in a better position than he to make such statements—the Manicheans had both meeting places and temples, which lead him to make a distinction between the two. It is assumed that Manichean temples were very simply constructed and bare of any decoration. The idea seems to have been that through bareness direct contact with the spirit of light could be made. It is thus permissible to think that these temples were primarily locations selected according to certain criteria that remain quite mysterious but that were connected to light and thus the sun—similar to druidic sanctuaries in totally natural surroundings. This is why people have been able to talk of solar temples and claim that Montségur was once was once a solar site, if not a temple. We do know that the eastern orientation of the fortress matches the average sunrise throughout the year along the Pech de Bugarach.

As we've learned, according to Manichean myth, the sun was what remained of the spiritual substance that was not contaminated by Ahura-Mazda's imprisonment in matter. But, in addition, as in Mithraism, the sun remains the symbol of the most perfect form of spiritual light, just as the cross represents perfect sacrifice to Christians. But let us not forget that the cross, which we find in Occitania as a legacy of the Gallic people of the Volques Tectosages, is a very ancient symbol of solar origin, as are the swastika and the Celtic triskele. Among the Manicheans prayers were always recited facing the sun. All of this makes it is easy to understand why so much effort has been expended to connect the Cathar cult to the worship of the Grail (which is described by Chrétien de Troyes as a vase from which a marvelous light emanates) or to an ancient sun cult that considered the sun to be both a symbol of spiritual light and a visible manifestation of the deity.

Manicheaism thus appeared as a high spiritual doctrine and as an attempt to provide a coherent explanation of a world subject to contradictions, including that of good and evil. The assertion can be made that it was an entirely separate and specific religion. But curiously enough, Manicheaism attracted savage repression during several eras. In A.D. 297 Diocletian gave the signal to commence the struggle against the Manicheans, who were beginning to spread throughout Italy, Gaul, and Spain. And in 389, Theodosios condemned them to death.

Manicheaism as an organized religion did not take long to disappear. Orthodox Christians delivered the final blow. But a religion never really disappears. The ideas take shelter in the shadows and reappear sometimes in new formulations. And because the problem of evil always remains current, one day or another the Manichean solutions would make their way back to the surface.

9

The Bogomils

During the period known alternately as the end of antiquity or the Dark Ages, the widest variety of religious sects appeared throughout the Christian world and its neighboring regions. The dualist theory, which hung on, often emerged through these sects alongside dogmas inherited from every possible tradition. The so-called barbarian invasions and the mixing of populations encouraged these kind of syncretic systems. In the midst of a world that was completely unstable and changing daily, it was quite hard to find sure, universally recognized values as benchmarks. Yet such values were the aim of a desperate search for answers to the troubling questions posed by the world.

The Christian Church obviously appeared as the most capable of assuring this universality of values. But it too was seeking. The dogma it professed remained quite fragile, for it resulted from a series of compromises made among the great theologians of the time, each of whom had his own way of perceiving and evaluating the evangelical message. It was no easy task for them to find a common view in which each could still recognize his own interpretation. It was only when facing those regarded as heretics that the Church could find some cohesion, first to fight off any material threat (the Church began as a secular institution and the stake of its material interests was always a key factor), then to clarify a doctrine that was seen as confused and lacking any unimpeachable foundation.

But the adversaries of the Church were numerous and existed principally within the Church itself, which they accused of being corrupt both spiritually and morally. Foes of the institutional Church claimed, and rightly so, to be reformers and keepers of the truth. To demonstrate this, they based their ideas on every piece of support they could find in sacred texts, philosophical systems, and moral treatises. This was the context in which Priscillian appeared (d. 385), a pious Spaniard who preached an ascetic monastic lifestyle modeled on the hermit tradition that had come out of the East and was beginning to spread. Priscillian had his own interpretation and created his own synthesis by incorporating into his original Christian doctrine elements that seemingly were part and parcel of paganism, ancient druidism in particular. But contrary to the Celts, he believed in the presence of two opposing principles in the world, good and evil, and his doctrine, which gathered adherents for a short time, was eventually revealed to be dualistic.

Around 660, an Armenian named Constantine, whose land was subject to conflicts among different cultures and religions, founded a new sect, the Paulicans, distinguished by the special admiration he displayed for the apostle Paul. For almost a century the Paulicans existed as a group of savage warriors against whom both Byzantium and the Arabs fought. Toward the end of the seventh century their extremely active missionaries reached Bulgaria, where the sect remained quite influential until the twelfth century.

Little is known of the Paulican doctrine because they avoided divulging it to noninitiates and even went so far as to maintain the appearance of conforming to the rules and worship of the Christian Church in order to allay suspicion and avoid persecution. But we do know this doctrine was based on a belief in two antagonistic principles. For the Paulicans, it was the demiurge, meaning the Prince of Darkness, who created the world and all living things. They completely rejected the Old Testament and considered the sacrament of the Eucharist to be a meaningless gesture. The cross, in their eyes, had no particular value, either as the instrument of the suffering imposed on Jesus or as a solar symbol. Despite all this, they sought close ties with Christianity, if only to "infiltrate" it and to discover in the Scriptures arguments in favor of their hypothesis. It was a convenient means to proselytize without becoming overly marginalized, and especially to form a more effective force than if they remained in the shadows. The Paulicians were thereby sufficient in number by the beginning of the twelfth century to influence the policies of the kingdoms in which they lived.

Earlier, along the Upper Euphrates they founded a colony that survived through force of arms in the middle of a land that was, even then, Islamic. Defeated in 878 by the Byzantines, a good number of them became soldiers in the imperial armies, and others were deported to the Balkans. It was here that the Paulicians would find a favorable terrain for spreading their dualistic doctrine.

The Slavs had begun establishing themselves in the Balkan peninsula around A.D. 500, setting up widely scattered and independent colonies. The Bulgarians were responsible for assuring the later cohesion among the different Slavic settlements and imposed their name on the country thus created south of the Danube. In the middle of the ninth century Christian missionaries began spreading the gospel in Bulgaria, which until then had followed a Slavic neo-paganism. But for obvious political reasons, the patriarch of Byzantium, upset at the sight of Rome taking an interest in regions he considered to be under his jurisdiction, sent in his own missionaries. There was thus a declared rivalry in Bulgaria between the Christians who followed the Roman ritual and those who followed the Greek ritual (the schism finally separating the Eastern Orthodox Church from the Church of Rome had not yet occurred), and sects with Manichean tendencies—most of all, the Paulicans—profited from the situation. In this new mingling of traditions and taking into account the region's heteroclite influences—Byzantium was more or less the sanctioned refuge of all the heretics of that time—a new sect made its appearance, the Bogomils.

In Bulgaria during the second quarter of the tenth century, in an inaccessible, mountainous region of Macedonia, a village priest named

Bogomil started preaching before the minor nobility, the lower clergy, and the peasants. He did not advocate revolt against the high nobility or clergy, but instead resignation and a search for peace in the monastic life, the sole means of finding consolation in this world that was base and troubled and at the mercy of the forces of evil. It was this precept that the priest's disciples, called Bogomils, strove to put into practice. Testimonies all concur that in the early days the Bogomils were ascetics and hermits clad in simple garb, who preached humility and compassion and spent much time praying and meditating. They rejected as useless and purely formal the pomp of the Church and all its sacraments, as well as any celebration of ostentatious worship. Most important, they were fiercely iconoclastic, which was not taken as an affront in Byzantium during this time. On a more secular level, Bogomil and his disciples denounced the power and wealth of the various states, which they viewed as vanity and emptiness. That which is veracious, modest, and humble was considered to be in Christ's image, but a Christ who is more symbolic than real, and who can expect nothing from this world but injustice, persecution, and sorrow.

The Bogomil doctrine appears somewhat confused to us because we know it only from their enemies, who did not always agree on the points they were seeking to refute. We do know there were two tendencies existing in this doctrine, one of absolute dualism and another of mitigated dualism.

In its absolute dualism, matter was considered the work of the demon and spirit the work of God. It was thus necessary to reject everything concerning the physical, practice strict asceticism, abstain from any sexual activity, drink no wine, eat no meat, and lead a life of penury and renunciation. Bogomils rejected the cross because it symbolized only cruelty. They refused to accept any organization that was earthly, thus evil, and rejected all hierarchy. This radical position led to complete marginalization, even intense persecution, but Bogomils considered that this should be tolerated and accepted with resignation in imitation of Christ, whom they recognized as model and exemplar.

The doctrine's mitigated dualism reveals more complex thought: In the beginning there was a spiritual world over which God ruled. The Trinity existed within God, with the Son and the Holy Ghost being only appearances of the Father. This constituted a negation of official Church doctrine and earned the Bulgarian Bogomils the name of Monarchiens. But Satan was also considered to be the son of God—the eldest son who had been given the mission of administrating the heavens, aided by a multitude of angels under his command. This is somewhat connected to the Lucifer of Christian tradition and to some of the Grail traditions. Out of pride, Satan rebelled, and was joined by some of his angelic host in this rebellion. However, the revolt of Satan and his angels failed, and they were hurled down from Heaven. It was at this point that they created the earth and a second heaven, the one with the stars, to avenge themselves.

According to this aspect of the doctrine, there was originally but one God and necessarily one principle. It was only following a rebellion that evil appeared on the scene, unleashing the creation of matter. But the doctrine clearly refrained from explaining *why* Satan rebelled. The proponents of a mitigated dualism always collide with this enigma, which they are incapable of resolving. It is clear that a radical dualism eliminates this question by asserting the eternal coexistence of the two principles of good and evil. But within this type of dualism there is no hope of ever getting free: The world will always have the liability of Satan and all religious life is futile.

Returning to Bogomil doctrine, inside this world Satan created a human being out of earth and water. He breathed his own spirit into him but asked God to breathe into this being as well, so that they might have a common bond. This myth is quite bizarre and any explanation for why Satan placed so much value in man being the link between him and God, or for why God accepted this arrangement, is lacking. It will be noted that an embryonic form of this myth can be found in the legend of the conception and birth of Merlin as recounted by Robert de Boron under the influence of the Cluny monks in the twelfth century.

In this telling Merlin, son of a devil and a saintly woman, benefits from the powers of both worlds. But as in the case of Merlin, who, endowed with "satanic" powers, used them for good, there existed in the Bogomil myth a very clear allusion to the possibility that humans, through the gift they received from God, could void the principle of evil and this return to the state that existed prior to Satan's rebellion. Some hope, then, was left for salvation, not only of the individual but of all creation, including Satan himself.

In the Bogomil myth God accepted Satan's proposition and placed a piece of his spirit in Adam and in Eve after she was created. But Satan, in order to gain more power for his creations, encouraged the serpent—in other words, consciousness—to convince Eve to have sexual relations with Adam and procreate. As punishment, God stripped Satan of his divine appearance and took away all his power to create. But he left him free to run the world he had already created.

Here original sin is interpreted as being a work of flesh. It is not by chance, perhaps, that the biblical text says "Adam *knew* Eve." There is a curious connection between knowledge as science or awareness and as sexual relations. For instance, the tree with the forbidden fruit is the the Tree of Knowledge of Good and Evil, thus on a symbolic plane, knowledge of the difference between the two sexes. This can spawn new interpretations of Original Sin, which the Bogomils did not introduce. They were simply satisfied with denouncing sexual relations as a manipulation by Satan for perpetuating his creation. Hence the taboo cast on procreation, at least for the category of believers who have achieved a certain degree of spiritual maturity and sufficient knowledge allowing them to practice chastity.

The Bogomils, like the Manicheans, had two kinds of adepts. The Elect or Pure, who had achieved a higher level, strictly observed all the commandments and prayed seven prayers during the day and five at night. All others were simple Believers who had not yet succeeded in eliminating the temptations Satan had placed within them.

But each believer could become a Pure, an achievement that was acknowledged at a ceremony analogous to one observed by the Cathars and somewhat resembling the Manichean laying on of hands. Somewhat different from the Christian baptism, which the Bogomils categorically opposed and deemed to have no value, it was instead a kind of baptism of the Holy Ghost. This "sacrament," if it can be called that, was most likely conferred following a long period of preparation or initiation. The new Elect had to confess, spend a set amount of time in prayer and meditation, and observe a fast. Following these, in the presence of an assembly of the Elect and Believers, he received the definitive consecration that moved him to the level of the Elect. It appears this ceremony was simply the placing of the Gospels on the new Elect's head followed by the recitation of the Pater Noster while the other members of the congregation sang hymns and held hands.

The Bogomils' metaphysical mythology was accompanied by a belief in reincarnation. While it is not explicitly stated in texts concerning them, as with the Manicheans, this belief cannot be tossed aside because it resolves the problem of the Believers' irredeemable comdemnation. Had they not had the possibility of reincarnating, they would not have had the opportunity to purify their divine spiritual element at each well-lived materialization. Some Bogomil sects who professed radical dualism denied the Resurrection of the Flesh and the Last Judgment. But while it is true that the dogma of reincarnation is contrary to the Christian dogma of Resurrection and the Last Judgment, the Bogomils overall accepted the transmigration of souls, not for the Elect, who would be definitively liberated, but for the Believers, who would have to complete their Purgatory in successive lives on Earth.

Though they were hunted down and persecuted by the Christians, the Bogomils maintained a presence in Bulgaria and around Byzantium for quite some time in regions controlled by the Byzantine Empire as well as those captured by the Muslims. They filtered throughout the Balkans in a westerly direction, especially after 1140, the date on which the Emperor Manuel Comnene took energetic measures against them and their influence in the Byzantium. They could then be found in large numbers in the territories that now form part of the former Yugoslavia, the Dalmatian coast, and northern Italy. They soon infiltrated the Italian cities and began moving toward Occitania and northern France. A document copied in the files of the Inquisition of Carcassonne mentions "the secret of the heretics of Concorezzo, brought from Bulgaria by the Bishop Nazaire." For in the Middle Ages in the West there was no mention of the Bogomils but of Bulgarians or Bougreans, after the country in which they had established their most long-lasting presence.

Did the Bogomils reach Montségur and did they inspire the beginnings of Catharism? There is good reason to see a direct line of descent from the Bogomils to the Cathars. Their respective doctrines offer more in common than obvious points and both sects are dualist. In addition, the name Bugarach in the Razès certainly attests at least to a connection between the Bulgarian and Albigensian heresies if not to the actual presence of Bulgarian Bogomils in the region. Indeed, some monuments discovered in Occitania are irresistibly reminiscent of Bogomil art, if only in the use of the discoid cross. Quite a few of these stone crosses have been counted in Occitania as well as in Bulgaria. But then, there are also such crosses in Sweden, the native land of the Visigoths.

It is difficult to come to any solid conclusion concerning these stone crosses. We know that the Bogomils refused to honor the cross in the way imposed by the Roman Catholics. To them, the cross was neither an instrument of Jesus' torture nor even a geometrical representation of the man Jesus with four branches that are the head, the two arms, and the legs made one by the single branch of the cross on which they were nailed. For them, he was a *living Christ* and not a God who died on an instrument of torture reserved for the lower classes. For them, as for the Cathars later on, Jesus could not be depicted as anything but a living man, his arms spread wide, and perhaps his head replaced by a solar symbol that implies an entirely different meaning. When the Bogomils and Cathars did use the Latin cross, they never depicted the body of Jesus, thinking that such a depiction was somewhat humiliating and base, as did the Protestants in a later time. Among the Cathars, the rosace, signifying the solar Christ, was sometimes used.

While we cannot deny for certain any possible Bogomil influence on some of the crosses discovered in Occitania, why should we strive to see them at any cost as either Cathar or Bogomil symbols? It should be noted that their existence is to be expected in a land ruled by the counts of Toulouse. The four-branch cross inscribed within a circle is part of their coat of arms and is quite old, existing long before the Cathar period. Numerous exegetes have tackled the problem posed by these crosses. Esotericists and hermeticists of all stripes have poured rivers of words over them. Certainly they are intriguing, but if we visit, for example, the Cabinet des Médailles in the Bibliothèque Nationale in Paris to look at the Gallic coins of the Volques Tectosages who occupied Languedoc at the time of Caesar, we would see that a large number of these coins include the famous four branches inscribed within a circle, the mysterious discoid cross. In the Toulouse region of Occitania, it is indubitably Celtic, as archaeologists and numismatics have informed us. In fact, it has nothing to do with the Bogomils or the Cathars, save that it is part of both the Bulgarian and Occitanian cultural heritage. And once again, we should not overlook the Swedish culture from which the Visigoths came.

All of this aside, it appears impossible to deny that contacts occurred between the Bogomils and those who would become Cathars. Their doctrines are too similar, and certain monuments depicting symbols other than the cross reveal, as René Nelli has noted, that "there are between Bogomils and Cathars the same contacts on the plane of figurative symbolism as on the philosophical and religious planes. We naturally cannot claim that the Bogomils invented these themes but we believe that the Cathars borrowed these themes from them."* The argument in support of their contact appears to have been made.

Regardless, however, the doctrine of the Bogomils is itself essentially

---

* René Nelli, *Le Phénomène cathare* (Toulouse: Privat, 1964), 188.

an original mélange representing a serious effort to realize a reformed Christian morality in this world and a dualism that was first lived in daily life before becoming a dogma:

> Bogomilism is very closely related to the extraordinary heretical movement of the West and brought to it the dualist teaching. But Bogomils and Cathars are not absolutely identical. The West is in no way a carbon copy of the East, and neither are its heretics— which, for the most part, it persecuted—simple copies of their Eastern counterparts. The teaching, the Scriptures, the missionaries might come from the East. But heresy in the West, since the beginning of the millennium, had laws and a face all its own.*

We should in fact distrust appearances and avoid superimposing upon each other cultures that are vastly different in origin and essence. If similarities are evident and real between two different religious approaches, it is not automatically implied that one has been derived from the other.

While the East had a great number of heresies, the West was certainly not lacking them. There were countless discussions in councils and everywhere else; new ideas inspired movements that lead sometimes to the formation of sects and sometimes only to preaching of no consequence. The great fear of the year A.D. 1000 only encouraged small-time prophecy, and something of this fear remained in everyone's mind, even though they knew the end of the world was not scheduled for the next day.

In the first years of the eleventh century, a peasant returned home from his fields one day, chased out his wife and, after having broken the crucifix in the church, refused to tithe the priest and instead made eloquent speeches repudiating the books of the Old Testament. He soon found adepts among the peasants, but finally abandoned by everyone,

---

* Arno Borst, *Les Cathares* (Paris: Payot, 1974), 65.

he cast himself down a well. Was he crazy? Some very familiar elements of the Bogomil doctrine can be recognized in his madness.

In 1019 an important group formed in Aquitaine contesting the power of the cross, baptism, and marriage, and refusing to eat certain foods. In 1022, on the outskirts of Toulose, heretics with mysterious teachings gathered from various Western regions. A Perigord peasant attracted some noblemen and several priests of Sainte-Croix d'Orléans with his preaching, and they would carry the good news to Rouen. What they allegedly proposed for reforming the Church were quite simply Bogomil theories. To them, matter was impure and marriage, baptism, confession, and the Eucharist should be rejected, as should the ecclesiastical hierarchy, so-called pious works, and prayers. "True Christians,"they said, lived on celestial food and the believer was purified by the imposition of hands. Condemned to the stake by King Robert II, they went to their execution smiling and endured their fate like men confident of going directly to the paradise of light.

Heretical examples of all kinds abounded in this era. The former Provencal priest Pierre de Bruis traveled through the south of France, declaring that it was necessary to demolish churches, burn crucifixes instead of worshiping Christ's torture instrument, and pray anywhere, even in a stable. Pierre de Bruis was burned in 1126. In Flanders it was a lay priest named Tanchelm who unleashed his wrath against the Church, which he contested had become a veritable brothel. He claimed that every human being is as close to God as Christ himself is, because every individual possesses the Holy Ghost and is the bridegroom of the Virgin Mary. During the same era, a former Clunisian monk, Henri the Heretic, an extraordinary orator, performed his missions in southern France. He raged against the Church, and after his inflamed sermons his adepts, who considered him an angel from Heaven, profaned churches, burned crucifixes, thrashed priests, and forced monks to marry, generally with prostitutes, who would then subsequently have to lead an honorable existence. In Brittany, the strange Éon of the Star considered himself "he who will come to judge the living and the dead."

He gathered a group of faithful and went on to pillage churches, castles, and monasteries, after which he distributed among the peasantry some of the riches he had gained. His activity was centered in the Brocéliande Forest, not far from the famous Barenton Fountain. His adepts called Éon Lord of Lords. He maintained that he had magical powers, sometimes using them on strangers, and he claimed that he would judge by fire the world God had entrusted to him. His scepter was in the shape of a Y. When the two branches were pointed toward the sky, it meant that two-thirds of the world belonged to God the Father. These same two branches pointed toward the ground signified that two-thirds of the world belonged to Éon. Of course, Éon of the Star played on the homophonic likeness of his name with the *eum* from the liturgy *(Per Eum qui venturis est judicare vivos et mortuous)*. In 1148 he was hauled before a council presided over by the pope and was condemned to prison, where he died. Was he crazy? We should note the undeniable connection between his name and the *eons* of the Gnostics, those demigods who ruled over the intermediary worlds.

In fact, the majority of these heretics were visionaries, sometimes of good faith and often convinced that they would achieve deep reforms in a Church that set an example that was far from perfect. They all sought a certain barren lifestyle within a world where injustice flourished and the wealth of the few stood out starkly against the poverty of the overwhelming majority. They all collided headlong into a strong opponent, and all ended up either burning on the stake or languishing in prison.

These, however, were not intellectuals. The arguments they advanced were of a great simplicity, if not completely elementary and perfectly obvious, and they had nothing to do with theology. But the time had come when a heresy could not endure if it was not based upon a dogmatic *corpus*. This corpus is what the Cathars would bring.

10

The Cathars

It was in the twelfth century that the Cathars truly made their appearance in Western Europe as representatives of a specific sect, rather than as Bogomils. They were in fact no longer Bogomils, having in some way been transformed into something different, for while the Bogomil heritage is important, it does not constitute the sum total of Cathar beliefs and practices.

Catharism, however, did not present itself as a coherent, organized system encompassing all spheres of religious life within a traditional framework. Nor was it the point of contact of heterogeneous sects thrown together by the accident of history. It was instead a vague linkage of lived experience and aspirations that, little by little, became condensed into a dogma and moral practice. The unity of Catharism resided in the commonality of experiences that, in the beginning, were only attempts to give a profound meaning to life in an incoherent world scarred by evil.

The foundation of this spiritual experience was obviously the irremediable contradiction between man's pure soul and the evil world. In the different schools of thought that made up Catharism, mainly the radical dualistic position and the mitigated dualistic position, there exists the same postulate to stumble upon: In the beginning there were two principles, that of good and that of evil. From the principle of good comes all that is light and spirit; from the principle of evil comes all that is matter and darkness.

These words were part of a profession of faith made by Florentine

Cathars. It is clear that the Cathars picked up the dualistic theme of the Manicheans and the Bogomils. But the part of the story that has never been truly explained or resolved is the fall of the angels. Why did Satan rebel, dragging with him the other angels (some say *all* angels), which are now human souls imprisoned in matter and subject to imperfection and evil?

The Bogomils spoke only of revolt as the reason. The Judeo-Christian tradition leans toward Satan's pride, the sin against spirit. These explanations are quite vague. The Cathars, while not saying so, returned to Genesis 6:1–3:

> And it came to pass, when men began to multiply on the face of the earth and daughters were born unto them, that the sons of God saw the daughters of men that they were beautiful, and they took them, wives of all that they chose. Whereupon the Eternal One spoke: "My spirit cannot endure forever in man, for man is of flesh, and his days will number one hundred twenty years."

These verses are far from being clear. They no doubt come from an archaic tradition that was no longer understood very well at the time of Moses and thus their position in the chronology of Genesis was moved. But the essential point is that the sons of God, meaning angels, were seized by lust. It remains to be known just what these "daughters of men" were in the reality of the myth, for it is obvious that in the Cathar view, this fall of the angels could have taken place only before the creation of the world.

Moderate Cathars recalled, as did the orthodox Christians, that the handsome and good archangel Lucifer had been taken advantage of by an evil spirit. But with this affirmation, they are maintaining an absolute dualistic position, posing the existence of evil itself. The radical dualists provided a more logical explanation: Satan/Lucifer rebelled against God out of jealousy, but did so by himself and was therefore repelled. But he wished to avenge himself and attract the other angels, so he waited thirty-two years at Heaven's gate and then hid within God's kingdom the following year to secretly extol to the other angels his treasures, particularly the charms of females. The curious angels did not know what a woman was, so Satan brought them one whom he had just shaped—who may be the Lilith of Jewish tradition—and presented her to them. The angels, inflamed with wild lust, broke the sparkling celestial vault and fought at Satan's side to ensure his dominance over the paradise of light. But their bodies were overwhelmed and their souls fell. This is all very reminiscent of the combats described in Indo-European cosmogonies, but the Vanir who attack the godly Aesir in Germano-Scandinavian mythology are not natives of the divine world; they have come from elsewhere. Furthermore, following this inexpiable war, the Aesir and Vanir make peace and form a single group, which was not the case in the Cathar myth. Only the adventure of Prometheus, the Titan who rebels against the other Titans of Olympus, presents certain similarities to the fall of the rebel angels, and it ends with Prometheus shackled upon Mount Caucasus.

According to the Cathar myth, nine long and heavy days and nights descended from the heavens, thicker than blades of grass or drops of rain, until finally God, full of wrath, took note of what had transpired and made the decision that never again would a woman pass through the gates to Heaven.

Here a fairly anti-female sentiment is quite visible, which is somewhat surprising given the numerous women among the Cathars, including many Perfects, who took their faith to the limit. We can interpret the nine days and nights as days by the world's reckoning, meaning centuries as they were spoken of in the Vedas (one of Brahma's days corresponds to four billion years) or by modern science's understanding of them as the Paleozoic Age.

To make sense of the Cathar myth, we must turn to Genesis 1: 6–7:

God said: "Let there be an expanse in the midst of the waters, and let it be a dividing between the waters and the waters. And God created the expanse, and he divided the waters which were under the expanse from the waters which were above it. And it was so.

The nine days and nights that fall are comparable to drops of rain and blades of grass. They are referring in fact to this famous separation of the waters of Heaven from the waters of Earth or, in other words the creation of a different space that will be the domain of Satan. It turns out that these mythological notions are somewhat in tune with modern scientific observations. In fact, the position of the earth some ninety-three million miles from the sun places it almost at the center of a zone where temperatures permit water to exist in a solid, liquid, and gaseous state. This zone is quite small, only about 2 percent of the solar system. Man's existence appears linked to two conditions: water in all three forms and universal gravity—which says something about the importance of water in mythology. It is not a coincidence that water plays an essential role in all religions. But what we primarily need to retain from the Cathar myth is that it makes the fall of the angels coincide with the appearance of life on Earth.

Of course, the myth resolves nothing, and it is satisfied in posing insoluble questions. How did the rebellious Satan manage to gain entry into Heaven? Did God know—was he informed of what had taken place? Was God an impotent bystander or did he *want* evil to exist? How could the angels sin if evil was not within them? What is sin? The strong point of the Cathar myth is certainly not logic. But the same can be also said of Genesis.

The conclusion remains that the demon created all things visible and perishable, among them the human body, while God created that which endures, the invisible and the incorruptible human soul. The moderate Cathars then added another detail: When Satan had finished creating the world with his defeated angels, God sent to the earth an angel who had remained loyal to him. This was Adam, whom the Cathars claimed as their direct ancestor. This angel was unfortunately captured by Satan and forced to assume human form, but because he existed in this form involuntarily, he would ultimately be saved, and all his descendents with him.

In other versions of the Cathar myth, Satan painfully attempted to breathe life into the inert forms he had created, which went on for thirty years. But the bodies he had made from mud dried in the sun; the water in them—in other words, the blood—evaporated. God, who knows all, ordered the angels lurking in the world below not to sleep during their stay there. Of course, the angels succumbed to sleep and Satan seized them and introduced them into the lifeless forms he had shaped.

As a variation of the principal myth, this version is tightly connected to it. It does involve, in more ontological language, the capture of the divine archetype by the human archetype, but this cannot be presented without sexual overtones. The sleeping angels were subject to nocturnal concupiscence. (Incidentally, in certain Cathar texts the constellations were viewed as perpetuating lust at night. This cosmic lust is called *coitus* in astrology.) On a more psychological level, and in a medieval context, we find here the famous belief in incubi and succubi, those male and female demons who take advantage of humans' sleep in order to couple with them at night. Merlin the magician is a perfect example of the product of such a union between a demonic incubus and a human woman. It goes without saying that beyond the introduction of incubi and succubi, we may note certain erotic physiological reactions during sleep that lead to those nocturnal emissions against which all good Christians are put on their guard.

Another important reason to consider this version of the Cathar myth is that it provides evidence for the bond between the human being and the cosmos. The human body may be made of mud, but the soul is angelic and belongs to the world above. All human behavior was considered a constant quest for balance between the gravity of matter and the lightness of the celestial element that animates it.

A problem, however, still remains unresolved: How could a soul that is naturally subtle, heavenly, and immaterial have been caged so easily in a heavy, coarse human body? The Cathar supporters of absolute dualism offered a solution to this question. The angelic soul, which is definitely a prisoner of the human body, has left its angelic body in Heaven. The angelic being that has become human is thus torn, separated. He will inevitably long to quit his body of flesh to rejoin his angelic body. The solution is a skillful one, for it explains the human being's need for spirituality, his innate transcendence. But the same radical Cathars imagined a third component to what was becoming a prime example of dialectical reasoning: There is, they maintained, a link between the body and soul of the separated angel: the spirit, which floats between Heaven and Earth, searching for the soul it recognizes as its double. When it finds it, enlightenment immediately results. At this moment the human becomes *cathar*, meaning "perfect," and because he is no longer separated from himself (which is the meaning of being sexual), he no longer experiences any sexual desires or lust and finds himself ready to reenter Heaven.

We find here the triune notion of our existence: Human existence is due to the three principles elements of body, soul, and spirit, whatever particular meaning each is given. This explanation has the merit of offering a solution to the problem of the Resurrection of Jesus.

We know through recent scientific studies that the famous holy shroud of Turin did in fact once envelop a deceased tortured man. This is beyond question. Currently, scientists of all opinions who have examined and analyzed the shroud have come to this observation: A corpse was wrapped in this grave cloth, but it was never unwrapped, and the cloth no longer contains the corpse. This implies that the corpse was able to remove the shroud without unwrapping it. Make of it what you will, for it defies all natural laws and the most current definition of logic. The scientists have drawn no conclusions, nor is that their job. But if we return to the Cathar hypothesis according to which the angels captured by Satan left their bodies in Heaven, we may assume that Jesus, who was only an angel to the Cathars, came down to Earth not enclosed within a carnal, demon-spawned body, but within his celestial body.

The status of Jesus Christ was fundamental to the Cathars: The place and essence of Jesus was actually the point on which they were most radically at odds with other Christians. Generally speaking, they did not consider him to be the Son of God, or the Son of Man, or the cornerstone of the Scriptures. His role between the primordial Fall and the return to Heaven was no more meaningful than his life: He was a preacher not a savior. The radical dualists claimed that Christ was an angel who, unlike the fallen angels, had no connection to sin, meaning the carnal body. Hence his Resurrection—which was thus not really a resurrection—and ascension to Heaven. As for Mary, she was an angel and not the mother of Christ in the carnal sense of the word. Jesus was content to *enter through Mary's ear* and take on a human appearance devoid of any carnal weakness. This is the famous theme of fertilization through the ear, meaning by the Word, that can be found as well, oddly enough, in the Celtic depiction of Ogma-Ogmios, god of strength and eloquence.

The moderate dualists took this notion of Jesus' appearance in human form as their own. For them, God was nevertheless the creator of matter, and they were not opposed to the incarnation of Christ. From their point of view, the angel Christ was made man in Mary and was stripped of his fleshly body upon his ascension. The Resurrection could therefore be considered real.

But the Cathars do not seem to have found agreement on the figure of Jesus. That he came to Earth, some said, showed that he too had sinned and was subject to all human weaknesses. Others believed that he had appeared on Earth in a physical guise, but in reality with his angelic body. There was even a suggestion that there were two Christs leading a parallel existence. The earthly Christ who died in Jerusalem was no doubt evil, and the licentious and adulterous Mary Magdalene, whom he defended, was undoubtedly his concubine. The true Christ, however, the celestial Christ who neither ate nor drank, was born and crucified in an invisible world. Strange concept. The assertion of the existence of an earthly Christ who was the sexual partner—or husband—of Mary Magdalene inspired, much later, strange stories centered around Rennes-le-Château and the church dedicated to her there.

According to obviously unverifiable stories, Mary Magdalene, wife of the earthly Jesus, moved to the Razès region with her children—thus with the children of the earthly Jesus—who united with a Frankish line to become the ancestors of the Merovingian lineage.* Cathar mythology sometimes leads to mysterious domains.

Ultimately, the real issue is knowing what Jesus—terrestrial or celestial—came to do on Earth. Some said that having himself committed sins of the flesh, he had to perform penitence for his misdeed and at the same time redeem the crime of all the other angels. Another theory claimed that the sacrifice of Jesus on the cross served no purpose; it was simply a mythological event, and while Jesus was crucified on Earth, Satan was crucified in Heaven. Dualism was always capable of meeting a challenge and eventually conceived the idea that Jesus and Satan were both sons of God: the good son and the bad son. It is this opinion that the restorers of the church in Rennes-le-Château preferred by presenting two images of the infant Jesus on either side of the altar. But as time passed, the Cathars were increasingly likely to accept the orthodox Christian doctrine stating that Christ was both human and God. It should be said that from so much discussion on the subject, which led to the emergence of so many varied and bizarre opinions, they no longer knew where they stood.

In any event, all Cathars, whether radical or moderate, accepted that Jesus bore a message and that he showed the way of renunciation, a way that was truly necessary to assure salvation. While the fall of the angels constituted the departure point of the Cathar doctrine, the return to Heaven and the complete liberation of matter were its clearly expressed supreme goals. Thus the human being lives on this earth to pay penitence, to expiate his rupture from God, and to win back his angelic status. On this point there is no divergence among the different

---

* See M. Baigent, R. Leigh, and H. Lincoln, *Holy Blood, Holy Grail* (New York: Delacorte, 1982).

currents of Cathar thought, which leads to an eschatology and the formation of a morality.

Human beings are the descendents of fallen angels and are thus angels themselves, either by heredity or by the transmigration of souls. The radical dualists arrived at this proposition: "My soul is the soul of an angel that, since the Fall, had transmigrated through numerous bodies as if through numerous prisons." The moderate dualists claimed that these multiple generations of soul and body would continue until the end of time. Only the perfecti were spared the need to reincarnate; their souls waited in a kind of temporary paradise for the Judgment Day when God would separate the good from the wicked. But on this point the moderate dualists themselves divide into two camps, for some claimed that time would not end until all souls had been saved. Radical dualists maintained that the liberated souls of the perfecti would immediately enter Heaven, while the soul of the person who was not yet a perfecti would have to reincarnate until completely purified. Radicals also visualized the possibility of reincarnations into animal form as punishment for a dissolute life, for example, or for lack of effort toward purification.

The end of the world would thus be a terrifying experience for the moderate dualist. The earth would be the victim of fire unless it was transformed into a fiery hell or simply decomposed to its state of divine chaos. Here again similarities with Norse mythology are evident. But the radicals asserted that nothing on Earth would change once Heaven had attained the final number of reintegrated souls. We see from all this that the eschatological vision of the Cathars was rather confused, and that as it evolved, it incorporated the eschatology of orthodox Christianity—but this in no way invalidates the Cathar's fundamental doctrine.

Their concept of morality was much clearer, more precise, and much simpler. It started from the perception that there existed only one sin: a rupture with God. All specific errors were simply particular forms of this sin. The sole problem lay in knowing whether this first sin was committed voluntarily or involuntarily. The moderate dualists supported free will; the radicals denied it. But both sides were in agreement that the person who refused to belong to this world thereby demonstrated that he or she did not in fact belong to this world and was thus not dependent upon Satan. To a Cathar, therefore, to sin was to submit to the world. There was no distinction between venal and mortal sins; all sins were mortal.

This is how the Cathars appear to have taken an original position in the context of sexual relations. Every sexual union involved the flesh and ran the risk of prolonging Satan's work indefinitely; therefore it was a sin. Under these conditions, sexual relations in marriage were no better than those that took place outside of wedlock. There was not a bit of difference between them. It was for this belief that the Cathars were accused of laxity and permissiveness. Actually, they made no distinctions between legitimate and illegitimate unions, free love, homosexuality, adultery, incest, or even bestiality. But their accusers should have been able to recall that in the early days of the Church, which was heavily influenced by Saint Paul and the other Church Fathers, the same concept existed. It was both the need to ensure the survival of the species and the need to take into account basic human nature that eventually caused the Roman Catholic Church to preach tolerance of marriage while at the same time reducing it to its procreative role and considering as anathema all other forms of sexual behavior. Again it should be specified that the Church only *tolerated* marriage. It was not the Church who wed the couple. It was not the priest who joined them. *It was the couple themselves* who effected the union, who conferred upon themselves the sacrament of marriage. The priest was there merely in the capacity of a witness, to record the act. Contemporary Catholics, completely intoxicated by the moralistic speeches of the clergy, no longer take into account this reality, which, it needs to be said, represents a beautiful piece of hypocrisy on the part of the Roman Catholic Church.

In any event, this seeming laxity among the Cathars was not evidenced by the deeds of the Perfects, for they observed strict continence. They had attained a stage of spiritual development that no longer permitted any weakness. It was a different story, however, for the simple credenti. Because they were too strongly attached to the physical world, they could still either marry or form free unions. In fact, in certain Cathar groups it was almost preferable to have sexual relations outside of marriage; because such unions were not intended for the purpose of procreation, they amounted to the committing of only one sin instead of two. It is easy to see how that line of thinking could inspire excesses which the Inquisition did not fail to denounce.

The perfecti had many other obligations in addition to continence. They were required to abstain from any foods that came from generation: meat, which was diabolical flesh, was strictly forbidden. But they also stayed away from cheese, eggs, and milk. Curiously, fish was tolerated because, according to Cathar belief, fish were not the fruit of generation but instead were spontaneously produced by water. Both fish and wine, however, were avoided on fast days, when people had to content themselves with bread and water.

Another major prohibition according to the Cathar precepts, at least for the perfecti, was that against killing under any pretext. This ban extended to animals, who might, under the doctrine of transmigration, contain the souls of certain men and thus certain angels forced to be reborn as lower life forms because of sins committed in a previous life. This was taken to quite an extreme, for disavowed as well were any acts of self-defense that might kill or even wound an aggressor. The Cathars were staunch partisans of absolute nonviolence. The death penalty was viewed as murder because the punishment and execution of evildoers was God's business and not that of the pope, the emperor, or any king.

This prohibition created many problems for the Cathars, especially during those times when they were heavily repressed. During the Albigensian crusade, while the perfecti never took up arms, numerous credenti, who were not compelled to scrupulously observe this ban, took part in combat and even committed assassinations, such as that of the Inquisitors in Avignonnet. But most often it was mercenaries and unconverted sympathizers who assured the defense of the Cathars, as was the case at Montségur in 1244. Further, it is likely that the Templars, whose role was officially very discreet during the Albigensian crusade, intervened in their favor on the battlefield on certain occasions. The Cathars' adversaries in fact claimed that the Templars were the secular arm of the perfecti.

Beyond these prohibitions, Cathar morality broadly coincided with orthodox Christian morality and that of the majority of the other heretics. The essential point was not to forbid certain actions but to show that they retarded or even prevented the process of humanity's return to its angelic origins. The greater a Cathar's awareness of his or her angelic status, the more he or she avoided opportunities for sinning. Cathar morality was unique in that it did not issue edicts made up of negative rules. On the contrary, it was a positive morality encouraging perseverance in the quest for purity. This is the aspect that attracted men and women who were met with the Perfects' example. The Cathars were numerous, proof that this example was convincing and that their moral example was satisfying.

In addition, their extremely simple religious ritual attracted the faithful who were satiated with the abundant ceremony of Roman Catholicism. As with the Bogomils and all other dualists, the rites observed by the Cathars were kept to a strict minimum. They involved prayers, songs, fasts on certain weekdays, and, most important, sermons. The perfecti were held to be above all men of the word. It is probable that the sermons were followed by discussions in which all those in attendance could take part. The prayers and sermons might take place anywhere, outside in the woods or in other completely natural surroundings, in castles, or in private homes. With all due respect to the fans of mystery who view Montségur as a Cathar temple, a Manichean temple, or even a solar temple, it does not seem that the Cathars had temples. As was true of certain other places, Montségur played a distinctive and very symbolic role, perhaps as a spiritual "pole" much like Mount Meru in India or the Hill of Tara in Ireland. But it cannot be considered a temple proper, through this in no way diminishes the importance of this incontestably sacred site.

Like the Bogomils, the Cathars rejected the sacraments of the Roman Catholic Church, including baptism. Because they considered all humans to be angels in a "dormant" divine state, the Cathars believed they had only to perform a ritual gesture to allow them entry into the divine community. It was each individual's responsibility, they believed, to become aware of this "dormant" status and put it right. They of course rejected marriage for the perfecti and were satisfied with a vague marriage ceremony—which at that time had to be Catholic to be considered official, for there was no secular civil authority—for the credenti. This meant that in the eyes of the Inquisitors, the married Cathar credenti women were considered concubines. Finally, without accepting the sacrament of penance, the Cathars practiced a kind of public confession. The perfecti confessed their faults before an assembly of perfecti and credenti, somewhat similar to the practice of the Manicheans.

One sacrament, if we can call it that, that was practiced by the Cathars was the famous consolamentum. It appeared in two distinct forms depending on the set of circumstances. There was the consolamentum given to a Believer who thought himself worthy of the rank of perfecti and wished to enter that group. The new perfecti had to commit to respecting the rules binding those who claimed to have attained a sufficient degree of wisdom and purity. This was an act of extreme gravity, for an individual could be received by the perfecti—or *don* himself—only once in his life. This explains the rigor, austerity, tenacity, and faith of the perfecti and their tranquil acceptance of death when they were condemned to burn at the stake. To deny their faith was forever to deny their consolamentum, to regress and risk finding themselves in an inferior position in a future incarnation.

Another form of consolamentum could be conferred upon credenti by perfecti on simple request, but only when a Believer found himself in danger of dying. It was somewhat equivalent to the baptism that any

Christian can administer to any unbaptized individual who is threatened by death. But this consolamentum had no lasting value; though it could be bestowed several times, depending on circumstances, it was rendered invalid in the event the individual survived.

In both forms of consolamentum the ritual was identical. The credenti was asked if he wished to become perfecti and devote himself to God and the Gospel. If he answered affirmatively, he was asked to promise that in the future he would abstain from all forbidden or frowned upon foods, that he would no longer devote himself to sexual congress and no longer lie and curse; and that he would never abandon the Cathar community, even out of fear of death by fire, water, or any other means. Once these promises had been made, the candidate recited the Pater Noster, the only acceptable Catholic prayer and reserved only for perfecti because it was viewed as the prayer spoken by the angels before the throne. It was used, however, in its heretical version: Instead of *panem quotidianum* (daily bread), the Cathars said *panem supersubstantialem* (bread beyond substance) because to them material bread was only a diabolical construct, like everything else in the world. After this recitation, the perfecti laid hands on the new Elect and placed the Book, without a doubt the Gospel, on his head. Finally they gave him an accolade and the entire congregation prostrated itself before him.

There was another very distinctive rite that we know of because of the siege of Montségur in 1244: the *convinenza*. It is a variation of the consolamentum used in the event of war, should soldiers be mortally wounded and lose the ability of speech. Before leaving for battle, they would agree with the perfecti that the consolamentum be administered to them without having to make the usual promises and without reciting the Pater Noster. But this convinenza seems to have been an unusual exception.

There remains the practice of the endura. The Cathars had such a pessimistic conception of the world that their adversaries did not hesitate to present them as candidates for suicide. Logically, men who believe they are angels imprisoned within a physical casing could be tempted to cut corners to escape their prison by the quickest means possible.

Furthermore, the courage they exhibited when faced with death, even by the horrible means of fire, and the hunger strikes some of them began while incarcerated in the dungeons of the Inquisition, could lend credit to the hypothesis of some sort of ritual suicide. But there is not a trace of any belief in suicide in the Cathar doctrine. Suicide would actually have been an obstacle to the process of purification that occured through penitence and the endurance of suffering in this world. But the practice of the endura does remain mysterious.

Found only among the Cathars of the fourteenth century, it was not an ancient practice. Thanks to the files of the Inquisition, we know that the heretics, principally women, meditated in endura, that is, entered a state of prolonged fasting, even to the verge of death, ordered by the deacon of their community. The fact seems to be proved historically. There are also examples of Cathars going into the mountains in the middle of winter and allowing themselves to die of hunger and exposure. But this practice was limited to the beginning of the fourteenth century and only to the region of Ussat-les-Bains and the upper Ariège Valley. We know of no examples elsewhere, and none in earlier times when the Cathars were strongly organized. No doubt the endura should be viewed as one final, desperate manifestation of the Cathar faith at a time when it was a foregone conclusion that Catharism was a lost cause. This has not prevented some of our contemporaries who claim to be twentieth-century Cathars from emphasizing the endura as an authentic ritual, even to the point of advocating it and making it one of the most important elements of the doctrine. We should recall that the famous Otto Rahn, author of the book *The Crusade Against the Grail* and an incontestable Nazi who vanished mysteriously in 1939, was credited with having performed the endura in the mountains on the Austrian-German border.* The sacred

---

* Christian Bernadec has advanced arguments that because Otto Rahn was of Jewish descent, which was viewed as an abomination and as incompatible with his S.S. membership, he did not commit suicide but was instead taken away by his superiors to emerge later under a new identity.

aspect of this well-known form of suicide, practiced, for instance, by elderly Inuit who have outlived their usefulness to their tribe, has fueled numerous legends.

The endura reveals, in any case, that around the year 1300 Catharism was on the road to extinction and that each group who had managed to escape the Inquisition at that time led an autonomous existence. There was no longer any cohesion among the scattered Cathars. However, this cohesion and unity was significant at the end of the twelfth century and beginning of the thirteenth century. The Cathars formed dioceses within which, beyond the large mass of credenti, there were perfecti, the Elect who claimed to be the sole Cathars or, in other words, the Perfects. But among these perfecti were some bearing the title of deacon, who were most likely charged with special responsibilities, in particular preaching among the populace in order to seek converts or among the credenti in order to strengthen their faith. There should be no misinterpretation of the word *deacon,* however; the Cathars rejected any sacerdotal hierarchy, even the idea of priesthood. It was only due to of contact with orthodox Christians and because of the necessity to oppose them more effectively that they borrowed a vague hierarchical system from the Church, for it allowed them to coordinate their efforts and organize their defense against repression.

Normally, it was the credenti and perfecti gathered in a single congregation who selected those who would be entrusted with responsibilities. Certain Cathars lived in isolation as veritable hermits, and these individuals did not share in community life. Others who generally lived in towns were therefore established as deacons. It was from their ranks that preachers, sages, and theologians were recruited. They were in some respect the spiritual guides of a community, but the congregation of perfecti was also charged with the election of a leader responsible for a diocese. He was given the title of bishop, but this was nothing more than a convenient name. If the bishop did not perform his duties satisfactorily, the congregation could revoke his title and choose another in his place. In this way he was at the service of the entire

Cathar community but had no right to sacerdotal prerogatives. He was only the first among equals, and only temporarily, depending on circumstances. The bishop was chosen in a somewhat democratic fashion and could be assisted by two coadjutants, a major son and a minor son. If the bishop died, the major son would succeed him, as long as the community had not selected another bishop. In this way a cohesion was maintained, unthinkable at first glance, within groups of men and women of different origins who sometimes professed divergent ideas, groups that were totally accepting of free discussion and never refused contradiction. We cannot attribute this to tolerance; it is rather out of a concern for a constant search for truth that the Cathars left the example of men and women of a great piety and intellectual honesty. But this was also the reason they constituted a danger for the Roman Catholic Church. The Church considered them a bad example for its faithful, as did the Capet monarchy for the populations it was seeking to draw into its sphere of influence.

So they had to disappear, by any means necessary, which is exactly what happened.

Part 3

THE CATHAR
ENIGMA

11

The Cathars Among Us

It is commonly believed that Catharism died when Montségur was taken and the pyre was lit, when 205 perfecti* perished, unwilling to renounce anything, knowing they were purified angels certain of entrance to the paradise of light. This is a reality. Following the tragedy of Montségur, the Cathars were scattered or fell victim to the dreadful claws of the Inquisition. There were obviously sudden bursts of renewed activity during the following century; such a religion based on profound and unshakeable convictions will not disappear in the stroke of a decision made by a court, even an ecclesiastical court. But normal wear and tear played a role in their demise, as did terror. The royal Capet adminsitration put into action by Alphonse de Poitiers, brother of Saint Louis and husband of Jeanne de Toulouse, had spun its gigantic web over all of Occitania. From 1321 to 1335 there were still numerous condemnations for heresy, but they were beginning to be less common. Ultimately, at the end of the fourteenth century, after the first tragedies of the Hundred Years War, the Inquisition no longer operated in Cathar territory, proof that the heresy no longer existed.

But this may be difficult to accept, for we know religions always leave behind traces. Nonetheless, Catharism simply disappeared as an organized and practiced religion. Druidism followed the same scenario after Caesar's conquest: Forbidden from teaching, the druids first

---

* [All credenti who would not renounce his faith would, with that gesture, become perfecti. —*Trans.*]

sought refuge in forests and other inaccessible places, but their disciples became increasingly rare and eventually they melted into their surroundings; they became integrated into new ways of thinking and new modes of spirituality; they became Christians. It is easy to imagine that an identical fate met the Cathars. Deprived of their teaching and cultural gatherings, scattered and dispersed in hard-to-reach places, they eventually lost all means of recognizing their fellows and melted away into an era that no longer lent itself to speculation on the fall of the angels. This does not mean that the Cathar spirit was dead. Just as the Celtic druidic spirit remained fairly vital in medieval civilization—even within Christianity, especially in the churches of Ireland, Britain, and Brittany—the Cathar spirit seems to have maintained its permanence in a large part of Occitania. Generally speaking, the Occitains have always displayed a bias in favor of heresy. In the sixteenth century a large number of the populace brandished the standard of the Reformation, and the history of Occitain Protestantism covers almost exactly the same regions where Catharism had a lasting influence. This is not to say that Protestantism was the heir to Catharism—that would be a false conclusion—but that Protestantism found in this region favorable soil for its own development. Furthermore, certain points of detail indicate not that Protestantism descended from Catharism, but instead that the two share a common source in the depths of the ages, if indicated only by the famous Hugenot cross, which is the Occitain cross over a dove. It is difficult to deny some more or less vague connection among the symbolism of the Hugenot cross and certain Cathar motifs.

But this connection concerns only epiphenomena, which is why it is appropriate to consider with extreme circumspection the numerous testimonies and pseudo-testimonies that have been published over the last century on the survival of Catharism in the regions of Montségur, the upper Ariège Valley, and the Razès. When we meet an individual who, in all seriousness, claims to be one of the last Cathars, it is hard to take their claim at all seriously. I have personally met so many individuals who are absolutely convinced that they are druids and say so quite loudly, wearing outfits that are more colorful than authentic, that I feel qualified to talk with any member of any sect, even one that existed before the Flood. The druids disappeared long ago, but since the end of the eighteenth century, more or less, esoteric groups have reinvented druidism, its doctrine and its ritual, even though in all honesty we know next to nothing about these matters. The "druids" of today, who are quite numerous, are in reality neo-druids, and whatever their sincerity or true motivations, it is impossible to acknowledge any actual connection between them and the druids of the past. Some of them are perfectly aware of this and will say so openly and honestly. Unfortunately, others are lacking such scrupulousness, and while their wild imaginations impress an audience eager to believe, they shout loudly that they are authentic druids—inspired by Heaven, of course. There are even those who, with no respect for the sacred and no sense of the ridiculous, perform their grotesque ceremonies surrounded by polystyrene menhirs. They have formed hierarchical druidic orders dressed in white, with bards dressed in blue and ovates dressed in green. The truth is that in no Celtic language we know is there a distinction made between blue and green; one word always serves to indicate both colors. So how can this dress code be genuine?

I imagine it is much the same today in Cathar Occitania. There must currently lurk a certain number of Cathars on the winding roads that cut through the passes and follow the valleys between Ussat-les-Bains and Rennes-les-Bains. Are these authentic descendents of the original Cathars? It is a question that I will refrain from answering. These new Cathars have one advantage over the neo-druids: They can always pride themselves on reincarnation, which the druids did not believe in. A contemporary Cathar can logically claim to be the reincarnation of a Cathar from the past, which would be doctrinally appropriate, something an individual claiming to be a modern druid cannot take advantage of, unless he fantasizes about transmigration of souls (and some have not hesitated to do this).

It would be more honest to speak of neo-Cathars. The link to the

Cathars of the fourteenth century has long been broken, and any attempt to reform Cathar worship could only be neo-Catharism. This was, incidentally, the intention of Déodat Roché, the reformer of Cathar studies in Occitania, whom René Nelli said was "much more cautious, and much more philosophical" than the majority of apprentice treasure seekers and Grail questers who have been swarming in the region since the beginning of the twentieth century. Roché did not give credence to all their wild imaginings, but he did believe in the *ideal* existence of a Pyrenees Grail.

Déodat Roché was born in the Aude in 1875. Interested in philosophical inquiries from an early age, he had first sought in ancient traditions, then in the Manichean religion, for the links leading to Catharism, which he sentimentally considered to be the very spirit of his native Occitania. He had made his career in the magistracy, but once freed from his duties, he moved back to live in Arques in the Razès—the territory where the mysterious tomb identical to the one in the Nicolas Poussin painting is located—and it was under his impetus that the Société du souvenir et des études cathares was founded. This organization would develop into an invaluable instrument of scientific research on Catharism, even after the death of Roché. It made no secret of its intention to rediscover the sources of Catharism as well as its visible and invisible extensions. But this was all done both with a respect for scientific methods and with the caution, even when the organization might have put forth bold theories.

Déodat Roché directed his personal quest toward what he believed was an initiatory path consisting of the substitution of certitude for faith, thanks to spiritual exercises that opened up horizons of which the vast majority of people were unaware. In this quest, he based his efforts on the philosophy of Rudolf Steiner, a fascinating and inspiring figure who had founded the School of Anthroposophy following disputes of an intellectual nature with the Theosophical Society. We should be grateful to Rudolf Steiner not only for his very real gifts and his inner

---

* [The Association for the Remembrance and Study of the Cathers. —*Trans.*]

vision, but for his great honesty, which caused him to insist on the utmost scrupulousness. He had not approved of the vexing tendencies of the Theosophical Society to accept straight off all so-called secret doctrines and the submission of theosophists to the traditions of the Far East. He claimed that the West had its own tradition and all that was required was to find it again. We can see that Déodat Roché, a product of this school of thought, had the intention of contributing to the understanding of the Western tradition by studying Catharism and restoring some if its relevance. Roché, who, like Steiner, was convinced that everything lies within, labored for the renaissance of Catharism in so-called occult circles, in the mind of the public at large, and in the region itself in a way that was extremely useful. By virtue of this he deserves the admiration and respect of all who are honestly seeking to learn who the Cathars were.

Such is not the case, however, with Antonin Gadal, president of the Ussat-les-Bains Tourist Bureau and a modest retired teacher who had been heavily influenced by theosophy, a doctrine this former agnostic did a poor job of assimilating. Certainly he was in love with his native region and ready to do anything to place it in the spotlight with no thought of his own material benefit. He was also one of those unrepentant dreamers of whom René Nelli speaks.

Antonin Gadal was born in the Sabarthes, in the upper Ariège Valley, where caves hold the memory of so many bygone eras. In his youth, before World War I, he had made the acquaintance of Adolphe Garrigou, who had devoted his life to archaeological and scriptural research on the Cathar question. Enthused by Garrigou, Gadal became his zealous disciple. But he was not satisfied with simply researching, exploring caves, and speculating on medieval Gnosticism. He "invented" the Pyrenees Grail based on several vague studies of Wagner and *Parzival,* and published both a biography of Adolphe Garrigou and a kind of historical novel on Cathar initiation that he pulled from his imagination. He later published a work entitled *De l'heritage des Cathares* in which he explicitly names those he feels are the modern heirs of Catharism: the Rosicrucians of Holland, who are currently known as the Spiritual Church of the Golden Rose + Cross. The extraordinary poet Maurice Magre had already connected the Rosicrucians to the Cathars and claimed that Christian Rosenkreutz, the founder of the Rosicrucians, was a Cathar initiate who had been taught by Albigensian refugees in Germany. Outside of the fact that Christian Rosenkreutz is a mythical figure, this connection does not have anything that is *a priori* absurd. This is why there is a rest and meditation center of the Golden Rose + Cross in Ussat-les-Bains.* The members of this philosophical society even today see their role as continuing the work of Antonin Gadal, who died in 1966, and carrying on the Cathar legacy. They have formed a Gadal Museum in Ussat and never miss a chance to pay homage to the memory of the "faithful and tireless revealer of the Cathar mysteries," the "beloved brother," and "old servitor of the previous fraternity."

This is very telling regarding the role played by Antonin Gadal. He was not content simply to dream but was compelled to share his dreams with others, and thereby contaminated an incalculable number of naïve souls who, despite the most objective archaeological findings, have taken part in a gigantic operation of mystification that borders on outright dishonesty and is, at the least, obvious intellectual dishonesty.

Once in this mode, people began to see Cathars everywhere. Cathar graffiti were discovered in every cave and every castle. Even the Grail has been discovered. Christian Bernadec laughably recounts how one day he brought Antonin Gadal some fragments of pottery dating from the end of the Bronze Age. Gadal then made a long speech to him about these "precious fragments confirming that the Cathars celebrated their worship in this place. After crossing through the symbolic and sacred wall in procession, [the Cathars] came into this nave. In each niche hollowed

---

* This society has nothing to do with the more important Rosicrucian group of the A.M.O.R.C. [Ancient Mystical Order Rosae Crucis —*Trans.*] whose very official seat is located in Eure.

† Christian Bernadec, *Le mystère Otto Rahn* (Paris: France-Empire, 1978), 34.

into the walls there was an oil lamp or candle."[†] That is what he would like to think. Bernadec adds that Gadal "always had the same attitude: complete disdain for the texts that contradicted his exaltations."[*]

Antonin Gadal seems also to have passed on to his disciples his disdain for texts. Christian Bernadec also recounts an anecdote he heard from his own grandfather concerning Joseph Mandement, who was president of the Tarascon-sur-Ariège Tourist Bureau (which at the time included Montségur and was rival to the bureau of Ussat) and also an ardent seeker of the Cathars but little disposed to indulging delirious fantasies:

> One day, Mandement had caught red-handed a young German who was drawing fake "authentic" Cathar carvings, at Sainte-Eulalie, I believe. It did not turn out at all well for the bloke. A short while later he found himself in the hospital in Sabart. Mandement had punched him right in the nose. This did not stop him from writing a book on Montségur and the Cathars once he returned to Germany. His name was Otto Rahn.[†]

This story reveals how seriously we should take Otto Rahn, an author whose work has inspired so many vocations on both sides of the Rhine. But we should render unto Caesar his due: Otto Rahn would never have written a word without Antonin Gadal, who was his initiator and primary informant. This only increases Gadal's responsibility for the diffusion of pseudo-revelations on Catharism and the Grail. Christian Bernadec, although he denounces the deceits of Antonin Gadal, whom he knew in his youth, cannot help but display a certain indulgence toward him and defines him as a "poet" in order to excuse his conduct.

This is an insult to all poets who claim to create nothing other than poetry. Gadal claimed to be an archaeologist, historian, philosopher, and spiritual reformer. I never knew Antonin Gadal personally, but I

---

[*] Christian Bernadec, *Le mystère Otto Rahn* (Paris: France-Empire, 1978), 110.
[†] Ibid., 11.

have read everything he has written. It requires a stout heart, incidentally, to read his work because his mind is so muddled that it is necessary to attack each text twice to follow the thread of his bizarre reasoning. All of Gadal's writings, widely distributed by his faithful disciples after his death, concern Catharism and the actual presence of the Grail in the Pyrenees and are fully stocked with diverse observations on heretical or simply esoteric sects scattered throughout the world.

Having studied these texts attentively, I can say that there is, in my opinion, not one line worth remembering. Each is an inextricable blend of stupidities pulled from who knows where and presented any old way, most likely in the order they came to the author's mind. The citations he sometimes uses are truncated or incorrect. He has never read a medieval text or any Celtic work. He does not even have a full knowledge of Wolfram von Eschenbach's *Parzival*, the keystone of the concept of the Pyrenees Grail. He knows *Parzival* only through the vague fragments cited by other authors who have few scruples about the exactitude of their sources. Gadal could have read the excellent translation of *Parzival* by Ernest Tonnelat but that would have risked ruining his personal fantasies. So he mixed episodes from Wolfram's work with those pulled from other versions of the legend, which he likewise did not take care to read. There exists a very good translation of Chrétien de Troyes's *Perceval* by Lucien Foulet, as well as two acceptable transpositions of *The Quest for the Holy Grail* by Albert Pauphilet and Albert Béguin. But these likely posed too many dangers to his theories.

In addition, he displayed a total misunderstanding of even the most elementary archaeology and could not tell the difference between a novelist and a historian. He claimed to be restoring to honor the spirituality of a dualistic doctrine, but he never posited the basic problem of dualism and did not have a clue about metaphysics and theology. His naïveté was so great that he believed pebbles worn away by time to be Cathar talismans and would likely have believed that the moon was made of green cheese.

It would be appropriate to classify him once and for all as a good tourist bureau president. He managed to lure crowds into his small domain; this is sufficient for his glory. Unfortunately, Antonin Gada remains the primary person responsible for all the wild imaginings that have been uttered or written about the Cathars and the Grail over these last fifty years. Was he manipulated, like Father Bérenger Saunière at Rennes-le-Château, by the Theosophical Society during the thirties, or by the mysterious Thule Group? This would not excuse everything, especially his delusion regarding the analogy between his name and that of Galahad,* the discover of the Grail, or the ridiculous monument—named the Galahad Monument—erected in Ussat-les-Bains. While I don't mean to be malicious, I cannot help but feel that Antonin Gadal profaned both the Grail and the Cathar spirit by putting both within reach of so-called intellectual and spiritualist groups, all bearing the imprint of the most dubious kinds of racist ideologies.

That said, it is not by chance that over the last one hundred years so much interest has been expressed in the Cathars and what they represent, and in the secrets that are no doubt somewhat too hastily attributed to them. It seems that the Cathars have something to say to us and it is this "something" that has motivated all the research undertaken by historians, philosophers, and archaeologists as well as by serious occultists and crackpot prophets. The fact that the Cathars were persecuted makes them sympathetic at first glance, aside from any esteem for their doctrine. We have at present acquired if not a sense of real tolerance (that is still a long way off), at least an acceptance of the plurality of opinions, and it seems to us that any repression in the realm of consciousness is an attack on the dignity of man.

On the other hand, ever since the Enlightenment there has been ceaseless denunciation of the dictatorship of the monolithic churches over the spirit. The example of the Cathar repression finds itself among

---

* He made his name an anagram of Galahad [Galad in French —Trans.]. But he clearly never realized that the figure of Galahad is completely absent from the German version of the legend upon which he claimed to base his wild ravings.

these denunciations. At once, without even questioning the deep motives behind this repression, hasty construction of a monument to the Cathar faith has been undertaken, for the sympathy they inspire, like that felt for all who are persecuted, has a tendency to transform itself into unconditional admiration.

We should not delude ourselves, however: The Cathars, whether they called themselves perfecti or the Pure, were neither better nor worse than any of their contemporaries. Among them could be counted exceptional men and women who distinguished themselves by their faith as well as by their charitable spirit or intelligence. But deeper probing will reveal brutes, profiteers, and fakes as well. Certainly they denounced the turpitude of the Roman Catholic Church that was quite visible during the twelfth and thirteenth centuries, including the hypocrisy of the priests and their immorality. They no doubt were right to do so. But the Inquisition often accused them of things that we would rather pass over in silence. There were all sorts among the Cathars, just as there were all sorts among their adversaries.

We should not forget that a society organized in the prevalent style of the twelfth and thirteenth centuries, based on the structures of an active, conquering monarchy and those of a very deep-rooted Church, could tolerate the Cathar model no more than the Romans could put up with the Celtic model that threatened to destroy their own social structures. The refusal of the world and thus the works of the world, which the Cathars preached and practiced, constituted a danger for Christian society that threatened to topple it. It was therefore understandable that the Church and the Capet monarchy would put everything to work to destroy what they called a heresy. Is this such a shocking declaration? From the perspective of the twenty-first century the Inquisition is an indefensible monstrosity. In the context of the thirteenth century it was fully justified and the people who vigorously took odds with it were precisely those who risked falling into its clutches.

Could we ourselves be potential "clients" of an Inquisition ever ready to be reborn from the still-glowing embers of a weakened Church, or of any church claiming to hold the one and obligatory Truth? There is such a possibility. In fact, heresy seduces us because we all feel somewhat heretical. This is why we feel so much sympathy for those who were victims of the pyres. But they are crocodile tears we are spilling. They interest us because they represent our subconscious tendencies: to dive, as Baudelaire said, to the depths of the unknown in order to find something new there. But Baudelaire was careful to specify: "Hell or heaven, what does it matter?" The unease of the last one hundred years, the metaphysical anguish that has seized us ever since physicists first admitted they do not know what matter is, the collapse of traditional values once thought eternal, the more or less conscious millennium fever that still has us in its grasp at the dawn of the twenty-first century—all combine to give us the feeling that we are close to heretics of all stripes. After detecting an emptiness in ourselves that the official churches—both religious and secular—have not managed to fill, we are striving to discover its cause and especially how to fill it. And because we have the sense that over the course of history men and women have been eliminated for bearing other answers, it is to them we turn to for help. They might know something that was if not forgotten, at least scorned and concealed.

Every era attempts to rediscover the past. Every era devotes itself to a re-reading of tradition. This is the way human progress declares itself. We believe we have the duty to overlook nothing from the past, and therefore we closely examine everything exiled from official thought. Such is the case with Catharism. And it is all the more exulting because the Cathars have the reputation, justified or not, for having held secrets. Lost secrets always excite the imaginations of people, who are all more or less treasure seekers or knights setting off in quest for the Grail.

It is therefore hardly surprising that the contemporary interest displayed in the Cathar phenomenon is accompanied by an equally enthusiastic interest for everything concerning the mysterious Holy Grail, especially since Wagner spread throughout the entire world the enchanting harmony and haunting rhythms that accompany the triumph of Parzival the Pure, the "perfecti," who began as a somewhat naïve, simple believer and became King of the Grail after straying momentarily in the fairylike gardens of Klingsor, where the Flower Girls gave off an aroma so mellow that it could not help but leave an aftertaste of sulfur and brimstone. There is food for thought here, and I perfectly understand those who have gone seeking the Grail at Montségur, hoping to rediscover the winding path that leads to the secret castle of which Montségur is only the visible facade.

In Cathar mythology there is both an earthly Christ, who is the husband or consort of Mary Magdalene, and a heavenly Christ, who is the Pure among the Pure and an archetype of the radiant angel whose light Parzival/Perceval spots escaping from the Grail. But Perceval does not ask any questions during his stay at Montsalvaesche/Corbenic when he sees the mysterious procession with the bleeding spear, the silver platter, and the "cup" held by an extremely beautiful young girl. Perceval is the classic example of the man who no longer knows he is an angel slumbering in the diabolical snares of matter. It is necessary for another angel, female in appearance, to reveal to him where he has failed. She bears different names: In the Welsh text of the legend she is the empress with many faces; elsewhere she is the hideous lady on the mule, or Kundry the sorceress. But Perceval does not know that she is also Melisande.

In all the texts of the Grail legend, we are told that it is difficult to discover the castle where the wounded king guards the mysterious vessel. Sometimes an individual passes in front of the castle without seeing it, blinded by the illusions sent by Satan or his pet sorcerer, whatever his name (except for Merlin, who is quite different and over whom the devil has no hold). Sometimes the reality is so obvious, so apparently luminous that it is impossible to see. Many curiosity seekers have gone astray on the Tabe Massif or in the caves of Ussat and many devotees have sought the discreet path leading the the cave of Mary Magdalene. It is proof that many are interested in something that is living and rooted in this arid land. It is never a waste of time to chase phantoms, and if phantoms are to be found here, they are simply a reflection of something that exists somewhere else.

The problem lies in avoiding the dead-end roads. In a land charged with history, memory does not fade; it permeates the countryside and gives it a certain color and a specific perfume. But memory is faithless. It resembles those fairies who spy on travelers and subject them to tests before deciding whether to show them which way to go or to imprison them in some kind of trap.

In these prophetic times in which we are told the twenty-first century will be mystical or that it will not be, there are prophets crowding every crossroads. The sad truth is that they are speaking a language that is incomprehensible to ordinary people, and when by chance they put themselves within the grasp of those they meet, it can be seen that their predictions are contradictory.

This is the game.

In Wolfram von Eschenbach's *Parzival,* the young hero, following his failed visit to Montsalvaesche, seeks to be "initiated" by the hermit Trevrizent, who tells him, among other things, that the Grail was formerly guarded by "angels who were neither good nor evil." But then Trevrizent tells Parzival that he has lied, that this information is not true—which is a specific admission demonstrating that the initiator does not necessarily point out which road to follow; he only gives a few crumbs of what it is necessary to know and blends truth with lies. If the new elect is worthy he will find what is true and disentangle it from what is false. An initiator can never take the initiate's place; it is up to the initiate to achieve his quest.

In the discordant concert of the sycophants of the Grail and the Cathars, who can tell true from false? Testimonies are not lacking, and each claims to bear the truth. We should avoid being taken in. The *secret* of the Cathars, the Cathars' *treasure,* the *Grail* are only words through which somebody can say anything he wishes. It is like the Spanish inns of legend: We find there only what we have brought— exactly the case regarding the quest for the Cathars in the meccas of Montségur, the upper Ariège Valley, and the Razès. What if Montségur was only a prism in which all the rays of human intelligence converged?

This hypothesis at least has the merit of making the fortress a kind of solar temple.

But as I've pointed out, in folktales, when the devil builds something—a bridge, for example—he leaves it unfinished. Oh, it may be missing only a trifle, sometimes just a single stone, but that is enough to cause the whole structure to crumble. For the bridge is the work of the devil, and even if you are a radical dualist, you know that the devil is not God. Only God is capable of placing the missing stone where it should go.

In Chrétien de Troyes's *Perceval*—a text that those studying Montségur have a tendency to overlook, dazzled as they are by Wolfram von Eschenbach—the passage corresponding to the episode of the hermit Trevrizent is much more sober and not at all encumbered with philosophical speculations. Let's recall that this version was composed much earlier than that of Wolfram and follows more closely the legend's archetype. In this episode, Chrétien tells us that the hermit;

> [spoke] an orison in Perceval's ear and [Perceval] repeated it until he knew it by heart. Many of the names of God were included, among them the greatest, those that should never pass the lips of man, for it is to his life's peril that he utter them. Also, once he had taught him the orison, he forbade him from speaking it, save in the event he needed to escape an even greater danger.*

Here's a pretty tale. Perceval is now in possession of a prayer that will permit him to escape death. He has therefore obtained quasi-immortality. Chrétien de Troyes (who never finished his work—intentionally, it seems), refrained from showing us Perceval as king of the Grail, and we do not know if he proposed to go that far in his book. But what is there to say about this dreadful and secret prayer including the names of

---

* Chrétien de Troyes, *Perceval*, translated by Lucien Foulet (Paris: Stock, 1947), 153.

God? This scene is reminiscent of the Hebrew tradition's Lilith, who, hounded by the angels of God for abandoning Adam, refused to obey the orders of the Eternal One *because she knew the ineffable name* *of God.*

Despite the Christian vocabulary used by the author, it is not certain that this episode of *Perceval* illustrated exemplary orthodoxy. This secret prayer resembles a little that missing stone in the bridge built by the devil. It is probable that the Cathars were on the verge of discovering the ineffable names of God. Perhaps they even knew them. But was this a secret they passed on? Did they leave it somewhere in Montségur, in Quéribus, in the Lombrives Cavern, in the castle of Montreal-de-Sos, or in Rennes-le-Château? Or perhaps it was in Rennes-le-Bains, in Granès, in the castle of Usson, or even in the castle of Puivert, where graphic depictions of the Arthurian legend can be found. How to know, if not through the hermit?

12
Catharism and Druidism

On the day of the seven hundredth anniversary of the pyre of Montségur—March 16, 1944, during the Nazi Occupation—Joseph Mandement, president of the Tarascon-sur-Ariège Tourist Bureau, which oversaw Montségur, inaugurated in the company of a few friends a small stele erected on the side of the pog in honor of Maurice Magre, the first president of the Friends of Montségur who died in 1939. After having requested authorization from the proper authorities to erect the stele and alerted the German authorities of their gathering, Joseph Mandement and only six frinds found themselves at Montségur. We know the list of the six: Antonin Gadal, Paul Salette, René Dlastres, Maurice Roques, Paul Philip, and the writer Joseph Delteil. Their small ceremony went off without a hitch, and nothing noteworthy took place except that a small German airplane flew over Montségur and drew a Celtic cross in the sky with its white smoke.

The Celts at Montségur! And through the intermediary of a German aircraft! This is better than a legend, all the more so because the event was confirmed by the testimony of those who were there. Unfortunately their testimonies differ on the interpretation regarding the airplane's movements. Here is what Paul Philip, who was president of the Tarascon Tourist Bureau at the time, said: "Toward noon a small plane came toward us, tracing a circle of white smoke that started drifting away, and then it returned to draw two very vague diameters. We arrived at the conclusion that he had intended to draw a Celtic cross."

This is too good to be true. The nationalist writer who conceals his identity behind the pseudonym Saint-Loup has written some pretty things on this incident, his casual embroidery rendered all the easier by the fact that he was not there, but what wouldn't be done to glorify the Germano-Celtic friendship? What a nice present the Germans gave to the Gauls of Montségur on this occasion. It should be noted, however, that since then the Celtic cross, although a very simplified version, has been used for philosophical and political ends that the Celts never foresaw and that are, in any case, absolutely contrary to the Celtic mind-set.

But the testimony of Joseph Delteil does not agree with that of Paul Philip:

So on this morning of March 16, 1944, a small propeller airplane circled the ruins of the castle of Montségur, where we were gathered, physically present but minds elsewhere, as if in a dream on this day commemorating March 16, 1244. This small airplane, which, someone wrote later, carried Rosenberg (ideologist for the National-Socialist Party), circled for several moments, but I have to testify that I did not see a cross inside a circle, as some have suggested or written.*

Delteil is explicit: He saw no Celtic cross. Philip was vague; he saw something and it was following discussion that the group concluded it was a Celtic cross.

Obviously, with Antonin Gadal in the group, we can be certain that the undeniable—and normal—flight of a small German reconnaissance plane was transformed into a affair of state requiring the transit of a high Nazi official saluting his Gallic (Aryan) cousins with a stream of smoke resembling the Celtic cross.

All of this is grotesque on its own but is even more intolerable for

---

* Christian Bernadec, *Le mystère Otto Rahn* (Paris: France-Empire, 1978), 260–61.

the way it completely distorts the historical truth and creates a relationship—rather irritating in this instance—of close intimacy between the Cathars, the druids, the Grail, and Nazism. This is not the first time that someone has introduced the druids into the debate. Gadal saw them everywhere, and of course, as predecessors of the Cathars. Most important, making Montségur the site of the Grail Castle could not help but push wide open the doors of Celtism. It was necessary at any price to find druids at Montségur, Ussat, and Rennes-le-Château.

And they were found. But it is important to clarify matters: It is not that there never were druids in this territory at the same time that it was occupied by the Gallic Volques Tectosages or Rhedones. In fact, it would be surprising if there were not, for this very remote land with its forests and high peaks would lend itself magnificently to druidic worship. The problem is that the druids left even less of a visible trace than the Cathars. Indeed, if these druids left any souvenir of their presence, it was not in writing—they refused to use writing—but in a few archaeological objects and place names. That is all.

If there are connections between the Celts and the Cathars, they exist only on the planes of doctrine, system of thought, and of course religious tradition, which form the framework of every ancient civilization. In this regard, the partisans of amalgamation risk being greatly disappointed, for it is not merely a ditch that separates the Celts and the Cathars but one of those fabulous crevasses that abound in the Pyrenees in the neighborhood of Montségur whose depths are incalculable.

In fact, from an ontological point of view, Cathar dualism was fundamentally opposed to Celtic monism. From everything we know, the druidic doctrine insisted on "the dark and profound unity" that exists between beings and things, between creatures and creator, *between matter and spirit*. This was not even the famous formula from the Emerald Tablet: As is above, as is below.* It was a more direct formula in which

---

* [The Emerald Tablet of Hermes is the original source of Hermetic Philosophy and Alchemy. —*Trans.*]

the comparative element gave way to identification: What is above *is* what is below.

Consequently, to the Celts the world—our visible world of appearances, the world of the living—was exactly identical to the Other World, the world of the gods, heroes, and the dead. The feast of Samhain, November 1, which was the great Celtic festival of the New Year, was recuperated by the Christians and later became All Saints Day, the day of the communion of saints (living and dead alike), when the world of the living could communicate—symbolically—with the world beyond. On this day individuals could pass from this world to the next, thus attesting to the essential unity of the visible and invisible. For the Celts, terrestrial society, guided by the druids in alliance with the king, was to have conformed closely to the image of the world beyond, that of the deity.

This assumes a view of the material world that is diametrically opposed to that of the Cathars. For the Celts, the individual was not imprisoned in matter; he blossomed in matter because the world was in a state of perpetual becoming. This excluded any idea of a Fall, any idea of Satan as the evil spirit who created an imperfect world in caricature of the work of God. Satan is not Celtic; he is Persian. And while the Christians gave him the appearance and attributes of the Gallic Cernunnos, the horned god, it was because they were incapable of ridding themselves of this burdensome figure who expressed strength and fertility.

And if there were no Satan, there was no evil. The Celts did not acknowledge any metaphysical evil; evil was simply the imperfection of individuals, imperfection being normal in a perpetual evolution. It was the perfect, meaning the *finished,* that was the equivalent of nothing. Consequently, evil in all its forms—injustice, violence, suffering, illness—amounted only to a series of incidents on the necessary journey to a superior level. The absence of a principle of evil did not lead to laxity; quite the contrary, for the the heroes of Celtic mythology, followed by the great saints of early Celtic Christianity, revealed human life to be a constant effort toward something higher. There was no need to explain the world as the malefic creation of a rebellious angel and no need for the coming of a messiah who would reveal the return road to the paradise of light. If the Celts converted easily to Christianity, it was because the Resurrection of Jesus proved to their satisfaction that their doctrine of rebirth in another world was valid.

And they did believe in rebirth in another world and not any kind of reincarnation in the Cathar sense of the word. Despite all the inventions of the critics who have never verified their assertions in an authentic Celtic text, the doctrine of the transmigration of souls was completely unknown to the druids and the mythological tradition of the Celts. "Death is the middle of a long life," were the words the Roman poet Lucan put in the mouth of a druid. Here is one of the rare points shared in common by the Cathars and the Celts: Death was not feared because both groups knew there was an *after,* although they did not conceive of it in the same fashion. The Celts, however, instead of considering life as a punishment, made it the leaven of individual evolution.*

This had obvious repercussions on the social plane. For the Cathars the world, with its structures and societies, was a diabolical creation, and the best possible reaction to it included disdain for the world, austerity, continence, and the refusal of all physical pleasure. There was none of this feeling among the Celts, who, on the contrary, exalted this world, *a world that was divine* in all its manifestations and considered as an instrument of perfection. For them, morality simply acted as a series of rules that could help guide individuals to the best possible solution. Good was everything and evil was simply an imperfect good, as is the case in orthodox Christianity, where it was even the basis of Augustinian thought. This view amounted to a refusal of any

---

* For more on the religious thought of the Celts, their metaphysical concepts, and their morality, see Jean Markale, *The Druids* (Rochester Vt.: Inner Traditions, 1999). For more on the transition from druidism to Christianity and the specific attitude displayed by the early Christian communities of Ireland and Britain, see Jean Markale, *Le Christianisme celtique* (Paris: Imago, 1984).

Manichean attitude: There is neither good nor evil, heaven nor hell, night nor day, life nor death. There is only one reality, but this reality presents numerous aspects.

The differences between Cathar and Celt are no less evident with respect to nature. For the Cathars nature was stained with every defect—they were not vegetarians out of respect for nature. In fact, the Cathars were content to ignore the natural world. To the Celt, on the contrary, nature was sublimated because it too was divine manifestation. It was within the framework of nature that individuals communicated with God because it held nothing that was opposed to absolute transcendence. This belief could not have existed without respect for nature and an attitude that we might term *ecological*.

But for the druids nature was not only mountains, landscapes, rivers, forests, and little birds. It was also the human being in its most physical manifestation. The flesh was not cursed; it was exalted exactly as spirit was exalted, for body and soul were merely two faces of one reality. Improvement of the body was considered improvement of the mind, and, as the Greeks also believed, you could not have one without the other. Consequently, there were no sexual prohibitions or guilt. The prohibitions—they exist in every religious system—were magical in nature and referred to a holistic vision of the subtle relationships between the individual and his or her surroundings without any moral connotations.

It is therefore quite difficult, unless we imagine a druidic system made of whole cloth—which some have not hesitated to do—to establish any connections between the radical or mitigated dualism of the Cathars and the integral monism of the Celts. It is on only a few points of detail that a certain similarity between the two can be noted. The most significant concerns the conception of Jesus.

We know that the Cathars believed Mary had been inseminated through her ear. This allowed for the complete elimination of any sexual relations on the part of the Virgin Mary while at the same time it conformed with orthodox doctrine, which considered the Holy Ghost to be the genitor of Jesus and that symbolically this Holy Ghost was depicted as a dove. In fact, this dove seems to have played a role in the plastic arts (if we can use this term) of the Cathars before being recuperated by the Huguenots.

We should not, however, stop at this standard interpretation, which is valid in both Catharism and orthodox Christianity, for it is simply the face value of the symbol and serves merely to establish a meaningful image. This interpretation allows for the elimination of the sin inherent in all procreation. The dove of the Holy Ghost is quite practical, and if it had not existed it would have been necessary to invent it. But it did exist long before, if only as the dove that brought the olive branch to Noah, a symbol of peace, it is said. It became a symbol of peace because in the text of Genesis—and still simply on the surface—it was a symbol of rebirth and regeneration. But if we consider that Genesis is the reworking of a mythological episode that was clearly much older than its verses (as is everything concerning the Flood, moreover), our judgment should be revised.

We know in fact that Noah and his ark, holding one pair of every living species and floating upon the waters, is the clearly rationalized and historicized depiction of a primitive goddess whose name was probably Nuah. If we go back to the very essence of this myth, it is quite meaningful: The goddess Nuah—a virgin, of course—floats upon the primordial waters. At a certain moment, a dove appears, holding in its beak a branch, which it deposits upon the ark. There is no need to turn to psychoanalysis to grasp the meaning of this episode: It involves the fertilization of the virgin goddess and suggests that a new humanity will be born from this union.

Simply put, the dove represents the Holy Ghost, God's spirit. But how did it manifest? Through language, of course, by *the Word*. The Gospel of Saint John, so honored by the Cathars, says exactly this: "In the beginning was the Word, and the Word was with God, and the Word was God" (John 1:1–2). And again, "the Word has been made flesh and has dwelled among us" (John 1:14). The Word, therefore, appears as the instrument of creation, or more exactly, as the absolute and abstruse God in his role as creator. God, in himself, is undifferentiated. For the possibility that the human spirit may be conceived, this spirit must be presented in a form that will translate its action. Hence the image of the dove.

And if the dove is the Holy Ghost, therefore the Divine Word, the act of fertilization thus put into operation can take place only through the ear. It is not so much for eliminating the sexual aspect of creation that this method is employed; it is to signify something much more important: the omnipotence of the Word. The Cathar myth of the insemination of the Virgin Mary through her ear forms a variation on the orthodox episode of the Annunciation by the angel who appears to Mary, but its meaning is clearly much stronger: It is not an angel who is at work, but God himself, as the Word.

This same concept can be found in druidism, essentially in the role that had been devolved upon the written word. The druids forbade the use of writing for several reasons; the spoken word was instead in great favor. It was with the spoken word that a druid could take action on both spirit and matter (for they are one). The druid could transform the world with his incantation—his spoken word. And the druid in Celtic guise was by nature the god manifested, because all the gods of the Celts were druids and all the druids gods—in other words, all were functional manifestations of a deity who is one and unknown outside of his actions. We know, thanks to a passage in Caesar's *Commentaries,* that a Gallic priest held the title of *gutuater.* The passage is confused and shows that the writer, in this instance Caesar's lieutenant Hirtius, understood the term to be a proper name whereas the inscriptions confirm that it was a common name. But the *gutuater* is the "father of the word." The name derives from the word *guth*—"voice" or "word"— which can be found in the term meaning, in Ireland, the preeminent incantation, the *geas,* a dreadful procedure that confers upon the word the power of absolute creation.

It so happens that the word enjoyed great favor among the Cathars. Outside of several extremely simple rituals such as the consolamentum, the activity of the perfecti that we think of as sacerdotal (which is actually an improper use of the term, for the Cathars had no priests) was primarily preaching. The Cathars wrote little, but they spoke and left lasting memories of impassioned and remarkably skilled orators. It was through the spoken word that they converted the Occitains to their faith and it was how they transmitted their doctrine. It is through the spoken word that they officiated and were thereby in perfect accord with the Gospel of Saint John, to which they ceaselessly referred. The authentic Cathar, the Pure among the Pure, was believed to be an angel who manifested the voice of God and spread it around for the use of those who have not yet attained a sufficient level of purity to hear God speaking to them directly. The Virgin Mary had attained this level; she heard God, hence her particular position and the trigger of all the speculations on her nature that would later lead to the Catholic doctrine of the Immaculate Conception.

But how many humans still have their ears covered?

Here, then, is a very significant point on which the Cathars and druids share common ground: the importance of the spoken word, which was the manifestation of God in his creative or re-creative functions. And let us not forget that, in the Cathar view, Satan usurped this power of creation when he made the world. So Satan too owned the art of the spoken word. But there was something missing and thus his creation could be only a caricature. It was therefore up to God to re-create the world. This belief even existed in the myth of the Flood, but there it was historicized and thrown back into the past when it actually concerned the future.

There is yet another point of concordance between the druidic doctrine and the symbolic mythology of the Cathars: the light. The God of the Cathars, like that of the Manicheans and especially of the Mazdeans, was King of the Paradise of Light. We return to the Gospel of Saint John: "In it (the Word) was the life, and the life was the Light of men. The light gleams in the darkness and the darkness never received it" (John 1:4–5). John took advantage of this to declare that he was sent by God as witness to this light. More precisely: "This light was the true light, that by coming into the world, lit all men. It was in the world, and the world had been made by it, and the world knew it not" (John 1:9–10). If I understand these verses correctly, they say that the light and the Word are identical.

The issue is a subtle one, to say the least, and in order to understand it, we must return to the theory of creation as the Cathars conceived it at the beginning of the thirteenth century:

> Whereas the Catholic theologians ordinarily oppose the action of "making" *(facere),* which means fabricating one thing from another, to that of creating *(creare),* which is properly to make something out of nothing *(ex nihilo),* the Cathars saw no difference between *facere* and *creare.* The two terms are generally associated as equivalents. God is *creator sive factor,* to create or make always meaning to create from an earlier, pre-existing substance."*

This concept is hardly comprehensible in the framework of traditional logic positing the principle of an independent third party: if A is not A, not-A is not A, and there can be no identification between what is positive and what is not.

However, the Cathars asserted the eternal existence of what may be called substance, which remains nothing only in its absolute state, as long as it has not been set in motion by a creator, who is also a shaper. At this point, the Cathars were forced to borrow the Mazdean image of eternal and incorruptible light, from which derived all that existed. The reference flowed from the source, as emphasis was placed on the paradise of light that caused the creation of the fallen angels, or in other words, human beings. Thus, all transpired as if the original light had spread around itself, creating and shaping forms that, although each had their own distinguishing features, necessarily retained a particle of the luminous energy that prompted their existence. This creation theory

---

* René Nelli, *Le phénomène cathare* (Toulouse: Privat, 1964), 27.

of the Cathars could therefore be compared to the very scientific theory of the Big Bang, the initial explosion that gave birth to the universe. The "one hundred thousand suns" of a nuclear explosion have become the terms of a terrifying image whose reality cannot conceal its mythological connotation. In this gigantic explosion, the particles that were dispersed through space were not created *ex nihilo,* for they belonged to the original mass formed by the potential light waiting to manifest. So the Cathars thus came back to the Gnostic theory of emanation. Creation, according to the Cathar Jean de Lugio, was inseparable from the creator just as the rays of the sun were inseparable from the sun itself; its creatures *emanated* from the original light.

The consequences of this theory were visible in the eschatological vision of the Cathars, their morality, and their vocabulary that abounded with references to whiteness and light. Was there also evidence of this theory in their worship? This is less certain; the Cathars were not Mazdeans.

On the other hand their mythology is solar, which connects them to Celtic tradition. But here too we must be cautious and restore things to their true place. There are a great many people in the present day who claim to be druids and perform ceremonies honoring the sun as well as the solstices and equinoxes. They even make Saint John's Day into a great Celtic festival that has come down to us from the dawn of time. The *dawn of time* is actually the right choice of words: Saint John's Fires are a legacy of the ancient civilizations that preceded the Celts on the European continent but have absolutely nothing to do with the Celts themselves. There are no references to a solar festival celebrated on the solstice in any document concerning the Celts. The Celtic festivals are well known; they always take place forty days after a solstice or equinox, at the beginning of November, February, May, and August. The monuments that can be classified as *solar,* for example the circular temple of Stonehenge or the megalithic alignments of Carnac, belong to a civilization that predated the Celts' arrival. It is irritating all the same that people claiming to be druids could overlook such a historical reality and that this alone should discredit their alleged druidic affiliation. In fact, in the Celts' worship, as in their mythology, everything connected to the sun clearly appears to be a legacy of an earlier civilization that was more or less integrated by the Celts into their own.

For there are solar elements in Celtic tradition, though of a very discreet nature with ontological significance. Certainly there is a god whom Caesar compares to the Greco-Roman Apollo. But Caesar does not speak of him as a solar deity. He is a healing god, a deity of springs who furthermore conforms to the vision the Greeks had of him. However, this Celtic Apollo carries characteristic titles in Gaul and Great Britain: Grannus and Belenus. The significance of the name Belenus (Belenos) is easy to grasp: It means "brilliant." In the name Grannus, meanwhile, the same root can be found that is in the Gaelic word *grian,* meaning "sun." Furthermore, it is very likely that Belenos is present in place names of the Cathar region in the form of *bel* (as in Belesta), this term often being confused with the adjective meaning "beautiful," though it is not of Latin origin. The name Grannus is quite recognizable in the village of Granès, near Rennes-le-Château. In reality, the solar function of the deity, its radiance, its emanating nature, is most often depicted in feminine form, as an ancient sun goddess whose aspects, somewhat altered, became those of the well known legendary heroine Isolde.

Belenos has in fact a kind of feminine equivalent in Gaul: Belisama, whose name (which is that if the town of Bellême in the Orne district) is a superlative meaning "very brilliant." We know it through several Gallo-Roman era inscriptions, particularly the one on a stone found in Saint Lizier in the Ariège region, which incorporates it with the Latin Minerva. As in Great Britain, this Minerva is identified as the goddess Sul, whose name leaves no doubt as to her role as a deity of the sun. Let us not forget that in the Celtic and Germanic languages the sun is a feminine noun and the moon is masculine, which can greatly confuse the interpretations of the great legends. Accordingly, Siegfried, the central figure of the Nibelungen saga, is not a solar hero but a "moon man," and it is the Valkyrie Brunhilda or Sirgdryfa, presented as a prisoner within a citadel surrounded by flames, who is the "sun woman."* The same holds true for Isolde.

The prototype for the figure of Isolde is in fact an Irish heroine named Grainne. It is not difficult to recognize the Gaelic word *grian* here. In the legend, Grianne, wife of King Finn, has fallen in love with the handsome Diarmaid—who does not return her affection. She then compels Diarmaid by means of a dreadful geas, a sacred and magical spell, to follow her and love in such a way that he can no longer live without her. If we analyze the legend of Tristan and Isolde we find the same outline: In the beginning Tristan is not in love with Isolde. It is she who forces him to love her by virtue of the love potion (the equivalent of the *geas*), and this works so well that Tristan can no longer live without Isolde. We are also told in the thirteenth-century prose romance that Tristan would die if he did not have physical contact with Isolde at least once a month. This is easy symbolism to understand: The sun Isolde gives life and warmth to the moon man Tristan. Every twenty-eight days the moon man loses his strength and disappears. This is the time of the dark moon; the sun no longer illuminates it and it becomes the equivalent of nothing—it melts and dissolves into the eternal night. But through the sexual act Isolde restores strength and vitality to Tristan. The moon man emerges slowly from the night on his journey through space. But the legend of Tristan ends tragically: Isolde arrives too late to cure him of his wound; she arrives too late to transmit to him her energy and Tristan, deprived of this energy, can no longer hold on to his life.

It would perhaps be an exaggeration to claim that the legend of Tristan and Isolde is the expression of a Cathar myth. Its origin clearly appears Irish, even if certain connections can be established with a Persian tradition. But there is an incontestable similarity here, and Occitain troubadours, extremely knowledgeable about Catharism,

---

* See Jean Markale, *Siegfried, ou l'Or du Rhin* (Paris: Retz, 1984).

knew Tristan's story quite well, as is amply evidenced in their work. For it is in the spirit of their work that the connection exists, through the angle of solar symbolism. All that is required to be convinced is to decipher the legend according to Cathar doctrine, and to recall that among all the Indo-European peoples there was the image of a female deity of light, the famous Scythian Diana spoken of by the Greeks, who subsequently became "lunar" through the reversal of values and introduction of patriarchal society.* It is probable that the Persian Ahura-Mazda was originally a luminous being who materialized in the form of a female goddess.

Isolde the Blonde thus becomes the original light, that of the original paradise. Following their rebellion, the angels incarnate in matter. They feel imprisoned and aspire to return to the paradise of light, but blinded by Satan's traps, they no longer know the road that leads there. Furthermore, Satan himself obstructs the way ("obstruction" is the etymological meaning of the word *devil*), and it is fatal to encounter him when setting off in search of the sun. In the legend of Tristan and Isolde Satan is Morholt, a kind of monster or giant, whose true significance is vague and is similar to the Fomorians of Irish tradition. This Morholt is a devourer: He has come to demand a tribute of young men and maidens (Satan swallows up created beings in his hell in order to deprive them of the light once and for all). Tristan battles against him and kills him. At first the fallen angel Tristan, who vaguely remembers he belongs to the world of light, eliminates the troublemaker. The way is free for the present, but he still does not know where to go, and his struggle with Satan has weakened him. He has received an incurable wound. He thus by chance leaves on a boat, sailing over the sea—in

---

* This reversal of values appeared in Greece with the elimination of the Pythian serpent (the telluric mother goddess) by Apollo (the celestial male god), who took advantage of this to take possession of the solar nature of Artemis/Diana, now considered to be his twin sister and relegated to a lunar role. See Jean Markale, *Women of the Celts* (Rochester, Vt.: Inner Traditions, 1986).

other words over the primordial waters that separate the world of appearances from the world of realities.

It is at this point that he lands in Ireland, the Other World, where Isolde lives, and she cures him. Smitten with Tristan, Isolde waits for him to declare his love. But Tristan has not recognized in Isolde what he is searching for so confusedly. He makes no move. He returns home, and still not understanding what has happened, seeks to wed Isolde to his uncle Mark. To do this he needs to struggle against another appearance of Satan, the great crested serpent of Ireland, a monster that devours its victims. Tristan is victorious but is once again wounded, poisoned by the monster's breath. He is healed a second time by Isolde, who thereby confirms the double duty of the ancient solar goddess: She brings both light and healing. But Tristan still has not recognized what he is seeking. It is then that Isolde takes action: On the boat she arranges for her maidservant to choose the wrong container, and in the company of Tristan she drinks the "herbed wine," the elixir of love, which in reality is a draught of wisdom like so many others in Celtic tradition and which the French writers used to remove all guilt from Tristan and Isolde's liaison. Henceforth, Tristan, who has recognized in Isolde the unique dispenser of light, can no longer live without her or her radiance. The human soul, remembering that it belongs to the divine world, realizes that it is an angel and can no longer go backward. The Cathar who had become a perfecti could never renounce his redis-covered angelic nature.

Interpreting the Tristan legend in this fashion is not to claim that it is a Cathar creation. It merely traces in the legend mythological elements that illustrate the Cathar assumption. And it is surely because the legend can bear this reading that it enjoyed so much success in the twelfth and thirteenth centuries. Fables are remarkable in that they can serve as supports for numerous religious or metaphysical themes. All that is required is the modification of a few details while leaving the original outline intact.

Beyond illustrating the perfecti's attitude toward the god of light, the love of Tristan and Isolde can also be understood as a narrative depiction of the theory of emanation. The moon is nothing without the sun; the light of the moon emanates from the sun and the moon is visible only when the rays of the sun strike it. Tristan, the moon man, truly exists only through his contact with the radiant Isolde. In short, Tristan is pure emanation, and emanation implies the permanence of a bond between the one who emanates and the one who receives this emanation. The Cathars often stressed this bond, without which the imprisoned fallen angels would be permitted no hope. But because it was impossible to express this theory of emanation without resorting to images, the legend of Tristan was found to be quite relevant. The love story served to mask even more the heretical content of the message. In the same vein, the troubadours who sang of the ideal woman, the perfection embodied by the lady, that is to say, the *domina,* "the mistress," used the same subterfuge. It has been said too often that the troubadours were indicating the Cathar Church beneath the features of the lady. This was not the case. In fact, there was no Cathar Church; there were only groups of Cathars who, to survive, organized and formed hierarchies but with no intention of creating a monolith mirroring the Roman Catholic Church. If she were Cathar, the lady of the troubadours was nothing but the personification of the primordial light to which each believer owed exclusive and passionate worship. Hence the odd eroticism that can be discerned in courtly love. But don't be fooled: Courtly love was not an invention of the Cathars. They were merely content to use it as they used the terms *diocese, bishops,* and *deacons.*

This exaltation of light both by the Cathars and the Celts leads to the question of dualism. Whatever their position, radical or mitigated, the Cathars were always vexed by the problem of what rank to attribute to Satan. His position never appeared the same in the various schools of thought. Sometimes he was the son of God and equal to Jesus; sometimes he was a rebel angel but subject to God; or he was the incarnation of a principle coexisting with the principle of good, for which God himself is the incarnation.

One of the explanations for the fall of the angels seems particularly ambiguous. If the angels rebelled, fell, and took on a demonic or human form, it is, as noted by René Nelli, because "by losing themselves *they only changed into what they already were.*" This is indeed a surprising explanation coming from dualists. It leaves the impression that evil and Satan were therefore contained in the totality, for the angels overtly took on a form for which they held the potential within themselves all along. Does this mean that the Cathars were false dualists and that their doctrine instead aimed to prove, at least to those capable of following their reasoning to its logical conclusion, that everything returned to a deep, dark unity? Were they claiming that Satan was in God? Or did they mean that the God of light, the primordial God, contained both good and evil?

It could be said that Catholic theology is not too far from this same conclusion. But the whole edifice was saved through the introduction of free will. If God left his creations their freedom, then the fall of the angels and Adam's Original Sin are the consequences of this freedom and, under these conditions, God is not both good and evil; he has merely made available the choice between the two. Of course, Saint Augustine reduced the scope of this choice by subjecting it to divine grace as the only sure guide capable of showing the way, but nonetheless the emphasis was placed on individual responsibility.

The Cathars rejected the concept of free will. They believed that there was in fact no choice. As René Nelli writes: "For a doctrine that taught that the good remained eternally with the true God and the wicked with the demon, this establishment of heavenly hierarchies excluded freedom absolutely." Therefore, the evil angels were created as evil for all eternity. But, by the theory of emanation that posits a hierarchy that goes from the least nullified (Jesus) to *absolute nothingness* (Satan), certain Cathar theologians came to make the claim that Satan himself would be saved at the end of time, for the end of time would not come about until there was no soul left to be saved. According to this reasoning, then, there was no eternal hell or any evil existing independently of God. God was both good and evil, but in the absolute state these were not antagonistic. It was only when relativity was introduced by creation that good and evil, themselves thus made relative and separate, confronted each other in a war that would conclude only with the end of the relative and a return to the absolute.

This was a heretical position that no Catholic theologian dared support. The Cathars themselves were quite careful to express it in a way that did not say too much. It is clear that the credenti and even some of the perfecti simplified the explanation and contented themselves with the classic image of a Satan who created matter and was surrounded by numerous demons, all clad in the same flashy garments, much as the Catholics conceived them. Only the theoreticians arrived at this vision of the doctrine. But it was an incontestably monist vision, and left nothing to envy in the integral monism professed by the druids.

So is there a possibility of Cathar and druid convergence here? Yes, but only when analyzed in depth. In fact, the Cathars were satisfied to have their doctrine remain an attempt to explain human misery and the world's imperfection. If we go back to the symbol of the solar light that spreads through space and emanates around a central point, we can conclude from it that evil is simply the consequence of moving farther away from this central point. Evil is thus an imperfection, a poorer impregnation of the light. We should not therefore speak of negation or of Satan as he who negates: Evil can be summarized not as the absence of good *but as the absence of the primordial light.*

In this case, the Cathar doctrine appears close to the druidic concept. For the Celts the world was a perpetual becoming in which there was neither good nor evil but only movements that were not always in harmony. Individuals taking part in this continuous creation, this perpetual becoming, lead it to its perfection or, in other words, its completion. At that time there would no longer be room for any internal contradictions. In fact, there would no longer be anything, for the world existed only through the sustained efforts by individuals to fuel the becoming. In druidic thought this becoming was eternal, and God, who is the total of beings and things, did not exist but was becoming.

The great difference between the Cathars and Celts is specifically the fact that for the Celts there was no primordial God. For them God was the end result of the collective activity of individual beings, and these individual beings simply came from a God who existed totally in potential. There was no fall of angels; instead, there was an evolution. Therefore, matter was not evil, and it was not even the medium of the soul's reascent to the paradise of light; it was one face of being, and the other face was spirit.

With these basic assumptions it is quite hard to detect any unity of views between the Cathars and druids. Whatever degree of dualism was displayed by the Cathars, even when it lead to a disguised monism (which was accessible only to theologians), a basic incompatibility exists between the two systems. For the Celts, God did not exist but *became* through the means of matter and spirit, which were essentially identical, differing only in form. For the Cathars, however, God did exist, and following the fall of the angels that weakened his light, he came into existence again through spirit, by denying matter, which was only an illusion.

Despite some commonalities, the two concepts are irremediably contradictory. No druid, if there was even one left at the time, could ever became a Cathar. To suggest otherwise is idle musing or delusion.

13

A Solar Cult?

Montségur is not only a site that attracts the fans of unsolved mysteries, those nostalgic for the Cathars, or those who are Grail seekers. Since 1244 the site has also become a kind of symbol of resistance for Occitain civilization against the encroachments of and finally its colonization by the langue d'oil civilization. This is a matter of historic fact and not a hypothesis or secret.

The monument erected at the base of the pog is quite revealing in that it memorializes an act of intolerance. In doing so it sends an appeal to humanity's moral conscience. It may not have been at Montségur that Occitania ceased to be its own country; that occurred at Muret. But the holocaust at Montségur speaks more to this moral conscience. Yes, it is certain that Cathars and Occitains of every persuasion, subjects of the count of Toulouse or the count of Foix, lost their independence at Montségur just as the Bretons lost theirs at Saint-Aubin-du-Cormier at the end of the fifteenth century. The pyre at Montségur has become the simplest and most complete image of the triumph of French hegemony over a *different* Occitain. In short, Montségur displays itself as a veritable monument to the dead. This explains the sorrow that clings to the place, and why Montségur has become a pilgrimage site at the present time for all those who have realized that their souls have been stolen.

The Occitains are a little like the Cathars: A devil surprised them when they were sleeping and imprisoned them in a material that was foreign to them. And so they have made a desperate pilgrimage to cast a nostalgic gaze over the mountains haloed in mist. Somewhere over the horizon the remaining shadow of a lost land causes suffering for those who can still discern it amidst the storms of memory. Yet the wind carries strange voices. And the sun emerges from behind the crests like a siren from deep waters.

On the Montségur pog, on the morning of the summer solstice and the two days preceding and following it, those who get up early—and there are many who do—and have the courage or passion to climb to the ruins of the castle are witnesses to an undeniable truth. The first ray of light that emerges from the darkness far in the east grazes the peak of Bugarach and directly enters the keep through the arrow loops.

This obviously does not occur by chance. At Stonehenge, England's strange circular monument on Salisbury Plain that is believed to be a solar sanctuary dating from megalithic times and completed in the Bronze Age, the first ray of the rising sun on the summer solstice strikes the central stone at the end of a kind of ceremonial aisle. Diodorus Siculus, who mentions the monument in his writings, recorded the local tradition that told how, every nineteen years, Apollo came down within the circle of Stonehenge. This length of time corresponds to a solar cycle that Celtic Christians made use of again. Another example of this is found in the alignments of Carnac in Morbihan. There then can be no doubt of the fact that the castle of Montségur was conceived and constructed in such a way that the keep can receive the first rays of sun on the summer solstice.

This has led to the conclusion that before being a defensive fortress and the mainstay of Cathar resistance against the oppression of the Church and the Capetian monarchy, Montségur was a sanctuary. This assertion is based on conditions that are just as mysterious as the capture of Montségur in 1244. The besiegers gave the besieged a reprieve of fifteen days, ordering that they leave the premises on March 16. This has led some to deduce that this deadline was given to allow them to celebrate one final solar ritual and feast, for calculations have actually confirmed that the equinox occurred on March 15 in 1244. But what does this prove? The equinox is not the solstice. Furthermore, this ritual has been described as a Manichaean festival, but the Cathars were not Manichaean, even if they did borrow some elements from Mani's religion. It is impossible to prove that solar ceremonies were celebrated by twelfth- and thirteenth-century Albigensians. It certainly appears that this interpretation is based on pure fantasy.

However, on closer examination the issue is not that simple and cannot be resolved so easily. First, Montségur occupies a singular geographic position and its orientation to the peak of Bugarach is not to be dismissed. Second, the military value of the structure—even if we do not know exactly what the real Cathar castle was like prior to the renovations that took place at the end of the thirteenth century—is subject to doubt. Montségur is better defended from the surrounding cliffs and precipices than from its own military architecture. The castle is small, its enceinte is too low, and the doors are more ornamental than effective. Furthermore, the structure on the summit of the pog does not entirely cover the platform it sits upon; two or three yards to the north and south are left to their own devices, unprotected. If the entire area had been used, as at Peyrepertuse or Quéribus, the fortress would have been better protected. But why was it left this way?

The search for answers to this question has led to the theory of a Cathar solar temple predating the castle, which would likely have been hastily fortified by the engineer Arnaud de Beccalaria on the orders of Ramon de Perella. Researchers such as Fernand Niels have taken precise measurements that provide evidence of the effort to orient the structure toward the sunrises. It is certain, then, that the architectural plan of Montségur relied on solar considerations. Each entry of the sun into a sign of the zodiac corresponds to a precise alignment with distinct points on the castle. In addition, the castle is oriented very subtly to the four cardinal directions, which can be perceived only by drawing a line from two corners to the center of the wall opposing it.

It is obvious that if someone is desperate to find correspondences between architectural elements and solar landmarks, he or she will always find them. At Carnac researchers—who are either somewhat absent-minded or singularly dishonest—have drawn astounding illustrations based on certain monuments and *have left out of these illustrations the monuments that interfered with their theories.* With this they have made the vast megalithic grouping of Carnac and the surrounding area say whatever they want them to say. There has been a little of this manipulation at Montségur as well. Fernand Niel's measurements will truly convince only those who were convinced before seeing them. A person can prove anything if he takes the time and trouble to do so, especially if he adds false or manipulated evidence to that which legitimately exists.

But there is no need to add up the evidence at Montségur to clearly grasp that the construction of the monument followed certain precise directions. It this exceptional? If we take the same measurements of all medieval monuments and all sites of a certain importance, we would come to this same conclusion. In the Middle Ages construction of a sanctuary, a fortress, or even a simple dwelling, whether Cathar, Catholic, orthodox, heretic, or related to an ancient tradition, was never undertaken without following certain religious, astrological, or magical criteria. This was a law of the time, and even the builders of a cathedral would follow, consciously or not, a solidly established tradition. Primarily reinforced by the successful completion of the work undertaken, these essential rules, transmitted from generation to generation, had a tendency to become esoteric—in other words, known only to members of the brotherhood. Hence their somewhat enigmatic nature. When a person knows a good recipe, he does not pass it along to just anyone. This is a perfectly normal phenomenon.

All of this means it is necessary to examine with the greatest care the theory that Montségur was a solar temple. First, no archaeological proof for the concrete existence of this temple has ever been discovered. The interior architecture of the fortress lacks any such characteristics, and the objects discovered in the enceinte or the village, including the famous pentagrams, have no precise meaning. Of course, the defenders of the Cathar solar temple hypothesis vainly try to explain that the

Inquisition caused the disappearance of all traces of a worship that was truly too heretical to even be preserved in memory. But the files of the Inquisition, although well stocked with testimonies and accusations, include no mention of any alleged solar cult. If there had been such testimonies, the Inquisition surely would not have failed to turn them to good use against the accused. If ritual ceremonies similar to Manichaean—or even Mazdean—practices had taken place at Montségur or other areas frequented by the Cathars, it would be known.

Of course, the partisans of the solar hypothesis reply that because of the need for secrecy, there was no trace left of these ceremonies, and that the perfecti, the only ones to take part in them, took great pains not to reveal anything about them. This represents the approach known as sophistry: Assert the existence of something with the simple argument that no one ever spoke about it.

But there is a more serious point here: Ceremony is of primary importance in solar worship of any kind. However, as all the documents on them make clear, the Cathars reduced ritual to a minimum. Prayers, the administration of the consolamentum, and the gatherings where sermons were heard were all carried out with the greatest simplicity and wherever they might occur, for the Cathars had no temples. Furthermore, the very idea of a constructed temple contradicted their doctrine: Matter was diabolical creation. To envision that Montségur may have been a sanctuary dedicated to the sun smacks of the most deluded kind of fantasy, for in being so, it would form a basic challenge to Cathar thought.

There remains the explanation based on the structure's solar orientation, and here the hypothesis can be supported with more likely evidence because it is precisely true that Monstségur was built according to certain solar orientations. It is also precisely true that the sun played a symbolic role in Cathar mythology: The sun was the image of the original light that engendered all creatures and was the still-visible testimony of the spiritual connection of every creature with that original light. The Greek or helicoid cross used by the Cathars is certainly a solar symbol, as is the ancient cross of the Volques Tectosages. There is nothing astonishing or exceptional about this. The Celtic triskel and the Germanic swastika (which is in fact an Indian symbol) are also solar depictions, and all traditions have viewed the sun as sacred.

We know that solar worship reached its apogee during the Bronze Age, that is to say between 2000 and 700 B.C., particularly in northern Europe on the shores of the Baltic. Numerous cult objects dating from that era, such as solar barks and chariots, emphasize the generative role attributed to the day star and its role as a psychopomp. This religion (or religions) of the Bronze Age was incorporated into new civilizations, which is why solar worship can be found almost everywhere among the different religious traditions of Asia and Europe. Among these traditions, we have seen that the Mazdean interpretation, with its simplicity and imagistic nature that placed it within the grasp of all, greatly permeated a current of dualistic thought culminating with Catharism after passing through the zealous worshipers of Mithraism, Manichaeism, and the Bogomilism. The followers of all these sects practiced worship honoring the sun in one way or another or used the solar image as the support for their teaching. Though the existence of a solar liturgy among the Celts cannot be proved, we know that that their mythological themes referring to a female solar deity were numerous and that these themes lived on beyond the Celts, if only in the Arthurian romances that took their basic outlines from the oral tales of the ancient Britons and Irish.

Neither did official Christianity fail to borrow elements from ancient solar liturgies. The radiant Christ was nothing other than the actualization of ancient beliefs. Jesus who died on the cross and was resurrected was the *sol invictus* of the Mazdeans and the worshipers of Mithra—the divine sun that dies and is reborn and carries with it all beings and things. Furthermore, the commemorative feast celebrating the birth of Jesus was placed on December 25 because this date corresponded to both the symbolic birth of Mithra, who emerged from the earth mother, and the Roman festival of Saturnalia, during which traditional values were reversed.* December 25 is in fact the time when the sun, following its slow descent toward winter, changes direction and heads back toward summer. And though it is considered a certainty that the word *noel* comes from the Latin *natale (die)*, it could be that the word is derived from the Greek *neo helios*, "new sun." If authentic, this etymology, which has always been held at arm's length by the official Church, would go a long way toward restoring things to their true place, the birth of Jesus being identified with the reascension of the sun. In any case, there is nothing contradictory in the birth of a divine child in a cave—a birth celebrated by angels, shepherds, and Magi—and the realization of a universal renewal at the moment when the sun, the visible star that dispenses light and heat—thus life—begins its climb back to the heavens.

With regard to the Cathars, though, the problem remains insoluble. Could they who were enemies of all excessive materiality, who loathed ceremonies that they deemed overly "pagan" and too "diabolical," have accepted the fact that at certain times communion could be established with the solar light, if only on a symbolic plane? If this were the case, it is to be expected that no mention of it appeared in the doctrinal texts; it concerned only individual practice and didn't warrant inclusion within the formal accounting of beliefs. There is always a gap between the doctrine of a religion and how that doctrine is applied, and very often the religious practices of the faithful seem profoundly at odds with theoretical teaching. So is it possible, then, that some Cathars, more aware than others of their connection with the Manichaean current, devoted themselves to solar-worship practices that were primarily considered ascetic?

The question deserves examination, especially if we recall at Montségur the distinctive nature of the keep (or what is called the keep), with its arrow loopholes that directly channel the rays of the summer solstice sun. In truth, this is the sole truly meaningful piece of

---

* [Saturnalia was a festival that presided over an entire reversal of values—slaves and masters traded places and people did the opposite of what was customary for them. —*Trans.*]

evidence, and through comparison with ancient traditions that are not Cathar, it allows us to sketch out a theory that should satisfy everyone.

We can recall the special place held by the Gospel of John in the Cathar doctrine, particularly where the Gospel text concerns the Word, which is identical to the light. For the Cathars, this text answers their search in the scriptures for a justification of their belief in the paradise of light. They also supported their views with *The Vision of Isaiah,* an apocryphal text from biblical tradition. Three Ethiopian translations of a now-lost Greek original of this text have come down to us. It is a kind of compilation centered on the figure of the prophet Isaiah and his ascent to the seventh heaven. It is probable that *The Vision of Isaiah* came from the same archaic model as the Mazdean tale known as *The Book of Arda Viraf.* In this text, during the course of a seven-day trance, the hero is carried off to the firmament and visits the spheres of the moon, the sun, and the stars, in other words, the purgatory, hell, and heaven of Ahura-Mazda.

In *The Vision of Isaiah,* a variety of influences can be discerned: Hebrew of course, but also Persian, Christian, and, without doubt, Gnostic. The emphasis is placed on a hierarchy of spiritual zones corresponding to different states, with each represented in the guise of one of seven heavens. This theory of seven heavens goes far back in time. It can be found in the religious culture of both Babylonians and Jews long before the Cathars picked up on it for their own use. But for the Cathars, as for the non-Cathar author of *The Vision of Isaiah,* only the sixth and seventh heavens were absolutely spiritual. In the lower heavens the angels were not as closely united with the deity or with each other. Furthermore, angels were curiously polarized there into angels of the right and angels of the left. As another Cathar text, *The Secret Last Supper,* claims, it was was for this reason that Satan succeeded in seducing only the angels of the lower heavens up to and including the fifth heaven. The sixth and seventh heavens were places where the light retained and perpetuated its integral purity: "And the eyes of my soul were opened, and I beheld a great glory, and its luster was so dazzling that I could no longer see the angel who was with me and all the angels I had spied praising my Lord."

This short passage indicates that the spiritual light of the seventh heaven was so exceptional that it banished all other lights. The same idea is expressed in *Perceval* by Chrétien de Troyes, specifically in the description of the light emanating from the Holy Grail: It was a light that eclipsed that of the candles as well as the rays of the sun. The idea to be grasped here is that there exists somewhere, symbolically at the highest point in the heavens, a privileged spot where the light is of absolute purity. It is possible, then, to consider the keep of Montségur, penetrated by the sun of the summer solstice—in other words by light in its purest, freshest, and most dazzling form—as a representation of this seventh heaven.

This well-known motif of the castle in the sky, or, in its most archaic form, the chamber of the sun, is present throughout folk tradition and was particularly used in Celtic mythology.

In a Breton tale entitled *The Saga of Yann,** the hero, guided by a horse who is really a magician—his own father—in animal form, goes through a series of adventures leading him to win the daughter of King Fortunatus on behalf of the king of Brittany. This situation is somewhat equivalent to the legend of Tristan, in which the hero plays the role of nephew going to win the bride for his uncle. Thanks to the magician and the intervention of animals to whom he rendered service, the protagonist in *The Saga of Yann* obtains the young woman. She, however, bemoans her fate during their journey back:

Goodbye my father, goodbye people of my land, goodbye my beautiful castle, which is held up by four gold chains and by four lions, the strongest in all the land! I was happy when I dwelled

* Jean Markale, *La tradition celtique en Bretagne armoricaine,* 4th edition (Paris: Payot, 1975), 148–68.

within you! Of what good to me now are your gold keys, except to increase my grief and pain?

But unlike Isolde, who makes Tristan drink a love potion, the princess hurls her gold keys into the sea.

Of course, once brought into the presence of the king wishing to wed her, she consents to the marriage only if someone will restore her "beautiful castle, which is held up by four gold chains and four lions." It is obvious that the princess, who belongs to the Celtic Other World, finds her place with the king of Brittany to be an exile. She demands the presence of this castle in the sky to serve her as a kind of link with the Other World from which she comes. The theme is very "Cathar": The fallen angel—the princess—remembers the primordial light and strives, through a symbolic ritual, to re-create this lost light.

The castle in the sky appears in numerous folktales not only in Brittany but in all regions of Europe. In *The Saga of Koadalan,* a strange Breton story,* the magician Foukes lives "in a gold castle, held between earth and heaven by four silver chains." In another Breton tale, *The Swan Women,*† the daughters of a powerful enchanter "dwell in a beautiful palace decorated everywhere in gold and crystal, a very beautiful palace that sits high in the sky, tethered by four gold chains above the sea." In the Languedoc version of this tale, *The Black Mountain,*‡ the daughters of the enchanter are duck women, and the castle is located on a very high mountain. The same is true in the Basque version of this tale.§ But the essential element is the presence of this sunlike castle in the sky—whether chains or a rocky peak hold it in its place. We must note, however, that the theme of the swan women seems the most

---

* Jean Markale, *La tradition celtique en Bretagne armoricaine,* 4th edition (Paris: Payot, 1975), 169–85.
† Ibid., 186–91.
‡ Jean Markale, *Contes occitans* (Paris: Stock, 1982), 223–33.
§ Jean Markale, *Récits de la mort des pays de France* (Paris: Charles de Bartillat, 1986.)

archaic: The swan is a Hyperborean solar animal, and Celtic mythology teems with women who appear in the form of swans. These women—fairies, deities, or, in Cathar terminology, angels—belong to the Other World. They are found elsewhere, including in Germano-Scandinavian mythology, in which the Valkyrie, in love with the hero Siegfried-Sigurd, also appears in the form of a swan, additional proof of her solar symbolism.

But it is in another Breton fairy tale, *The Castle in the Air,** that this theme takes on its full significance. The young hero, who is seeking adventure as a means to earn a living, finds himself caught in countless difficulties. He manages to resolve them, thanks to his will and skill, and eventually finds himself in a haunted castle under the spell of an enchantment, which he breaks. In the garden of this castle he comes upon a young girl stuck within a well. This theme is analogous to that of the Castle of the Dolorous Guard, where, in the thirteenth-century prose version, Lancelot of the Lake must perform his feats, in particular freeing the young maiden who is held close to the pits of hell. But in the Breton story, the hero must keep watch for three nights in order to deliver the young girl. He succeeds until the last moment, when he falls asleep. The young maiden cannot wake him. However, she still tells him, "You will find me in a castle held above the water by three gold chains, but you will not get there until you have worn out a pair of iron shoes." The young man then sets off on his quest for the castle in the sky, and finds it, thanks to an old man, three crows, a flock of screech owls, and a giant to whom, during his journey, *he must give a piece of his buttocks to eat.*

All these details are significant. The princess is none other than the angelic soul that remains in the paradise of light as the hope anchored in the heart of all living creatures. Setting off on a search for her is

* Jean Markale, *La tradition celtique en Bretagne armoricaine,* 4th edition (Paris: Payot, 1975), 262–66.

enough to restore the original soul that has been broken by the fall. But not everyone is capable of succeeding at this quest: In other versions of this tale the two elder brothers of the young hero fail for one reason or another, but in reality because they are incapable of seeing beyond their physical selves. The hero, who is always the youngest, perseveres to the final stage, but then he falls asleep because the weight of matter is so restrictive. It is at this point that the angelic soul indicates the road to take or at least gives the theoretical clue to this road. The hardest task still lies ahead for the hero: turning to those guides qualified to show the way to the rediscovery of the castle in the sky, which will be possible only if the young hero sacrifices a piece of his flesh—a fairly clear symbol of his abandonment of the material.

Within the very interior of the story's plot there is a *quest,* which obviously counts the most toward returning to the source. But if the original light remains abstract and too remote to be apprehended by human consciousness, it will be of no interest to the fallen angel and will inspire no desire on his part. Therefore, it becomes necessary to transpose this original light to the domain of palpable realities. Hence the image of the castle in the sky held by three or four silver or gold chains that gleam brilliantly. But what holds these chains to the mysterious heaven where light knows no limits? At times they are held by four lions. The lion is the sign of fire, thus light, and at the same time symbolizes strength and nobility. Through it we rediscover the nobility of our origins.

However, this castle in the sky has become an object of fantasy. It is the mirror that reflects what is on high, the prism in which all the rays of the sun converge. It is by this particularly spellbinding image that the fallen creature maintains his hope and commits to taking action. This theme has been in circulation since the Middle Ages and has become incorporated into numerous legends, which is why it can be seen in the story of Tristan and Isolde that is so closely linked to Catharism, especially in the episode known as "Tristan's Madness."

This part of the legend concerns one of Tristan's visits to Queen

Isolde right under the nose of King Mark (who represents night). The hero is disguised as a lunatic (hence the title of the episode), in other words, a buffoon, which allows him to spout nonsense with impunity before the court as well as to talk to Isolde in perfect anonymity. At one point the madman asks the king to entrust him with Isolde. Mark then asks him where he will take her. Tristan answers: to a crystal room on high, in the sky, where all the rays of the sun converge and where he and Isolde can experience total happiness.

This is not an image invented by the author of "Tristan's Madness." It can also be found in two very old tales from Irish epic: *The Voyage of Art* and *The Story of Etaine.** In the first story there is a "crystal chamber" in which the young hero regnerates; in the second there is a "room of the sun" in which the heroine, in the form of an insect who has been gathered up by the hero Oengus, will restore her strength that has been depleted by a violent magic storm. And in *The Voyage of Maelduin* there is, in the middle of a glass citadel, a crystal chamber containing vats filled with an inexhaustible drink. The hero is welcomed here by the queen of the mysterious island that clearly represents the lost fortress in the air.

We should also recall that Merlin, the magician from the stories of King Arthur and the Knights of the Round Table, was enchanted by the fairy Vivian, to whom he had voluntarily given his secrets. He then found himself in the middle of the forest, trapped within an invisible castle that is described as a prison in the air or as a glass fortress. The mythological image of Merlin's prison is identical to that of Tristan's castle, for they are both in the air: Each is simply a crucible, a place in which the rays of the sun melt, a kind of athanor in which takes place the metamorphosis of primal matter into the philosopher's stone. The castle in the sky or any equivalent image, which is always presented as the property of an enchanter or fairy or mysterious queen who is in fact

---

* Jean Markale, *The Epics of Celtic Ireland* (Rochester, Vt.: Inner Traditions, 2000).

the ancient goddess of the sun, is the site of the transmutation. If we describe it in Cathar terms, this is where the creature who is trapped in matter awakens and receives the beneficial rays of the original light. Following the passage into this castle in the sky, which is the materialization of a reality that is much more subtle and abstruse, is a necessary action toward the reintegration of the angelic soul into its original abundance. And this chamber of the sun can be found only in the sky, on an island in the middle of the ocean, or, if necessary, on the top of a mountain—as in the case of Montségur.

It is quite possible that the keep that receives the rays of the summer solstice sunrise could be the architectural illustration of this mythological theme, which itself overlies an essential ontological truth in the Cathar doctrine. There is no need to discuss solar temples, for this is certainly not one; the Cathars were most reluctant to erect sanctuaries in proper terms. More likely it was a place of meditation, a sacred place, certainly, but one that assumed value only within the context of individual realization. Here we might intrduce the word *initiation,* but only if it is stripped of all religious or magical connotation. The Cathars never integrated elements of magic into their belief or behavior. In truth, they definitively excluded the appeal to technical magic that characterizes a good number of religions, including Roman Catholicism and Byzantine Christianity. It is because of their refusal of any ritual or magic that the Protestants may actually be considered the remote descendents of the Cathars.

The chamber of the sun at Montségur was perhaps the sole secret of the Cathars, perhaps even their only "treasure." But there was nothing exceptional or mysterious about this secret, for it concerned an individual attitude, a simple meditation that any Believer could accomplish in order to reach awakening. There are obviously similarities between this chamber of the sun and the tomb in which the apprentice mason is received before being presented to his new brothers. But there is one fundamental difference: The tomb belongs to the mythological paraphernalia of a new kind of celestial religion, whereas the chamber of the sun is the domain of the mind, the subtle fire and immanent light in which takes place the mutation of the old man, the transformation of the sleeping angel into the awakened angel or new man. He then will acquire the desire to begin his ascent toward the immeasurable heights of the seventh heaven.

This is only a hypothesis, but it has the merit of restoring to Montségur its value as a sanctuary without allowing it to fall into the snare of those who would ascribe to them perfectly delusional solar ceremonies that no document on the Cathars can justify. The Cathars were certainly the heirs of the Manichaeans and Mazdeans, who did practice a form of worship that we can classify as solar—with all the customary reservations because we do not know its exact scope. But the Cathars always openly displayed their intention to weed out ritual and never to sacrifice spirit to matter. The so-called Manichaean ceremony of March 15, 1244, on the occasion of the spring equinox, seems to have existed only in the minds of twentieth-century commentators. We have not a shred of proof for its occurrence, and such a ceremony would have been contrary to the very spirit of Catharism, to its barebones nature and austerity.

So why couldn't the keep have been a meditation room, one of the chambers of the sun found throughout the oral tradition of Western Europe, the symbolic prism in which the rays of all suns—both physical and spiritual—and which myths and their offshoots, epics and fairy tales, have so many times cited as the goal of every human quest toward the light?

14

The Cathars
and the Norse

We oddly enough find among those who, over the last hundred years, have taken an interest in the Cathar question and its profound significance not just the Occitains, whose motivations for this interest are perfectly understandable, but also a great number of people from the north with connections, in one way or another, to the great themes of Nordic mythology. These are primarily German intellectuals, but Dutch, Anglo-Saxons, and Scandinavians can also be found among their number, as well as the usual crowds of hermeticists and esotericists from northern France who are seemingly heavily influenced by the symbolist and decadent milieus of nineteenth-century Paris. Some of the influential figures from that time include Huysmans; Mallarmé; Rémy de Gourmont; Élimir Bourges; Villiers de L'Isle-Adam; Maurice Maeterlinck; Claude Debussy; the Sar Péladan; the strange Jules Boise, the lover in name of Emma Calvé, who was the correspondent and no doubt mistress of Father Saunière; Saint-Yves d'Alveydre; Stanislas de Guaïta; the very Voltarian Anatole France (who was much less a realist than is customarily thought); the novelist Jules Verne (who is wrongly considered to be a writer for only young people); and many others.

All of these who discovered the Cathars subscribed to widely varying currents of thought, and it would be hard to find a unifying approach among them. The sole point they shared in common was the spell cast upon them by the work of Richard Wagner, even upon those who once adored him—such as Debussy—but then rejected him categorically. This shadow of Wagner is important to the rediscovery of the Cathars because it in part fueled intensive research that often yielded original observations, but it also completely distorted the motivations of this research by joining one of the most debatable forms of German esotericism with the metaphysical and mythological components of what was basically a Mediterranean heresy.

We should be wary of the Mediterranean aspect of Catharism. It certainly developed essentially in Italy and Occitania, and shared a current of thought of Persian origin that had existed in the Middle East, but what does this mean? It was actually northern Italy, not southern Italy, that was touched by the Cathar heresy, and it is well known that northern Italy, especially during the Middle Ages, was made up of a mosaic of people from the north: Celts from the Po Valley, Lombards and Ostrogoths, Venitians and Illyrians of even more obscure stock, and the Slavs (the Bogomils in particular) who came from the Balkans and who pledged allegiance to the Germanic Holy Roman Empire. Further, not all of Occitania was touched by Catharism, but only the former Septimania, or Visigothic region, in which German invaders originating in Sweden had merged with the authochtonous Celtic population that had been only marginally affected by the Roman conquest. These are the Germanic components involved in the birth of the Cathar heresy.

Furthermore, while Catharism was colored by Christianity, and while the doctrine of the perfecti was based on certain Judeo-Christian texts, it is difficult to honestly consider it as a deviant version of Christianity. It was in fact a separate religion and shared only its immediate surroundings with Christianity. It was not a heresy but the culmination of a dualistic system that hearkened back to the most ancient pre-Christian religions. What we must emphasize is that the system was fundamentally Indo-European, which was not unusual because the Persians were a branch of this mysterious people that proliferated almost everywhere and that we know primarily through its language and sociocultural structures.

There were, of course, mutations along the way. The dualistic system could hardly recognize itself in Greek theogony or Celtic mythology, though both share the same Indo-European source. On the other hand, it seems to have survived intact in Germano-Scandinavian mythology.

To be exact, we know the mythology of the peoples classified as Germanic only through what the Roman Tacitus wrote about them, through medieval German literature, and through the later but archaic sagas of Iceland. (It is customary to include the Scandinavian and Icelandic peoples with the group of continental Germans.) Accordingly, the German god Wotan is none other than the Wutanas of Tacitus, as well as the Odin of the Icelandic poems, and while the Germans speak of Siegfried, the Scandinavians know him as Sigurd. In any event, if we did not have the great texts set down in writing around A.D. 1000 by the Scandinavians who had been newly converted to Christianity, we would know nothing of the primitive mythology of the peoples of continental Germany.

Now that this has been made explicit, we can note the obvious connections between the principal elements of the mythology of the Indo-Europeans of Central Asia and those of Germano-Scandinavian mythology. It is not surprising to find points where the latter coincides with Mazdean tradition, which is essentially of Central Asian and Indo-European origin.

All mythology is expressed according to the distinguishing features of the civilization that codified it, and among these characteristics, climate conditions have their part. This is why we can observe, in the tales that were inherited from the ancient Scythians of Central Asia and that Georges Dumézil patiently reconstructed,* a clear tendency to explain the world as a perpetual struggle between the two antagonistic forces

---

* Georges Dumézil, *Romans de Scythie et alentours* (Paris: Payot, 1977).

of heat and cold. This is indicative of a harsh continental climate in which the opposition of winter and summer is felt to be the consequence of a gigantic confrontation between gods of opposite polarities. The origin of dualism is to be sought here, as well as in the combat between Ahura-Mazda, who is light and fire, and Ahriman, who is darkness and cold; both traditions translated into mythological terms the reality of everyday life.

A figure named Batraz appearing in these Scythian stories is a hero who was born under very odd circumstances: Because his mother dies before his birth, his father nourishes his embryo under the skin of his back. At his birth, Batraz appears as a man clad in iron covered with flames. He spreads an incredible heat around him and becomes the protector of his people by struggling against the forces of cold and darkness throughout his life.

Batraz can be seen again in Irish mythology as Cuchulainn, but Cuchulainn has lost his original character; he is a formidable warrior whose ardor must sometimes be cooled by a dip into a vat of cold water, which he subsequently brings to the boil. But in Germano-Scandinavian mythology, Batraz appears as the model of the absolute warriors whom the Valkyries search for on battlefields so they might be brought to Valhalla, for it is with such individuals, who are as hard as iron and burn like fire, that the gods can mount an effective opposition against the forces of darkness. These forces are made up of the giants, who, in the depths of the earth, are preparing to raise an assault against the divine domain, the fortress of Asgard with its rampart Valhalla, where the gods—the Aesir and the Vanir—take their stand. In short, the gods of Asgard are the Pure, the perfecti, and the warriors of Valhalla are the credenti who, though not entirely liberated from the yoke of matter, form an intermediary host between the world of evil and the world of good.

The difference between this mythology and Cathar doctrine is that Cathar eschatology is optimistic (Satan and his legions will be drowned in a lake of fire), whereas in Germanic mythology, the giants of the cold, by attacking the divine world, will unleash the final battle during which everything will be destroyed by fire, including the gods. One lone hope remains: Baldur, the son of Wotan-Odin, murdered as a result of Loki's betrayal, will be reborn and will bring about the rebirth of an entirely different world. But this notion remains particularly confused in the Nordic texts and one wonders all in all if Germano-Scandinavian thought might not be entirely conditioned by belief in the annihilation of beings and things.

There is, then, among the Norse as with the Cathars the expression of an undying struggle between the principal gods, between light/fire and darkness/cold. The souls of the fallen angels are sleeping and are numb in the chill darkness of Satan's kingdom—in other words, matter. Only the souls brushed by the divine fire emanated from the paradise of light could awaken and respond to the call. It is understood that perhaps the triumph of fire at the end of time, which characterizes Germano-Scandinavian eschatology, will be the final victory of the beings of light over the beings of darkness. Baldur, who is no doubt the same figure as Batraz, will be reborn from this heat like the phoenix of Mediterranean legend. But at what cost? At the cost of the supreme renunciation, the annihilation of all terrestrial substance, and even more, the complete extinction of the human race, which is merely the temporary, transitory, and corruptible prison of this primordial light. In one sense, in Germano-Scandinavian mythology the new man cannot be anything but different and will appear only at the price of a gigantic conflagration. This idea exists in Cathar doctrine: absolute purification can occur only through fire. This explains the perfecti running into the flames of the Montségur pyre while singing hymns to the glory of the light.

Purification is the key word. From the Cathar perspective this conclusion would seem to be the logical conclusion based on the belief that the world can be explained by a fall from an original angelic state to a diabolical state. But this notion is absent in Germano-Scandinavian tradition. In the beginning there is chaos. Consciousness slowly emerges from this chaos, but once it is set in motion, this consciousness cannot stop itself; it must continue to the farthest limits to free itself from that which covers it tightly and to purify itself over the course of confrontations that represent life with all its ups and downs.

Strange musings can be read in *Lucifer's Court,* the book by Otto Rahn that is something of a travel diary from the time of his stay in Cathar country: "I have come from the north. I am heading toward the south. Hardly has my journey begun when my gaze turns again toward the north, toward the 'midnight' where, it is said, sits the mountain of the Gathering and the Crown." Then again: "Tomorrow, around this time, I will thus be rolling toward the south, holding in my heart the desire to cast as much light into these shadows that I can. May it be granted to me to be a bearer of light!"

Words of either a visionary or a crank. The work of Otto Rahn is of no scientific or even esoteric value. It is a collection of confused musings and false observation but is nonetheless revealing. For the words of Otto Rahn are those of a man on a mission, someone who in good faith believes to have found an ideal place where the light will defeat the darkness. For him this place was Montségur, the fortress on the heights, where the rising sun of the solstice entered the "meditation room." There the purification, the regeneration, could symbolically take place.

The connotation is obviously suspect, especially when we remember that Rahn was a member of the S.S. We can make out some disturbing shadows behind his mission. First we find the strange Hans Horbiger, author of a somewhat woolly-minded theory on the origin and evolution of the world. For Horbiger's thought, with its assertion of the primitive existence of an enormous accumulation of cosmic ice, his history of humanity centered around a perpetual struggle between ice and fire and the force of repulsion and that of attraction, represents at the beginning of the twentieth century a reactualization of Germano-Scandinavian mythology with an added racial perspective that is not at all far removed from that of National Socialism. In addition to this we know that Horbiger was held in very high esteem by Hitler's entourage. A German author wrote this vibrant homage to him in 1935:

It is to Horbiger's undying credit that he powerfully resuscitated our ancestors' intuitive knowledge of the eternal conflict of fire and ice, sung by the *Edda*. He has revealed this conflict to the eyes of his contemporaries. He has provided a scientific foundation for this grandiose image of the world tied to the dualism of matter and force, the repulsion that scatters and the attraction that gathers.

We might think this writing to be a Cathar work. Wouldn't "the repulsion that scatters" be the fall of the angels and Satan's creation of matter? Wouldn't "the attraction that gathers" be the original light that draws angelic souls once they have awakened from their torpor in order to bring them to the great gathering point in that vast mythical north that haunted the imagination of Otto Rahn?

From the time of Romanticism, and especially in Germany, an entire current of thought called Nordic thought had developed—set in opposition to Mediterranean thought—with Madame de Stael incontestably acting as its initiator. The discovery of Celtic and Germanic mythological traditions during the nineteenth century demonstrated the actual existence of these two opposing systems, these contradictory patterns of logic, one Norse and barbarous, the other Mediterranean, Aristotelian, and, for centuries, dominant in the West, where it suppressed its opposite beneath the murky depths of the subconscious. Theories like those of Horbiger, which are totally antiscientific, shored up the movement of Nordic thought by giving it a dimension it did not possess at the start, focused exclusively as it was on mythology, sensibility, art, and literature. In fact, having acquired a scientific cover, this movement was converted into a political and philosophical instrument. Norse myths such as those of Hyperborea, Atlantis, and Ultima Thule thus became the symbols of a new way of thinking about humanity: Truth came from the North and this truth had been concealed for twenty centuries or more by Mediterranean thought extended by Judeo-Christian doctrines. Sweeping away Judeo-Christian doctrines and positioning the ancient traditions of the North in a place of honor once again was enough to restore this truth. Beyond this, all the doctrines that had been persecuted by the prevailing ideology, all the esoteric, religious, and philosophical ideas that had been classified as heretical could then be resuscitated.

It is quite certain that from this new perspective the Cathars, pursued by the Inquisition and massacred by secular power in alliance with the spiritual authority held by the Judeo-Christians, were held up as examples, all the more so because correspondences were found between Germano-Scandinavian thought and Cathar doctrine. This explains the interest that Germans—and, generally speaking, all Nordics—displayed in the Cathar heresy at the end of the nineteenth century and the beginning of the twentieth.

Added to this interest in the Cathars was the activity of numerous esoteric societies that claimed to be the keepers of "lost secrets" and thus to be directly in the line of descent from the great "initiates" of times gone by. Among these, the Golden Dawn emerged in Great Britain in 1867 out of the renewal of the Rosicrucian tradition. The expressed purpose of the Golden Dawn was the practice of ceremonial magic and the understanding of initiatory powers. One of its leaders was the Irish poet W. B. Yeats, one of the main forces behind the restoration of Celtic tradition. There was also the all-powerful Theosophy Society from which Rudolf Steiner would soon separate himself. One of the members of the Golden Dawn, Aleister Crowley, expressed fairly strange ideas concerning the permanent presence of an initiatory tradition passed down by a race that had retained its purity over the centuries. We know that Crowley later said: "Before Hitler was, I am." This is to illustrate that the secret societies of this time had certain tendencies to envision the existence of a pure and authentic tradition as linked to a pure race bearing all the hopes of humanity.

In Germany itself at the beginning of the twentieth century, through the awakening of interest in the visionary and through the ramifications of the Rose + Cross and the extensions of the Golden Dawn, there existed a large number of self-proclaimed philosophical sects who did not seek to hide their belief in the "pure race," meaning, of course, the Aryan race, and who loudly asserted the predominance of the Nordic tradition over the cosmopolitanism represented by the Mediterranean tradition. It is in this swarm of sects that the famous Thule Group was born, which had an undeniable influence on the formation of Nazi ideology.

The Thule group emerged out of the Order of the Germans, founded in 1912. One of the order's animators, Rudolf von Sebottendorf, was given charge of the "province" of Bavaria, and it was he who created a rift there that led to the formation of the group. The name chosen for this society is quite revealing: It is a specific reference to Ultima Thule, the mythical yet real island of the Hyperboreans, where the eternal combat between fire and ice (volcano and glacier) takes place. It is possible that the name Thule comes from an Indo-European root meaning "balance" (*tûla* in Sanskrit), which may have been used at once time to designate the position of the Pole Star in the sign of Libra. It is also possible to see in it the Greek word *tholos*, "fog," which would also characterize quite well the nature of this remote island. Whatever the case, the Thule Group exercised a profound influence on the men who came to found the National Socialist party in Bavaria. We should recall that Alfred Rosenberg, one of Nazism's most virulent theoreticians, wrote on the subject of the Thule Group: "The Thule Society? But everything started there! The secret teaching we drew from that source was of more use in our gaining power than any S.A. or S.S. divisions. The men who founded that association were true magicians."

The Thule Group's association with ceremonial magic has been widely studied as the origin of the Nazi movement in initiatory occult practices. It is important to recall the interest in the Cathars displayed by all the more or less secret societies whose philosophic appearance was based on a return to Norse symbolism. The Cathars may have appeared in southern countries, but the Nordic components of their doctrine are not in doubt and provide sufficient explanation as to why the Nordics of the late nineteenth and early twentieth centuries examined them so closely, seeking to determine the exact meaning of the Cathar itinerary, and if they did have secrets, just what these secrets were.

The invasion of the Polars* denounced in the March 6, 1932, Ariège edition of *La Dépêche,* is not a legend. In that instance Otto Rahn had arrived in the region of Ussat and Ornolac that same year. And the Toulouse daily also raised some questions: "What will these researches unearth and who will be the first to discover the Cathar treasures and manuscripts, the French engineer Monsieur Arnaud in Montségur, or the German Polar Monsieur Rams [this is Rahn] in Ornolac?" This illustrates that the purpose of all research undertaken in Cathar country, whether real or imaginary, delusional or symbolic, has always been related to a "treasure."

The Polars involved here in 1932 were, according to *La Dépêche,* "a band of foreign visitors belonging to a theosophical society whose seat was in Paris." But the Polar reference is not gratuitous. Germano-Scandinavian mythology definitely made a good match with Catharism.

The problem lies in not knowing what the Polars were looking for, not whether or not Otto Rahn found what he was looking for (confirmation of the claims made by the turn-of-the-century initiatory and philosophical societies). Anyone can find what he is determined to find. The real issue is knowing why Montségur and the other Cathar sites motivated the Nordic seekers so strongly.

Regarding the Germano-Scandinavian mythological view, the North is no longer a geographical marker but a symbolic site, the place where all the great forces animating the world converge. The idea of a *pole*—especially the North Pole, which is linked scientifically to the existence of a large mass of magnetized iron somewhere in that region of the world—represents the human desire to define a center of vital activity, a kind of pivot around which the world is organized, whether materially or spiritually. The pole is the equivalent of the omphallos,

---

* [Polars were the supporters and proslytyzers of Nordic beliefs. This nickname was coined by a French journalist. —*Trans.*]

the navel of the world, which is the point that was once symbolically in contact with the primary cause. The umbilical cord, however, has been cut and there is no longer an effective connection between the world and the mother substance. All that is left is a scar, which can always reopen, allowing new contact and fusion with what came before. Every initiatory doctrine needs to be nurtured by a primordial substance that justifies its existence and allows it to endure. Spirituality of any kind is not an *ex nihilo* creation and connects as best it can to an *illud tempus,** as Mircea Eliade says, without which it lacks all meaning. And while this *illud tempus* does not figure on any calendars or in any annals, it exists nonetheless through the unavoidable sequence that connects today's thought to that of yesterday. All doctrines, meaning all attempts to provide an explanation for the world, must be supported by a solid base, but this base is all the more solid and certain in proportion to its connection to an origins myth. The pole, like the omphallos, is the privileged site at which the myth of origin resides. This site was Delphi in Greek religious thought; Tara in the mythological thought of the ancient Irish; and for all the druids in Gaul it was the sanctuary in the forest of Carnutes, the place, according to Caesar, where these druids gathered.

In the case of Catharism, as in the case with Germano-Scandinavian mythology, the ideal spot, the most appropriate place to serve as a pivot, is the North Pole, absolute north. Lost in the midst of ice that covers a mystery concealed beneath the thickness of the glacier, it is, in essence, the domain of primordial purity and whiteness. The North Pole is easily seen as a place that excludes all physical or spiritual pollution. It is the place where there is no longer any evil, for evil is imperfection, pollution, and degeneration. The North Pole is a fairly good representation of what the human mind conceives of as the original angelic state. But the pole is ambiguous: The ice and cold are also

---

* [The moment before time starts. —*Trans.*]

representative of the numbing of intellectual and spiritual values. The cold is death, the impossibility of action, a kind of nirvana that extinguishes all desire to live. Thus it becomes potential energy—a virgin which, in being so, has a rich future.

It certainly seems that Montségur may have played this polar role. The bustle of life doesn't reach the summit of the pog. Instead the pog sits between Heaven and Earth, like the chamber of the sun of legend. But it is also the mythological fortress trapped in ice, a fortress that no one can leave once he is inside, and that no one can enter because its ice walls are as unbreachable as the stone walls of a real castle. This could be the picture of Asgard, the German Olympus where Wotan/Odin lives when he is not traveling; where, draped in his large cloak, his hat folded back over his forehead, he appears unexpectedly from the shadows with his eye flaming—that remnant of solar light connecting him to his origin.

In Irish tradition we are told that druidism was brought from the Isles of the North of the World. In this way Celtism connects to the Norse myth of the origin of the world, but we should not take this myth literally. The ideal North, the spiritual North from whence come the sciences as well as magic and religion, is only a simple clue. In fact the North can be everywhere and nowhere at the same time, because it is based more on emotion than on a logic that has no chance of being taken seriously. We know, and have always known, that the North is the direction of mystery, of what is troubled, misty, and inconsistent. But this North is what is intended for most mortals, because the audacious who dare cross the barrier of fog and ice, who dare assail the silence, can see what is on *the other side.* It is always the same quest perpetually starting over and perpetually questioned. Over there, far away, there is certainty, but only a few ever attain it.

This is why so many people assault the pog of Montségur. It is a symbolic pole, a mythological Olympus at the navel of the world. The presence of the Cathars and the search for the secret they may have hidden is only a pretext. The main goal is to scale the flanks of the mountain in order to emerge into full light. Among the majority of ancient peoples, orientation was determined based on the rising sun, and the left side of anything was the *sinister* side, the disturbing side, that of mystery. Toward the North there is never any sun; consequently it is in that direction that it must manifest itself in the most secret manner possible and only to those capable of seeing it in the darkness.

Such seems to be the meaning of the pole, and particularly the North Pole, which channels and pulls around it all the images of a purity found again. Montségur, the "beacon" of Catharism, cannot be anything else.

15

Montségur and the Grail

In 1933, shortly after Otto Rahn first appeared in the upper Ariège Valley, a curious discovery was made in a small cave located beneath the ruins of the castle of Montréal-de-Sos. It was a symbolic depiction painted on one of the smooth cavern walls, and was mentioned by Alex Coutet in an article in *La Dépêche* and examined later by the prehistorian Father Glory.

Here is Alex Coutet's description of the painting:

> It is a square about four centimeters in size, drawn in red. Two smaller squares are inscribed inside it, one inside the other. Double line crosses have been drawn, alternating Greek and Saint Andrew's crosses, forming a frame around the smallest square, inside of which other crosses alternating with red flames have been drawn. Outside and above the square a spear emerges; next to this spear a circle that is red on the outside and grey-white inside has been drawn. Six single line crosses are scattered outside the square.

That's all. But beneath the pen of Antonin Gadal they become something entirely different:

> There is in this cave, which has two or three entrances, a tri-colored painting: white, black, and red, a drawing that is directly connected to Chrétien de Troyes's *Perceval le Gallois*. An attractive drawing

can be seen on the rocky wall that has deteriorated slightly due to harsh weather conditions. It depicts red crosses, a broken sword, a spear, a decorated platter [*platter* is misspelled in the original French —*Trans.*] holding five drops of blood, and, in the center, the Grail in the form of a resplendent sun. This drawing is the only one of its kind in the world. Only a glance and the entire book of *Perceval* instantly files before your eyes.*

This commentary is based on several different expositions supposedly drawn from Chrétien de Troyes but in fact borrowed from any available source, in this case Wolfram von Eschenbach's text as well as the *Estoire du Saint Graal* or *The Quest of the Holy Grail*. It is obvious that Antonin Gadal read neither Chrétien de Troyes's text in its entirety nor any of the other texts. We can immediately perceive that the three colors of which he speaks (white, black, and red) are not in Chrétien de Troyes's text (only two are found there: white and red) but instead are in a Welsh text recounting the adventures of Peredur. This color combination is also a veritable cliché in the context of Celtic literature.†

Here we find the Grail in Montréal-de-Sos, after it was found by this same Antonin Gadal in the castle of Montségur! Saddest of all is that this painting is absolutely not Cathar, or Templar, or even contemporary to Chrétien de Troyes. It no doubt dates from the seventeenth or at best sixteenth century.

---

* A. Gadal, *De l'heritage des Cathares,* edited by the Rosicrucians of Haarlem (Ussat-les-Bains: n.p., 1980), 26 ff. In the middle of this pamphlet a color reproduction of the famous painting can be found, entirely retouched. A reader with any scruples for objectivity can see what is offered by reality thanks to the black and white photograph, fig. 14, facing page 129 in René Nelli's *Le Phénomène cathare* (Toulouse: Privat, 1964). The comparison speaks eloquently and provides proof positive that any means is good that shows what cannot be shown.

† I have provided a lengthy critique on this theme of three colors, with quotes and supporting references, in my book *The Grail* (Rochester, Vt.: Inner Traditions, 1999), 15–16. In this book I have systematically analyzed *all* the versions of the Grail legend, and we can easily see that they are *all* different.

Nelli writes:

It very well may have been executed during a relatively recent era by a village wizard or a contemplative shepherd whose drawing was simply inspired by what he had seen in church: the *mortuary sheet,* for example, with its silver tears; or some frescoes that decorated a chapel wall (a frieze of Greek crosses, scattered gold flames, etc.).*

Furthermore, since the discovery of this cave drawing, other examples of paintings in this style—with an even stronger folkloric character—have been discovered. It requires an extremely active imagination to see in their depictions the description Chrétien de Troyes provided of the famous Grail procession: The spear looks more like a fifteenth-century poignard; whether the platter is indeed a platter is debatable; and the so-called Grail as a solar disk is an oversimplified depiction of Christ's head rather than a sacred vessel. As for the drops of blood, contrary to Chrétien de Troyes's description, they do not seem to be running off of the spear. However, we should put things in their proper perspective: As René Nelli noted, if this painting truly depicts the Grail, "that would not be further proof that this is the work of a Cathar hand, because there is not one single text authorizing us to conclude that Catharism ever paid any particular attention to the myth of the Grail."†

We may reasonably ask, then: Why were the myths of the Grail held in such esteem in Cathar country, particularly in Ussat-les-Bains and Montségur? The answer is clear and precise: because of incomplete and confused information about the different versions of the Grail legend, primarily the German version by Wolfram von Eschenbach.

It would help here to sketch out a little literary history and to provide some exact dates. The first text to bring up the Grail Quest, though

---

* René Nelli, *Le phénomène cathare* (Toulouse: Privat, 1964),184.
† Ibid.

without actually naming the marvelous object, was an Occitain text, the *Roman de Jauffré,* dating from 1180. This story involves an Arthurian adventure during which the hero goes through all the stages of an initiatory quest. The first text to name the mysterious Grail and present the hero as Perceval is that of Chrétien de Troyes, a Champagne poet of Jewish origin who wrote around 1190. This *Perceval, or the Story of the Grail,* allegedly commissioned by the count of Flanders, Philippe d'Alsace, was left an incomplete work and no doubt intentionally so. In the period from 1190 to 1210, four different authors furnished a conclusion in several fragments, and an anonymous author deemed it wise to write a kind of preface to the whole thing, entitled the *Elucidation.*

Parallel to this fundamental series of texts, and at roughly the same time—1200—a Welsh-language tale appeared, *Peredur,* that is much more archaic in spirit. The adventures are almost identical to those experienced by Perceval—whose name here is Peredur—but the Grail is not mentioned. Another text, this one in French and betraying a strong Glastonbury Abbey influence, was written around 1195. It is a long romance entitled *Perlesvaux*—after the name of the hero—and the Grail occupies a choice place in the narrative. All of these texts may be classified as Franco-British and form a primitive version of the legend.

More texts were written between 1200 and 1250; these are quite elaborate versions exhibiting a very different mentality, and one clearly bears the imprint of a Cistercian influence. The first is Robert de Boron's *Joseph* in which a synthesis of biblical and Celtic elements appears for the first time along with the connection of the Grail theme to Christ's Passion. This was followed by a strange tale known as *Didot-Perceval,* an adaptation of a lost poem by Robert de Boron, and then by the *Estoire du saint Graal* (an adaptation of *Joseph*) and *The Quest for the Holy Grail.* These last two form part of what is called the *Prose Lancelot,* a large corpus of Arthurian legends also known under the name of the *Vulgate Lancelot-Grail.* In *The Quest for the Holy Grail* the discoverer of the Grail is no longer Perceval but Galahad, son of Lancelot of the Lake, a Christ-like figure entirely fabricated from the viewpoint of holiness as conceived by Cistercian theologians.

In none of these texts, neither Franco-British nor Cistercian, can a single detail be found linking the Grail theme to Cathar doctrine, or locating the Grail Castle at Montségur or somewhere else in Cathar country. But this is not true for yet another version of the legend, the one written by the German Wolfram von Eschenbach in both his *Parzival* and his "Titurel," two works dating from around 1210 that can be labeled Germano-Persian. Here the connection with Catharism appears certain, and the very specific details found in Wolfram's text provide a satisfying explanation both for the interest displayed by the Nordics in the Cathars and for their suggestion that the Grail Castle was located at Montségur.

In fact, by crossing the Rhine, the Grail theme found in the German context a completely original maturation from the original Celtic outline. Certainly Wolfram von Eschenbach's *Parzival* follows quite closely the plot of Chrétien de Troyes's *Perceval,* which is logical, considering that the author presents his own work as the adaptation—if not outright translation, in the case of certain passages—of the French romance. But the details of Eschenbach's work are far from concordant with the French version. In fact, there is a deep rift between the two works even regarding the spirit that animates them. What was a mythological legend inherited from the Celts and transposed, for the needs of the cause, by each of several French writers according to various aspects of Christian ideology then popular, eventually became a philosophical, truly hermetic work, or at least one charged with easily detected esoteric elements.

The Germany of the early thirteenth century was a crucible in which apparently contradictory influences met but from which emerged a spirituality that was as far from orthodox as Cistercian spirituality may have been at the time of Saint Louis. The German visionary tradition had already appeared in embryonic form in the poetry of Minnesinger (which Richard Wagner clearly revealed in his Master Singers of Nuremburg) and Jacob Boheme's profile was beginning to appear on the Germanic horizon. The taste for secret rites, for initiations—it is not clearly known into what—was developing and inspiring the birth of so-called secret societies in which occultism became a veritable mode. In parallel fashion, the number of alchemists was growing whose motivations were increasingly oriented toward understanding the great secrets of the universe through the philosopher's stone. In addition, because this was the time of the Crusades, people brought back from the East not only spices and perfumes, but traditions thought to have been long forgotten, and monastic orders such as the Teutonic Knights, who were created for these circumstances, behaved in a very "corporatist" manner. The end result was the formation of actual initiatory societies that combined elements borrowed from Roman Christianity, the Eastern Church and other sects, even Islam, and beyond that, the currents that stirred Asia Minor, Persia, and the borders of the Himalayas.

Wolfram von Eschenbach, no doubt a native of Bavaria, lived among the entourage of the Landgrave Hermann of Thuringia in a milieu where there was always a great interest in the occult. He wrote several unfinished works, but his finished *Parzival* is presented as a long poem the central part of which, by the author's own admission, is an adaptation of Chrétien de Troyes's *Perceval*. However the novelist from Champagne was not his sole source.

The entire first part of the book relates the adventures of Parzival's father, who had never been mentioned in Chrétien de Troyes's work. It is possible that Wolfram invented him on his own, seeking to provide a preface to his hero's adventures, but other elements, namely the introduction of Parzival's half brother, who is a European-Islamic halfbreed, or even the mention at the very end of the poem of Parzival's son Lohengrin, who himself becomes the founder of a famous lineage in both history and legend (that of Godefroy de Bouillon) appear to have been borrowed from very different sources far removed from Chrétien de Troyes and the Celtic archetype.

Conceding to the stylistic device of the time that called for ceaseless reference to a predecessor, even an imaginary one, Wolfram acknowledged his inspiration to a model that he opposed to Chrétien de Troyes: "Master Chrétien told this tale, but altered it; and Kyôt, who passed the true story on to us, was irked by this for good reason."* Throughout his work Wolfram quoted this Kyôt the Provençal who "wrote the French version." This detail is somewhat surprising, for a native of Provence in that era would write only in Occitain and never in French. Basing their arguments on the fact that Wolfram often cited Provins en Brie and the very name of Kyôt, which may be the German transliteration for Guyot or Guillot, critics have attempted to identify Wolfram's mysterious informer as the known poet Guiot de Provins, author of numerous poems and a satiric Bible that lack neither verve nor ferocity. But this similarity of names appears to be a coincidence.

It is not out of the question that Wolfram's attribution to Kyôt might be a ruse. In fact, the name Guillot or Guyot is connected to the root word *guille* (the Anglo-Saxon *vile* and the English *wile*), an old French word meaning both "deceit" and "foolishness." There are numerous examples in twelfth- and thirteenth-century literature of word play involving the term *guille* and the names of Guillaume[†] and its diminutives such as Guyot and Guillot. The most famous example can be found in the fifteenth-century work *La Farce de Maître Pathelin*, which concerns the draper Guillaume and the expression "Do you take us for Guillaumes?" meaning quite simply, "Do you take us for imbeciles?" I could also cite the famous proverb "Tel croit guiller Guillot que Guillot guille" (Littré).[‡] All of this means that during an era when the troubadours enjoyed practicing the *trobar clus,* meaning "camouflage," and various word games, Wolfram could very well be "taking us for Guillaumes" with his reference to Kyôt the Provençal.

It is hard, though, not to accept the existence of a source other than Chrétien de Troyes for the creation of *Parzival.* Here is what Wolfram says in this regard:

---

* Wolfram von Eschenbach, *Parzival,* vol. 2, translated by Ernest Tonnelat (Paris: Aubier-Montaigne, 1934), 324. All the citations of Wolfram von Eschenbach's work in this book are extracts from this translation by Ernest Tonnelat, the best one to date.

† [Guillaume = William. —*Trans.*]

‡ ["He thinks to gull (trick) Guillot whom Guillot gulls." —*Trans.*]

The illustrious master Kyôt found among some abandoned manuscripts in Toledo the substance of this story, copied in Arabic script.
He had to learn the characters A, B, C beforehand (the elements of
magic writing, according to Wolfram), but he was never initiated
into black magic. It was a great advantage that he had been baptized—otherwise this tale would have remained unknown. There is
not in fact a pagan wise enough to reveal the nature of the Grail
and tell us how one comes to know its secret virtues (Wolfram von
Eschenbach, *Parzival*, vol. 2, translated by Ernest Tonnelat, 23).

In short, the original outline of the quest and especially the great
secrets of the Grail had a precise origin for Wolfram: They came from
the East through an intermediary Arab manuscript. Numerous details
throughout the story would appear to confirm this declaration of an
Oriental source, for these details are neither Celtic nor borrowed from
Chrétien de Troyes.

There is first the wound of Anfortas the Fisher King (whose name,
incidentally, comes from the Latin *infirmitas,* whereas in the French
texts his name is Pelles, shared by the Celtic deity Pwyll Penn Annwfn).
Wolfram tells us that the king's wound is insupportable when the
weather is freezing. He is the only author to make this specific claim.
And when he cures the king, Parzival appears wearing the features of
Indra, a regenerative solar deity who, when the Aryans occupied the
northern lands before completing their migration toward the Indus
Valley, was regarded as the god who made the ice melt.

The Fisher King himself can be considered the equivalent of a
mythological Indian figure. The gold fish is the first manifestation
Vishnu embodies as a creator; it is a symbol that combines with the
image of the *icthus* of the first Christians as the representation of the
man-god Jesus Christ. In Tibetan Buddhist speculation, the gold fish
symbolizes the creatures immersed in the ocean of the *samsara,* the
infernal cycle of reincarnation, who must be lead by the fisherman to
the light of liberation. This theme is quite close to the Cathar doctrine

of the awakening of the angelic soul imprisoned in matter, which, under the direction of a perfecti, will regain the path to the original light.

In Wolfram's text and nowhere else, Parzival's father went to war in the East, in the neighborhood of Baghdad, which is where he was killed. But he had a son there, Vairefils (sometimes spelled Feirefils), meaning "gray son," with whom Parzival later achieves some of his adventures. There could be much said about the presence of this Vairefils at the side of the hero and about his fundamentally ambiguous nature. As a person of European and Islamic descent he should simply be colored, but as it happens, he is always depicted as black and white, and thus appears to the author to be a concrete representation of the dualistic principle. In any case, the author's reference to an Oriental source appears to be supported here.

Wolfram places some of Gawain's adventures in the magical palace of Klinschor, or Klingsor, a figure who later assumes considerable importance in Richard Wagner's opera. Klingsor's palace, minutely described by Wolfram, bears an astounding resemblance to descriptions of the Buddhist monasteries of Kabulistan, especially the palace of Kapisa with its fantastic wheeled throne, comparable to the bed of wonders. It is beyond doubt that the author knew well the Oriental model that served in the story he was telling.

The Grail Castle—which is not named in Chrétien's work and is called Corbenic in the Cistercian *Quest*—bears the name Munsalvaesche, or Montsalvage, in *Parzival*. The meaning of this is "Mount Savage" or "mount of salvation." But what is exceedingly strange is Wolfram's detailed description of this castle, which is impossible not to compare to the Manichaean citadels of northern Persia, in particular the fortress of Ruh-I-Sal-Schwadeha, on Lake Hamun in Sista on what is now the Iranian/Afghanistan border. Taking into account that Ruh-I means "mount," might Montsalvage be the exact correspondent of Ruh-I-Sal-Schwadeha, at least on the phonetic level? This resemblance is too close to be due to chance and would seem to indicate a Manichaean influence on the *Parzival* narrative.

That said, it is impossible to make Montsalvage and Montségur coincide. There is kinship only between the first syllables of each word. But this does make it easier to understand why it was principally the Germans who clung to the identification of Montségur as the castle of the Grail. In any event, Wolfram's text does have some connections to the Cathars.

In *Parzival,* but in none of the other versions, the Grail is a precious stone on which a dove identified as the Holy Ghost sometimes alights. This stone is called, or at least Wolfram declares that it is called, *lapsit exillis,* which might need correcting to *lapis exillis,* (*lapis* means "stone" in Latin). People are now convinced that Wolfram, who had no more than a working knowledge of French, made a number of misinterpretations when translating Chrétien de Troyes's story (the most famous being the French word for *platter,* which is translated as *knives*). This has led to the following explanation for his replacement of the vessel containing the blood of Christ, or the simple container described by Chrétien, with a precious stone: Wolfram had confused the precious stones that adorn Chrétien's Grail for the Grail itself. This explanation is hardly satisfying because the context of Wolfram's work justifies the selection of only a single stone. There is first an alchemical allusion—*lapis exillis* is quite close to *lapis elixir,* the term used by the Arabs to designate the philosopher's stone. Next, this Grail Stone of celestial origin automatically brings to mind the Ka'aba Stone in Mecca, and many other stories of this nature. In particular, there is the tradition according to which the Grail was carved in the form of a vase from a gigantic emerald that fell from Lucifer's forehead at the time of his revolt and fall.* Here the theme ventures close to Catharism: The stone could symbolize what remained pure and angelic in the human soul following its imprisonment in matter. In this regard René Nelli has suggested that this *lapis exillis*

---

* Not included is the Celtic reference to the Stone of Tara in Ireland, which was the royal stone or coronation stone. It would shout when a future king of Ireland sat upon it, thereby designating who was, or was not, destined for royalty. This also brings to mind the Seat Perilous in the Cistercian version of the Grail legend.

may be a deformation of *lapis e coelis,* meaning "stone (fallen) from the heavens." This hypothesis seems quite attractive.*

In addition, the Grail Stone of Wolfram bears great resemblance to the famous Manichean jewel, which is the solar symbol of liberation and is incorporated into Buddhist tradition as the *mani padme* present in the heart of the lotus. It is also related to the Tree of Life found in Hindu traditions and is spoken of in the Persian Avesta as the *chwarna,* a magical and multiform object "that causes the waterways to gush from their springs, the plants from the earth, that causes the wind to chase the clouds, compels the birth of men, and guides the moon and the stars in their courses." Wolfram's Grail Stone possesses the same qualities as the chwarna. Another analogous symbol is the dove in Mazdean tradition that alights on the stone bearing a *hanna* seed. It so happens that the dove that lands on the Grail Stone carries a sacramental host and appears on Good Friday, which is, by chance, the day of the resurrection of the Nordic sun. And what can be said of the Buddhist paintings depicting the divine virgin carrying the jewel that dispenses joy? In Wolfram's text, the young girl who carries the Grail Stone is named Repanse del Schoie, meaning "reconsideration of joy." All of these accumulated details constitute precise facts and not ingenuous hypotheses. We must conclude that Wolfram von Eschenbach consciously and intentionally transformed Chrétien de Troyes's "receptacle" into the stone fallen from Heaven, and that the meaning and functions of this stone undoubtedly refer to an Oriental/Mazdean tradition that also nourished Catharism.

But there are many other points of agreement to consider between Catharism and Wolfram's text. First is the obsession with purity that Parzival and Catharism share. Even though Parzival is not a virgin—or even chaste, except in Wagner's opera—he is nonetheless on a quest for absolute purity. This purity, which is difficult to attain, was only simple naiveté in Chrétien's *Perceval.* But for Parzival it is conscious and

---

* Another theory interprets this *lapis exillis* as the "stone of exile" (*exillis* being an adjective), which obviously brings us right back to the Cathar doctrine.

allows him to pass through all the stages of initiation and become the incontestable king of the Grail. Further, his son Lohengrin, the knight of the swan, that preeminently symbolic animal, will pursue this quest that will force him to part from his wife, the duchess of Brabant, because she has broken the terrible taboo concerning his name and origins. When an individual is pure, he no longer has need of a name. And purity leads to perfection, the supreme goal of Cathar asceticism. The Grail King has attained this level; he has definitively resolved the dilemma of good and evil by denying evil. It is the victory of Ahura-Mazda over Ahriman, God over Satan, the light over the darkness.

As for the Grail Bearer, she is in no way comparable to Chrétien de Troyes's nameless maiden, or to the disturbing, dual-sexed empress from the Welsh tale of *Peredur,* or to Elaine, the daughter of Pelles in the *Prose Lancelot,* who couples with Lancelot to give birth to Galahad. Repanse de Schoye is chaste and pure. She can die but will be reborn from her ashes like the phoenix.

There is, then, the question that Parzival must ask to cure the wounded Fisher King. In the other versions of the tale, the hero must ask about the mysteries of the Grail. Parzival simply needs to ask: "King, from what are you suffering?" This is the ideal of compassion, inherited from a remote Buddhist tradition whereby souls can finally awaken, free themselves from their corporeal prisons, and ascend to the ecstatic joys of nonexistence in the kingdom of light. The ritual mentioned here by Wolfram is not Christian. It is not even Celtic. It is undoubtedly Cathar and is reminiscent of the consolamentum. When Parzival heals the Fisher King, the King does not die as he does in the other versions of the legend. Anfortas, to the contrary, is rejuvenated and devotes his life henceforth to service of the Grail. He whose sexual organs had been afflicted because he had taken too much pleasure from them, finds himself suddenly regenerated by Parzival the Pure and he transcends his libido, to the wonderment of others.

It is from this perspective that we need to examine the figure of the Esclarmonde of Pyrenees legend, particularly in the Montségur region.

She is the White Lady, a synthesis of the ancient goddess of springs and the historical figure of Esclarmonde de Foix, who was burned at the stake in the 1244 holocaust. Under certain conditions, Esclarmonde will emerge from the lake where she resides and wander along the walls of Montségur. Not far from Montségur a curious story is told that is similar to a Welsh legend:*

> A peasant had married a fairy who procured for him all that he desired. But she had forbidden her husband from calling her *fado,* meaning "fairy" as well as "mad woman." Of course, one day the peasant broke the taboo and the fairy flew away in the shape of a dove. The peasant soon saw that she would return to their home each day while he was away, but immediately upon his entrance into the house, his fairy wife would again fly away in the form of a dove.[†]

The Melusinian prohibition is recognizable in this story, but the fairy, instead of being a serpent woman like Melusine, is a bird woman as in Norse tradition. And what's more, she is a dove woman. We know that doves carved in soft stone and ceramic doves have been discovered in the Montségur area—one in Ussat-les-Bains and two at Montségur itself.[‡] We cannot help but recall the dove in Wolfram's text that comes every Good Friday to the Grail Stone, bearing a sacramental host, as well as the depiction of the Holy Ghost in Cathar tradition and the Huguenot cross surmounted by a dove, all of which are connected with the dove who brought the olive branch to Noah in his ark. The elements that converge here are quite revealing.

---

* Jean Markale, *L'Épopée celtique en Bretagne,* 3rd ed. (Paris: Payot, 1985), 273–76. This concerns *The Legend of Llyn y Fan,* certain elements of which can be found in the Languedoc story of *The Black Mountain* (Jean Markale, *Contes occitans* (Paris: Stock, 1982), 223–33), but in that tale the young woman is a duck woman.

† Adelin Moulis, *Croyances, superstitions, observances en Comté de Foix* (Ariège: Verniole, 1975) 12–14.

‡ René Nelli, *Le phénomène cathare* (Toulouse: Privat, 1964), 162–64.

Wolfram also claimed that the manuscript found in Toledo by Kyôt the Provençal was written by a certain Flegetanis, a Jew in the line of Solomon but whose father was Arab. Could this be a masked allusion to Chrétien de Troyes's Jewish origins? The name Flegetanis is yet another play on words. It is "the clumsy translation of Falalk-Thani, an Arab expression designating the second heaven, that of Mercury-Hermes, placed under the invocation of the 'messenger of the gods with S. Aïssa,' meaning Jesus. This second heaven governs life and spiritual knowledge."* Wolfram was rather unsparing in his description of Flegetanis who "worshiped a calf in which he saw a god." This is an indication of a bull-centered worship of the Mithraic variety. But he also says that Flegetanis "knew how to predict the disappearance of each star and the moment of its return." Wolfram thus turned him into an astrologer, or perhaps this detail concerns an image involving the transmigration of souls, which conforms to Cathar belief.

There is still more: "There was, he said, an object called the Grail. He had clearly read its name in the stars. A band of angels had placed it upon the earth then soared off far above the stars. These angels were too pure to remain here below" (Wolfram von Eschenbach, *Parzival*, vol. 2, translated by Ernest Tonnelat, 25). These angels offer a curiously Cathar connotation. Wolfram then claims that Flegetanis, who was a pagan, understood nothing of this story, whereas Kyôt the Provençal, who was a Christian, realized, in considering the departure of the angels, that the Grail must be entrusted only to:

[Men] who had become Christians by baptism and were as pure as angels. It is at this point that Kyôt, the master sage, sought in Latin books the place in which there could have lived a people pure enough and with a strong enough tendency to a life of renunciation to become the guardians of the Grail. He read the chronicles of the

---

* Albert Ollivier, *Les Templiers* (Paris: Le Seuil, 1958), 72.

kingdoms of Britain, France, and Ireland, and many others beside, until he found in Anjou that which he had been seeking (Wolfram von Eschenbach, *Parzival,* vol. 2, translated by Ernest Tonnelat, 25).

Here is a very significant point: The reference to Anjou touches on the Plantagenet dynasty, sovereigns of Great Britain and protectors of Armoricain Brittany but also the propagators of the Arthurian legends and the Grail myth. They also sought to make Glastonbury both the mythical isle of Avalon and the Grail Castle. The predominance of these three countries—Britain, France, and Ireland—indicates, according to Wolfram, an obvious Celtic imprint on the Grail theme. But what are we to make of the people who are pure enough to replace the angels in their role as guardians of the Grail? Are they Cathars? Templars? Or a completely different *pure* and *elect* people? We can note that though there is no reference here to Germany, because of this elitist evocation there is no further need for surprise at the particular destiny of this version of the quest, its heretical connotations, and especially its ulterior extension toward an Aryan mysticism. The Grail guardians, whether Templars, Cathars, or an entirely different group, would become the ferocious keepers of a necessary racial purity, eschewing from the outset or even coldly eliminating any heterogeneous elements not accepted into the mysteries of the Grail.

Wolfram von Eschenbach's tale does apparently follow the same outline used by Chrétien de Troyes. Parzival, "son of the widowed lady," one day leaves his mother to have himself dubbed a knight in the court of King Arthur. He experiences almost the same series of adventures as Perceval—and the Welsh Peredur: He enters the Grail Castle, witnesses the famous Grail procession, does not ask any questions, learns the truth about the Grail, and multiplies his efforts to rediscover the mysterious castle and heal the Fisher King. And like Perceval, he receives the teachings of a hermit who is revealed to be one of his maternal uncles.

This hermit is named Trevrizent in Wolfram's book. Whereas Chrétien de Troyes was satisfied to have him repeat a host of banalities to Perceval, it seems that Wolfram took advantage of this plot element to load the hermit's speech with an unlikely number of notions, some of which are even contradictory. Trevrizent appears as an initiator: He recounts, he explains, and he also lies (by his own admission).

Wolfran's Trevrizent first develops the theme, already exploited in the Cistercian version of the quest, of the replacement of the tenth legion of angels (Lucifer and the rebel angels) by the human race. Adam is clearly presented as Lucifer's replacement. Constantly appearing in Trevrizent's monologue are more or less veiled references concerning the light. For example:

> Thoughts can conceal themselves from the rays of the sun; thoughts, though no locks enclose them, remain hidden and impenetrable from all creatures; thoughts are darkness where no light penetrates. But divinity has the power to cast light on all; its rays shine through the wall enveloped by darkness.

These considerations seem to agree with the Cathar doctrine. The human being, caged in his thought since eating of the Tree of the Knowledge of Good and Evil, awaits a ray of divine light to awaken him. This divine light may perhaps be the Grail. Trevrizent in fact reveals to Parzival what the Grail is, but he does so through reference to those who guard this sacred object, in this instance the Templars, "who often ride great distances in quest of adventures. Whatever results from their combats, glory or shame, they accept it with an untroubled heart as payment for their sins." Why the Templars? A German author would rather be expected to speak of a German order, such as the Teutonic Knights. It must be believed that during the time in which Wolfram wrote, almost a century before the condemnation of the Templars, they had acquired not only a reputation as excellent soldiers but as the keepers of secrets and upholders of a somewhat mysterious tradition. This is the point at which Wolfram describes the Grail, something Chrétien de Troyes did not do:

> Everything that nourishes them [the Templars] comes from a precious stone whose essence is completely pure. If you don't know it, I will tell you its name. It is called *lapsit exillis*. By virtue of this stone the phoenix is burnt to ashes from which he is reborn. It is thanks to this stone that the phoenix molts its feathers, only to reappear in all its brilliance, as beautiful as ever. There is no person so sick who, if placed in the presence of this stone, would not escape death for the week following the day on which he saw it. Those who see it cease to age. From the day this stone appears to them, all men and women regain the appearance they had at the time they were in the fullness of their forces. If they were to be in the presence of the stone for two hundred years, they would not alter in appearance save that their hair would turn white. This stone confers such vigor upon men that their flesh and bones immediately become young again. This stone is also called the Grail (Wolfram von Eschenbach, *Parzival*, vol. 2, translated by Ernest Tonnelat, 36).

All of this obviously brings to mind the numerous feasts of immortality described in various mythologies, in particular *The Hospitality of the Head of Bran* in the Welsh *Mabinogion,* as well as the same tradition's tale of Peredur, in which the Grail appears as a severed head on a platter.* But Wolfram's stone clearly has an alchemical resonance. It is the philosopher's stone, supreme objective of the Great Work; in other words, both a physical and spiritual quest that, starting from primary raw matter, leads to the manufacture of a purified matter full of strength. It is the perfect understanding of the great secrets of the world and is also the "universal medicine," which in this regard confers a quasi-immortality.

---

* Jean Markale, *L'Épopée celtique en Bretagne* (Paris: Petite Bibliothèque Payot, 1975), 51–53.

However, Wolfram wrote for a Christian audience, or at least one under the constraints of a Christian society. Somewhat frightened by the heretical or pagan aspect of what he was describing, he added some Christian coloration: "Every Good Friday [a dove] brings to the stone the virtue of providing the best food and drink in the world. Heaven has nothing that is more delicious. The stone also procures game of all sorts for its guardians." If we understand this correctly, the Grail guardians have both a privileged and enviable situation—who wouldn't want to be a member of this elite company?

Wolfram now precisely approaches the subject of the selection and recruitment of the Grail guardians:

A mysterious inscription appears on the edge of the stone, by which is announced the name and lineage of those—men and maidens—who have been called upon to make this glad voyage. There is no need to erase the name, for it disappears from sight upon being read. The elect are sought from the most diverse array of lands (Wolfram von Eschenbach, *Parzival,* vol. 2, translated by Ernest Tonnelat, 37–38).

This means that the brotherhood of Grail guardians constitutes a truly closed society. These guardians are chosen in a way that is both mysterious and *magical.* They are the elect, yet they have not been candidates for this position and no one knows what criteria has presided over their selection. But it is easy to see why these words put in the mouth of the hermit Trevrizent have contributed greatly to making the Grail into the pivot of a secret society reserved for initiates who are not volunteers but have been called. Richard Wagner, in taking Wolfram's themes as his own, emphasized yet further this aspect of the Templars guarding the Grail; hence the ambiguous nature of his *Parzival* and the notoriety this work enjoyed in Nazi circles. For, on further reflection, the brotherhood of Grail guardians can serve as the esoteric model for other brotherhoods. This cannot help but bring to mind the Thule Group and its extended branches in Germany and elsewhere. It might also be a good idea to ask certain questions regarding the famous "Ballad of the King of Thule," for the king, we recall, was the owner of a gold cup. The Grail is linked to the idea of blood, and in some versions of the legend, this cup holds the blood of Christ. But given the fact that in Wolfram's text the Grail is a stone, the idea of blood is to be sought elsewhere: in the purity of the Grail guardians who constitute an initiatic lineage bonded by a kind of blood fraternity—but of pure blood that is protected from any racial intermixing. Hitler's S.S. is not too far removed from this, and this pure initiatic lineage would justify the interest displayed by the Nazis—Otto Rahn being the first—for traditions that place the Grail in Montségur and in Cathar country, or in other words, among the Pure.

Let us not forget that Hitler's objective was not preservation of the race, but the creation of a new, entirely pure race through a biological mutation that only true Aryans would be capable of undertaking. In Hitlerian thinking, the S.S. formed this incomparable elite. There is too great a tendency today to consider only the role of the S.S. as a police force. But the group served quite a number of other roles. The S.S. was above all a religious and esoteric order, with a very strict hierarchy, extremely precise rules, and particularly difficult preconditions for recruitment:

> It was in the upper spheres (of the Nazi regime) that the leaders were positioned who were aware of a Black Order the existence of which was never officially recognized by the National Socialist government. Within the party itself there was talk of those who were "privileged members of an inner circle," but [this inner circle] was never assigned any legal standing. It seems certain that its doctrine, never fully explained, rested on the absolute belief in powers going well beyond those of ordinary human beings." *

---

* Louis Pauwells and Jacques Bergier, *The Morning of the Magicians* (New York: Avon, 1960), 358.

We know where this led on the plane of racial research, on the plane of the construction of a new world according to criteria that emerged at the dawn of time, on the plane of the so-called inferior races, and on the plane of biological research practiced on human beings that reached new heights in aberration.

We also know that the Hitlerian dream collapsed under a rain of fire in May 1945. All of this turned into a nightmare in which desperate measures have been taken in an attempt to alleviate its ultimate convulsions. But Hitler's dream of becoming a pivotal figure was not solely contained in the organization of the National Socialist state. It was contained elsewhere, and this "elsewhere" was not destroyed by the collapse of the Third Reich, for it was never an official part of the entity of the state. It should be known that the Black Order still exists and is present "elsewhere," in Brocéliande of course, but also at Montségur, Ussat-les-Bains, and the surroundings of Rennes-le-Château. The Black Order still takes a passionate interest in the Cathars and the Grail, which is now more than ever the stone that provides every power. And the Black Order, with all due respect to the skeptics, is the heir of a tradition animated by the strange guardians of the Grail described in *Parzival*.*

Here are Wolfram's words of the German poet: "In this castle

---

* The descriptor used here must be clarified: the mention of a Black Order in no way signifies that the members of this order indulge in *black* magic or practices classified as malefic or satanic. First there exists neither *black* magic nor *white* magic; there is simply magic. Next, the name Black Order refers to the uniform of the S.S., which was one of their very visible manifestations, but certainly not the only one. To truly understand this, we must go much further back than the time of Hitler and remind ourselves that the S.S. was only an epiphenomenon, a transitory phenomenon, albeit a regrettable one. Finally, including mention here of a Black Order is significant of its relationship to an overall group of societies, each member of which is considered to be "philosophical," though its principal characteristics are that it is nonofficial, obscure, and thus dark. This Black Order, which has always existed and still maintains itself in the present day, is visible only under appearances that are most often harmless. The main thing is knowing their intentions, without stopping at considerations that smack of Sunday School Manicheaism.

dwells a noble brotherhood. Those who are part of it have fought valiantly to prevent men from all lands from approaching the Grail save those whom the inscription at Munsalvaesche has designated may enter the holy band." When Parzival first visits Munsalvaesche, his name has not yet been read from the stone. This is why he does not ask the question: "From what are you suffering?" When he is driven out of the castle following his failure, an invisible squire shouts at him: "May the sun's hatred befall you!" These are truly strange words. What could this curse—hardly Christian and with an obvious Mazadean reference—possibly mean? Is it suggesting that by not asking the question, Parzival has not awakened and his soul still sleeps in the darkness of matter into which the sun cannot penetrate? Here we are in the presence of an element that would on its own suffice to definitively label Wolfram's text a Cathar work.

In the speech he makes to Parzival, Trevrizent talks of Anfortas's wound. It seems surprising that while merely the sight of the Holy Grail heals everyone for at least a week, it cannot cure the the Fisher King, Anfortas. A curse hangs over him. He is wounded and decrepit "because in his quest for love he did not respect chastity."

This seems bizarre. What exactly is this quest for love? Is the love to be sought some form of platonic love, hence the transcendence of physical love? What we know of courtly love, after analysis, hardly weighs in favor of this response. Courtly love, or fine love, is not at all platonic or chaste; it is above all a love quest with an initiatory semblance and very precise rules, the main one of which is that a knight or a lady should never love beneath his or her rank on pain of degenerating. Now, according to Trevrizent, "the king of the Grail who seeks the love of any woman other than she whose name appears on the stone is destined to pay a harsh penance. . . . His war cry was 'Love!' In a single combat his virile parts were wounded by a poisoned lance . . .," which occurred because he dared love a woman who was not accepted by the Grail, and thus not by the community of Grail guardians. He failed his trust. This is why Anfortas remains wounded and beyond the healing of any medicine. He can be delivered only by the knight who asks him the question, "From what are you suffering?" He will then be obliged to answer and to confess his sin. His healing is tied to a confession that will negate his guilt and allow him to recover the angelic status he enjoyed before his fall. All of this remains in perfect harmony with Cathar doctrine.

When Kundry the sorceress, messenger of the Grail, announces to Parzival that his name has appeared upon the stone, she expresses it in the following fashion: "An inscription has appeared upon the stone and commands that you are to become the king of the Grail. Your wife, Condwiramur, and your son Lohengrin have been summoned to the Grail Castle along with you." Kundry thereby takes pains to explicitly state that Parzival's wife is accepted; he is not at risk of ruin through the love of a woman unworthy of him. The sorceress then begins raving astrologically, bestowing upon the stars their Arabic names that "were known to the rich and noble Vairefils who, black and white all over, was seated close to her" (Wolfram von Eschenbach, *Parzival,* vol. 2, translated by Ernest Tonnelat, 298–99).

Now everything is in its rightful place. Parzival has disarmed the spells of Klingsor, Anfortas's malefic double, whose castle is a false Munsalvaesche. Klingsor, we learn, is a former duke of Mantua, castrated by a king whose wife he had seduced. His wound is incurable and he has devoted himself to magic in order to avenge himself on other men for the affront he has suffered. (He brings to mind Chronos, who was castrated and then chained by Zeus.) It is not Parzival, however, but Gawain as he appeared in the Welsh *Peredur* who—as a true solar deity—illuminates the murky zones of Klingsor's castle, awakens the sleepers, and frees the knights imprisoned there. And all of this paves the way for Parzival.

It is after all these adventures that Parzival can pose the important question to Anfortas. The latter answers and is cured. Parzival is enthroned as king of the Grail and his brother Vairefils weds Repanse de Schoie, the Grail Bearer, after which they leave together for the East. They will have a son who will become the famous Prester John, founder of a fabled kingdom next to Ethiopia. As for Parzival's son Lohengrin—

more exactly, the "Lorrain Garin," hero of several chansons de geste—he will become the renowned swan knight and mythical ancestor of Godefroy de Bouillon and the dukes of Lorraine, among whose descendents are the Guise, eternal pretenders to the French crown. It all plays out as it does because Wolfram von Eschenbach wished to establish a royal and divine lineage through the symbol of the Grail.

But the lesson to be drawn from this vast, composite work is that access to the mysterious castle of Munsalvaesche is not obtained through personal asceticism, as is shown in the other versions of the legend. Entry to Munsalvaesche is gained not through a choice that is dependent upon the hero, but through a kind of cooptation camouflaged as the miraculous inscription on the stone.

There is a very clear-cut tendency toward a fanatical elitism exhibited here, an exaltation of an elect race, chosen by God—or the devil!—to accomplish a sacred mission that is not merely the guardianship of the Grail but the regeneration of humanity. But by what means?

I must repeat that the Grail is a container—even when it appears in the form of a stone—and what it contains is blood. According to Hebrew belief, blood is the vehicle of the soul. This is an extremely ancient idea that has never been totally abandoned. In Indo-European traditions blood does not assume such a direct form but can be recognized in the concept of an elite corps, a sacred lineage meant to preserve its original purity amidst the vicissitudes of the satanic world, even if it means taking refuge from ordinary mortals and struggling ferociously for its survival. Accordingly, in following Wolfram's work to its smallest nooks and crannies, strange initiatory frameworks emerge whose primordial element remains blood—a blood whose purity must be preserved. This is the point at which the Grail myth meets the Cathar myth. But it can then be seen that the Grail is not at all an object and that the treasure of the Cathars is far from being a material one.

Wolfram von Eschenbach wrote a poem entitled "Titurel" that consists of seventy strophes and claims to explicitly lay out the broad lines of the Grail lineage. The work is incomplete, obscure, and even more burdened with esotericism than *Parzival*. But it is no less revealing of the objective pursued by Wolfram: Titurel is the name of the first Grail King, and Wolfram is striving to demonstrate that there is a Grail race. He tells of the love of Sigune, Parzival's female cousin, for a certain Shionatulander, and these two figures are presented as perfect exemplars of the Grail race, that elite seed spread by God himself in the knighthood. It clearly seems that this elite race was totally exempt from mystical or even simply religious concerns. There is no question of any kind about salvation in the Other World. In fact, the sense of sin seems totally absent from their spirits. In reality, all God requests of these elect is assurance of their strength and courage in battle, and their beauty and loyalty in love—all in absolute fullness: "The entire Grail troop is made up of the elect who are favored by fate in this world and the other, and who are ever counted among those whose glory endures . . .";* and, "Wheresoever this seed was borne from the land of the Grail, it was given to multiply and spare all those who received it from the scourge of dishonor . . ."†

These lines, written in the thirteenth century, are disturbing insofar as they integrally trace certain discourses of the first half of the twentieth century. But more than a long commentary, they allow us to understand why those who upheld certain schools of thought—particularly of German origin—exploited so well the Grail theme as revised and corrected by Wolfram von Eschenbach, and why these individuals expended so much effort to find a *real* site for the Grail Castle. Through the fog of Cathar tradition, Montségur, identified as Munsalvaesche, appeared as the ideal place not for the discovery of some sort of sacred object, but to become the pivot of a wide-ranging activity directed outward. Montségur would be the symbolic North Pole of a new humanity governed by the guardians of the Grail.

---

* "Titurel," translated by Jean Fourquet, *Lumière du Graal* (Marseille: Cahiers du Sud, 1951), strophe 44, 243.
† Ibid., strophe 45, 243.

This takes us far from the original version of the Grail that appeared in the Celtic texts—those stories in which the Grail is an inexhaustible cauldron of abundance and inspiration. We are also far from the chalice that held the blood of Jesus, the "precious blood" spilled for the salvation of the world—*of everyone in the world.* And finally, we are far from the Cathar vision of fallen angels striving to find the lost light again, but knowing that nothing can be done as long as a single soul remains to be saved.

This is a betrayal—in fact, a triple betrayal. First, it is a betrayal of the peaceful Celtic metaphysic. Next, it is a betrayal of Jesus Christ's message of love. Finally, it is a betrayal of the Cathar vision of a world reconciled with itself.

The question emerges: Why this betrayal and recuperation? Montségur must conceal an occult power, for so many divergent fantasies converge there, so many contradictory searches, so many double-meaning delusions. In the long run, it is no more aberrant to visualize the Grail in the keep of Montségur, than to find it in the Broceliande Forest or Glastonbury Abbey. The problem is that we still do not know what the true contents of the Grail are.

16

The Royal Blood

What still fires the imagination is the flight of the four perfecti from Montségur before the capture of the fortress and the holocaust of 205 "heretics." Given the resignation—and even tranquil joy—of the Cathars who perished in the flames, it is not thinkable that these four perfecti would have fled their execution in this way without an imperative that far outweighed them and involved the entire Cathar community. If they "fled" from Montségur, it was for the purpose of protecting something that should not fall into the hands of the Inquisition or those soldiers of the royal army. As we have no clue about the true nature of this trust, we can imagine anything. The least likely solution is that it was some sort of material treasure. It is difficult in fact to imagine four men, even stouthearted men with a full knowledge of the terrain, carrying a heavy burden along the precipices over goat paths.

In any event, the path followed by the four perfecti is as obscure as their reason for taking it. Several itineraries have been suggested, with several possible relays. Mention has been made of the castle of Usson, and the caves of Ussat, Ornolac, and Razès. What is the importance of all this? They did not remain there, and even if we accept that they may have met at a secure hiding place to deposit their "treasure," time has passed, and treasure seekers risk much disillusionment if they take everything said on this subject literally. The problem is not so much learning where the Cathars hid the "treasure" they carried away with them, but rather discovering what it was they carried.

A clarification is called for here. From time to time, apparently well-intentioned people incite the public with loud declarations that they are in the possession of secret documents or that, by the wildest stroke of chance, they have been informed of the existence of such secret documents. First, they carefully refrain from showing all or even most of these documents, or, in the event they do reveal them after long being requested to do so, it can quickly be seen that these documents are fakes. Perhaps they are truncated or after-the-fact retellings; perhaps they are maps and genealogies fabricated from unverifiable testimonies; or maybe they are drawings or paintings that are imitations or falsifications; or quotes that have been truncated or distorted by being taken out of context—there are swindles of all sorts.

When we are presented with secret documents, our first reaction is one of mistrust. The distinguishing characteristic of secret documents is that they are secret, which is enough to disqualify them at the outset, even though this causes much grief to their discoverers. But a simple exercise of good sense should prompt this observation: When someone seeks to keep something a secret, he or she arranges matters to leave absolutely no tangible or legible clues. Any reader of spy novels knows this: A secret is usually passed on verbally and only very infrequently in written form. What's more, any written evidence is not left hanging about; it is destroyed once it has been read. So spare us these miraculously rediscovered secret documents that show up in perfect time to shore up a theory that was previously defensible only with suppositions. In the domain of the occult sciences all of this is even more true than in the domain of history proper. Yet archivists are fully aware that a great deal of their material, devotedly preserved, is made up of forgeries manufactured from whole cloth over the course of the ages and in response to specific circumstances.

In the case of the four Cathar escapees from Montségur, the most logical and likely hypothesis would be to claim they had a mission to fulfill, and that this mission consisted of transporting a certain number of secret clues to specific individuals. They most likely accomplished this mission, transmitting what needed to be transmitted, and took great pains to leave no traces that might be found and decoded by the agents of the Inquisition or royal authority. That is all.

But this in no way prevents the establishment of connections between troubling or inexplicable facts, design of comparisons, and finally the construction of suppositions.

The troubling fact is the interest constantly displayed by the kings of France in the Cathar region and the Razès in particular, after they had done everything in their power to destroy the Cathar heresy and take possession of the country. This fact should be linked on the one hand to the fury the Capet monarchy directed against the unfortunate Trencavel—even if he had nothing to do with Perceval—and on the other hand, to the indulgence of Raymond VII by Blanche de Castille, the count of Toulouse, the lord high protector of heretics, and a hugely treacherous vassal according to feudal custom. It is perhaps significant that the legends of the Razès ceaselessly mention a White Queen who is confused with the fairylike figure of the Pyrenees White Lady, and that the so-called treasure discovered by Father Saunière in the so-called Visigoth pillar (Carolingian, in reality) was called the Treasure of Blanche de Castille.

The hypothesis that comes to the forefront is this: Blanche de Castille knew that Raymond VII, Trencavel, and no doubt a few of their vassals had in their possession documents or stories and testimonies from oral tradition concerning the French royal line. It is probable that these traditions had been passed down by the Cathars or at least by those in Cathar circles to clerics or individuals capable of using them for the purposes of blackmail.

Another troubling fact is the certain connection—one based on the texts themselves, as we have seen—between the Cathars and the Grail legend according to the German Wolfram von Eschenbach. In the thirteenth century, certain German intellectual groups heavily permeated by occultism were convinced that a link existed between the Cathar heretics and the Grail guardians, and that consequently the Grail could well be a Cathar talisman. This idea, somewhat forgotten, was revived at the end of the nineteenth century by German intellectuals and French occult groups and was subsequently picked up by a great many others.

The theory is this: The Grail, which since the time of Chrétien de Troyes became an ideological object recuperated by various currents of thought, offers a connection with the Cathar "treasure" or, in other words, with documents or traditions concerning French royalty. We know that the epic cycle of the Chansons de Geste, including a number of legends on Charlemagne, formed a kind of mythological justification of the Capetian monarchy, legitimate heir to the Carolingian dynasty. We know that all the romances of the Round Table form a similar mythological justification for the Plantagenet dynasty—claimed heir to the fabled King Arthur. But the Grail cycle, although belonging to the Arthurian group, emphasizes a parallel royal lineage, a secret dynasty that has been traced back to King David.

Royal and noble families make it a point of pride to include in their lineage an exceptional ancestor, and when one is lacking, they arrange matters to either artificially bond with a figure from the past or invent a mythological figure for their origin. For example, in Rome the *gens Iulia,* to which Julius Caesar belonged, claimed descent from the Trojan Aeneas, and thus the goddess Venus. In France the Lusignan family claimed a connection with the fairy Melusine, and the Plantagenets themselves, before making the connection with King Arthur, claimed to be the descendants of an Angevin fairy. As for the Merovingians, the "long-haired kings," strange stories were told concerning the birth, and especially the conception, of Merovech: When Merovech's mother, the wife of King Clodion, was pregnant, she went swimming in the ocean and while there, it is said, she was seduced by an aquatic creature "who came from beyond the seas" and who thus impregnated her a second time. This was how Merovech was credited with having two fathers.

Of course such stories are hardly a rarity in mythological narratives and generally disclose a double origin. In this instance, Merovech—or whatever figure is concealed behind this name—seems to have had Germanic ancestry (Clodion) and foreign ancestry (the aquatic monster) that perhaps came from overseas. Because historical documents concerning the first Merovingians are totally nonexistent, there is nothing more to be added. But we should emphasize some characteristics of their dynasty: They were never crowned (Clovis was baptized in Reims but not crowned), though were considered kings at the age of twelve; they stubbornly refused to cut their hair; and they were generally believed to practice magic and possess supernatural powers. In short, although the Merovingians, for the most part, were bloodthirsty tyrants and unscrupulous murderers, their family benefited from a singular reputation, a veritable aura that was if not mystical, then sacred in a sense that is much more pagan than Christian. The conversion of Clovis to Christianity was simply a deft political act with no repercussions on his personal life or, moreover, on the lives of his descendents.

In the tangled history of Clovis's descendents, in which the various kings were always at each other's throats, there appeared the figure of Dagobert II, who, after a period of exile in Great Britain, was assassinated in December 679, without doubt on the order of the palace mayor—a Carolingian—named Pepin of Heristal. This Dagobert II was buried in the royal chapel of Saint Remy in Stenay, in the Ardennes. In 872 he was canonized by the pope, an exceptional event for that time, and the power passed on to another Merovingian branch, those whom posterity has labeled the "lazy kings" and who were actually puppets of the Carolingian palace mayors before being eliminated once and for all when Childeric III was deposed by Pippin the Short in 751.

Dagobert II is therefore the last official Merovingian of the elder branch. He had taken as his second wife Gisela, daughter of Bera II, the count of Razès. And here is where history meets legend: Dagobert had a son from this union who found refuge with his grandfather and eventually fathered his own lineage, thus assuring the permanence of the legitimate Merovingian dynasty. We cannot help but be intrigued by this son, Sigebert IV. His historical reality is certain, but formal proof remains lacking, unless we count the alleged parchments found by Father Saunière in his church, the originals of which have never been seen by anyone. That noted, it is more than likely that the story of Dagobert's son assuring the permanence of the Merovingian line is based on fact and that Sigebert IV himself became count of Razès. Among his remote descendents in the thirteenth century are Count de la Marche Hugues de Lusignan and the duchess of Brittany, Alix, both of whom, for various reasons, took part in the feudal struggles against Blanche de Castille and Louis IX as allies of Raymond VII of Toulouse.

Whatever we make of this confused history, we may ask if an attempt at blackmail concerning the legitimacy of the reigning dynasty may have been associated with the "treasure" of the Cathars. To completely investigate this delicate matter, we should not overlook the strange Nicolas Poussin affair involving his painting "The Shepherds of Arcadia," and the alleged secrets the painter held in his keeping and passed on to Nicolas Fouquet, whose career ended in disgrace. All of this is vexing; we can sense the presence of a mystery—one which, at the outset, we cannot set aside—that prompts suppositions that are difficult to refute.

It is all the more strange that the legend of the Holy Grail includes its own share of mystery surrounding both the precise nature of the sacred object called the Grail and the context in which the tale is presented, in particular everything concerning the line of Grail guardians. While Wolfram made these guards Templars, we should not take this literally, even if the Templars indeed concluded a pact with the Cathars, for whom they were very often protectors, thereby contravening the most elementary rules of discipline inside the Roman Catholic Church.

Everything here takes place on two levels: The first involves the reality of the Grail and the notions that lie beneath it; the second calls into question the Cathars' conception of the figure of Jesus. The first level sheds light on one of the most common practices of poets and writers of the twelfth and thirteenth centuries: word play, or, if you prefer, the phonetic kabbala, of which Wolfram von Eschenbach's Kyôt the Provençal appears to be a striking example. But the word play involves the Grail itself. In the text written by Chrétien de Troyes, the Grail is not yet "sacred." It is only a simple container more like the cauldron of plenty that inspired the Welsh bards than the Cistercian chalice that holds the blood of Christ. With those who continued Chretien's unfinished work, and also in the Cistercian versions, the Grail clearly becomes the *Holy* Grail, with the sanctity of the contents (the blood of Christ) transferring to the container (the cup, the vessel, or the chalice). When described in French, in which the spelling was not firm, the variations that can be seen in the manuscripts reveal a combination of the two words *saint* and *graal*.* Accordingly, these can take the form of *sangral, sangreal, sangraal*. By the fifteenth century, in the English text by Thomas Malory, compiler of all the Arthurian legends, the term *sangreal* clearly prevails.

The play on words is based precisely on this form because we can easily substitute for the normal and standard caesura *san-greal* another caesura: *sang-real*. In modern French *sang-real* becomes *sang royal*, "royal blood." Would the Grail simply and esoterically be the royal blood, meaning the evidence of a royal lineage formed by the family of the Grail King that the majority of texts trace back through Joseph of Arimathea to the biblical King David?

This idea appears attractive. While it is only a hypothesis, it is based on one constant in every version of the legend: the "holy" Grail is in the exclusive possession of a sacred lineage going back far in time, very far, all the way back to King David. Whether it is Lancelot of the Lake and his son Galahad the Pure, whether it is Perceval, Perlesvaux, or Parzival, the hero of the Grail is the nephew of the Fisher King and the initiating hermit (Trevrizent in Wolfram's text) and descendent of Joseph of Arimathea, himself a descendent of David and owner of the celestial emerald that served to construct the vessel known as the Grail.

Certainly the evidence for this purely mythological lineage remains bizarre to say the least. It introduces biblical figures, fairly marginal bishops, and kings borrowed from Celtic tradition, such as Evallach,

---

* [*Saint* = "holy" and *graal* = "grail." —*Trans.*]

which is nothing other than the name of the Isle of Avalon, the druidic conception of paradise. But there is a continuity and Wolfram strives to make it evident by going so far as to prepare what would transpire after the time of Parzival. Lohengrin was the ancestor of the kings of Jersualem as well as the dukes of Lorraine, and the royal blood of the Grail lineage could even be found in the Guise family (who knew full well where to draw the line when making their claims to the French throne) and the Hapsburg family, one of whose last members would one day take a very close interest in Father Saunière and the Rennes-le-Château affair.

While this is all very perplexing, it is highly dubious that anything of value can be gained from the numerous "secret dossiers" that have been opened in the relatively recent past considering there is no proof of authenticity of these documents. All that remains is hypothesis, or hypotheses, and everyone will form conclusions based on their own interpretations or convictions.

All the same, however, there is a curious tradition around Rennes-le-Châteaus and the Razès concerning Mary Magdalene, whose worship has been confirmed in Razès and at numerous sites, and under whose name the church of Rennes-le-Château was consecrated. It is hard to deny the presence of Mary Magdalene in this region, and the famous Magdala Tower built by Father Saunière, supposedly to house his library, is there to declare loudly and quite clearly the truth of her presence.

In an attempt to find an explanation for this, we need to begin with certain Cathar conceptions about the figure of Jesus. Jesus has always posed a problem for the Cathars. He is not the Son of God, or if he is, as in the view of certain Cathar schools, then Satan is another son of God. Both in some way share the world between them and are the symbols of the difficult struggle waged by good against evil.

The majority of Cathars believed that Jesus was an angel who had come to "awaken" the souls asleep in matter. But in evidence of the subtlety of their understanding of this figure, they presumed the existence of a second Christ. In fact, the terrestrial Christ who died on the cross in Jerusalem could not be anything but evil and this Mary Magdalene who appeared as a favored figure at his side, was certainly his concubine or even his wife. The true Christ was born and later crucified in an invisible world. It is this higher world (which is still not heaven for the Cathars) that houses the real battlefield where the two principles of good and evil meet.* Accordingly, the earthly Christ led a man's life in its entirety, and thus could have had descendents. What became of these descendents of Jesus and Mary Magdalene?

We know that the real life of Jesus Christ—and not the watered-down life recorded in the Gospels—poses certain problems. First, it is unthinkable that he was a carpenter in Nazareth because that town did not exist in his era. This is a legend that has grown out of the fact that Jesus belonged to the sect of Nazarenes. Furthermore, he was certainly not born in a stable or a cave; this was simply a symbolic site. He was not poor; according to the words of the official Gospels, he belonged to the royal family of David. Between his puberty and the age of thirty, Jesus disappeared: What was he doing? The way he preached definitely demonstrates that he had completed his studies. But with whom? This remains a mystery. He was also called *rabbi,* meaning "master" in the sense of the Latin *magister* and not the Latin *dominus.* But this title was reserved for "doctors" of theology, who were obliged to be married. Furthermore, celibacy was frowned upon for any normal man in Jewish society during the time of Jesus. This implies that he should have been married. The Gospels completely erase the sexuality of Jesus, after having erased that of Mary. But what would have been so reprehensible about Jesus being married? The question bears repeating, especially because Jesus (still according to the Gospels) never condemned marriage, in contrast to Saint Paul, whose attitudes were quite the opposite.

So when certain episodes of the life of Jesus are analyzed, most notably the famous wedding in Cana, questions arise: Why did Jesus

---

* Arno Borst, *Les Cathares* (Paris: Payot, 1984), 142.

conduct himself as the man of the house during this wedding? Could it be, by chance, because he was the husband? And who might his wife have been if not the enigmatic Mary Magdalene, to whom he appeared first following his resurrection? There is much to be said on the matter of Mary Magdalene who is obviously in love with Jesus, who is a woman from a rich social milieu, who was probably one of Jesus' first disciples rather than the repentant prostitute, as is repeatedly drilled into our ears, and whose profession the Gospels do not even mention.*

It is onto these observations and questions that the tradition of the arrival of Mary Magdalene in the Razès has been grafted. After the death of Jesus and the persecutions of the Jews (Christians were then simply considered members of a Jewish sect), she was said to have left Palestine and landed on the Occitain shores, perhaps at Marseille, perhaps at Saintes-Marie-de-la-Mer. She then settled, *with her children,* either in Sainte-Baume, where she is openly worshiped, or in the Razès, where this worship is no less overt and important. Her children are said to have then engendered their own lines, and one of her descendents even married a Norse king, perhaps Clodion the Long-Haired, father of Merovech. In this way, Merovech, the issue of two fathers, in other words, having a double origin (the sea monster symbolizing the overseas contribution, his Jewish ancestry), would be the heir of the Frankish kings, thaumaturges and magicians, and sacred pagan figures, and of the lineage of Jesus and Mary Magdalene, a divine lineage if ever there was one, even if this Jesus was only the earthly double of he who battled evil in the higher world.

Therefore, the hypothesis, unfortunately too often presented as a certainty, is that the "treasure" of the Cathars, stored at Rennes-le-Château or elsewhere in the Razès, is formed by the proof of the existence of a Merovingian lineage, a divine and authentic lineage driven from power by the Carolingian usurpers and their Capetian successors.

---

* For more on this subject, see Michael Baigent, Richard Leigh, and Henry Lincoln, *Holy Blood, Holy Grail* (New York: Delacorte, 1982).

This would justify Blanche de Castille's interest in this "treasure," which threatened to call into question the legitimacy of her son Louis IX, and of course that of the entire Capet dynasty. Was this the secret known by Nicolas Poussin and passed on to Nicolas Fouquet? Was this the secret discovered by Father Saunière, the secret for which he received payment in return for his silence? Was this secret a matter in which the Church had played a leading role (for the Roman Church's role was hardly glorious in the replacement of the Merovingians by the Carolingians)?

The only answer we can give to these questions is, "Why not?" These are hypotheses as good as any others, and together have the merit of shaking on its foundations an official history that is too often truncated and filled with inexactitudes and lies. Unfortunately, the myth of the Great Monarch has been incorporated into this secret. This king of the world—who will come soon, no doubt, for we have just crossed the threshold of the twenty-first century—can belong only to a divine lineage and will emerge from the mysterious valleys of the Razès like a new Arthur from his peaceful slumber on the Isle of Avalon. In fact, why couldn't the Isle of Avalon be located in the neighborhood of Rennes-le-Château? And are people aware that the Cathars believed that Frederic II, the emperor long suspected of heresy and neo-pagan practices, was not dead but would reappear one day and save all the Perfects and believers, gathering them together into a new nation? This is the myth of Frederic Barbarossa, asleep in a German mountain. This is the myth of Arthur. It is a myth as universal as the one concerning the Great Monarch. But watch out—let's hope this Great Monarch is not the Antichrist!

As explained so well by Jean Robin:

[T]he folklore, the traditions of all countries grant the dark powers their own geography, just as there is a sacred geography of pilgrimage sites, for example. By considering the surrounding countryside of Rennes from this perspective, it has to be accepted that the landmarks—and there are plenty of landmarks—compel us to envision a logical choice, or rather a mysterious correspondence between the place—a mysterious crucible—and the alchemy performed there. This is so prominent it is hard to tell if the land served only as a favorable support for certain influences, or if this fateful site secreted its own *egregores** (to borrow the language of occultism) and in some way animated the *thought forms* (to borrow another occult term) of the hoaxers.†

These are harsh words. It may be significant that the name Saint Michael's Rock was given to a prominent elevation near Arques, a promontory that is 666 meters high (666 being the numerical figure for the Beast of the Apocalypse). But as Péguy‡ says, "Those who are good at sin are from the same kingdom as those who are good at grace." This is where dualism overcomes its contradictions.

There is yet another theory concerning this sacred lineage of which the Cathars were allegedly aware. If all the texts of the Grail legend are given close examination, with particularly close attention paid to Lancelot of the Lake, unquestionably the key figure of this story cycle, some strange observations can be made.

The true name of Lancelot of the Lake is Galahad, and he forms part of the sacred lineage of the Grail King—in fact, he is its culmination. If he could not himself become a king of the Grail, it is because of the sin of his adulterous relationship with Queen Guinivere. To put it more precisely, for Lancelot the Grail is Queen Guinivere, model of beauty, perfection, and absolute love,§ but it is his son Galahad who will successfully complete the quest for the Holy Grail and in doing so, secure the triumph of the royal blood.

---

* [*Egregores* is an occult term signifying a set of marginal ideas that becomes the core of a new culture. —*Trans.*]

† Jean Markale, *Rennes-le-Chateau: la colline envoûtée* (Paris: Pygmalion, 1988),163.

‡ [French poet Charles Péguy (1873–1914). —*Trans.*]

§ Jean Markale, *Lancelot et la chevalerie arthurienne* (Paris: Imago, 1985). In this book I have explained at length Lancelot's motives in the Grail Quest.

Galahad is heir to the sacred line not only through his father, Lancelot, who descends from Joseph of Arimathea and thus King David, but also through his mother, the Grail Bearer, who is the daughter of the Fisher King and is herself a descendent of Joseph of Arimathea and David. An invention of the writers of the beginning of the thirteenth century, precisely during the regency of Blanche de Castille, Galahad is depicted as the most perfect crystalization of this divine lineage. After seeing what lies at the bottom of the Holy Grail, he cries out that he knows all the secrets of the world and dies instantly, for his human nature is incapable of tolerating such enlightenment. Thus it can be concluded that Galahad realized Cathar perfection in that supreme moment; he was in some manner struck by the divine light. Why was he able to have this vision? It was because at that moment he became aware of the royal blood flowing through his veins.

Lancelot outlives his son and during the collapse of the Arthurian world and after the death of Queen Guinivere he becomes a hermit and lives to the end his life in a state of piety. It is thought by some that a very real figure can be recognized in this fictional character, a hermit of the Merovingian Age, therefore the time of Arthur: the mysterious Saint Framburg or Frambaut, who is regarded as the ancestor of the Capets.

The alternate theory is this one: The "treasure" of the Cathars is nothing other than knowledge of the sacred and mystical Grail lineage that goes back to King David by way of Joseph of Arimathea, and perhaps Jesus and Mary Magdalene, and ends at a Lancelot of the Lake who is the fictionalized depiction of Saint Frambaut. This, then, would be the authentic Holy Grail: the Royal Blood, proof of this sacred lineage. This is what Blanche de Castille was seeking to obtain.

All we can say to this theory is, "Why not?" It is the most logical and most likely of all explanations concerning the Cathar "treasure" that was carried off from Montségur by four perfecti on a March night in 1244, before the capture of the fortress. There is nothing magical or supernatural about it.

But it may not be well known that the liturgical service of Saint

Mary Magdalene includes a hymn with this as its second verse: "The lost drachma is hidden in the royal treasure, and the precious stone, once purified of its filth, will outshine the stars."

This seems like the description of the Grail Stone that we find in Wolfram's text, and beyond that, the indication of a purification of the emerald that has fallen from Lucifer's forehead. Once this task is achieved—the purification of the stone and the completion of the quest for the Grail—then the royal blood flowing through the veins of all the sleeping angels will be able to shine in all its splendor.

17
The Cathars and Memory

While the Cathars as an organized entity vanished at the beginning of the fourteenth century, this in no way means that the Cathar mentality also disappeared, definitively swallowed up by the triumph of the orthodoxy. The belief in the existence of two fundamental principles in perpetual opposition recurs in countless later theories. The idea of the fall of the angels still influences attempts to explain a world subject to the powers of evil in which the human soul feels itself imprisoned. The notion of a salvation obtained through renunciation of this world remains a constant, as does the idea that purification is a prerequisite for any spiritual advance. In fact, consideration of the broad lines of Christian spirituality since the time of the condemnation of the Cathar heresy will lead us to question exactly what the exact reasons behind this condemnation might have been. There is nothing in the Cathar doctrine that truly shocks the Christian conscience. Ought we to conclude that this merciless condemnation was aimed specifically at people who claimed they could ensure their salvation without going through the Church? The same question arises later in history, at the time of the Reformation.

To be explicit, the Reformers of the sixteenth century seem to have picked up for their own purposes certain ideas of Catharism and there is no doubt at all that they used the Cathar criticisms of the Roman Catholic Church, which were that it was guilty of being bogged down in the material world, of having forgotten its divine mission, and of having joined with the hosts of Satan the better to deceive the souls who still believed in the light. These criticisms were levied particularly strongly by the followers of Calvinism, with its austere vision of spiritual asceticism and its refusal to accept any form of salvation obtained by other means than that of personal enlightenment. Though Calvinism's efforts to define the righteous in the midst of a fundamentally evil world followed paths parallel to those taken by different Cathar currents, of course the belief in the transmigration of souls, which appeared in Catharism but was never officially codified, had disappeared completely. It was now in one single life that a human being could hope to obtain salvation; there is no other possible life. It is not by chance that the severe Calvinist doctrine, very northern in spirit and corresponding very little to the spirit of the south, spread so easily in Cathar country, and that it has often endured in those regions so heavily influenced by Catharism.

But this is simply intellectual speculation and only concerns a few elites, those who are generally classified as master thinkers. In the same way that Cathar clerics were subject, in one way or another, to earlier Bogomil, Manichaean, or even orthodox messages, clerics in later denominations took possession of the Cathar tradition, developing it and extending it into new areas. This is a constantly occurring phenomenon in the history of human thought. Of course, it should not be overlooked that Catharism was also lived in daily life by a large number of the faithful. It would be surprising if it had not left certain imprints on what can be called folk memory, at the level of everyday life.

Here we talking about not simply ordinary symbols, for they endure even when their evocative value has been lost and no one remembers their exact meaning, but instead symbols such as the Occitain cross, the Cathar cross, and the Huguenot cross, which obviously all came from the same mold. This endurance of symbols becomes clear in the case of the Huguenot cross, which incorporated the Cathar dove, even if it did not imbue it with the same notion. Among the Calvinists, the dove represented the Holy Ghost, and that alone.

Among the Cathars it symbolized the soul freed from the grip of Satan and awaiting the moment to take flight to the higher regions.

This same symbolism has been assigned to that legend from the Montségur countryside concerning the fairy (confused with Esclarmonde) who appears in the form of a dove. The fairy tries to save a man by bringing him wealth and happiness, but this endeavor can succeed only if the man respects one basic prohibition: not to treat her as a "fairy" or a "madwoman." In other versions the man is forbidden to become angry with the fairy or to strike her, even lightly. Or, as in the Poitou region's legend of Melusine, he must not know the true nature of the fairy, for he is incapable of supporting the sight of a higher being. If we make a stretch, Melusine could very easily represent the Cathar perfecti who strive to save individuals still imprisoned by the world's illusions, but she has been repressed in the depths of the subconscious in the Christian orthodox consciousness, and has been "blackened" as a demon. This is proof that the Cathar message—a message announcing the possibility for every individual to become purified—was misunderstood, and that the world is not yet ready to find the original light again.

The same is true for those traditions concerning mysterious women who can sometimes be encountered in the valleys near springs or rivers. In the Rennes-le-Château region these women, known as *mitounes,* are said to lie in wait for young men whom they then seduce. Sometimes they take the appearance of washerwomen at the edge of a water way. In fact, a very widespread folk theme is that of the night washerwomen, and those of Brittany are regarded as particularly malevolent. In the minds of country dwellers, these fairies, mitounes, and washerwomen, like the White Lady of the Pyrenees, are embodiments of heresy. What they represent are the heretical theories that can seduce those who do not pay attention to where they are venturing and especially do not rely on official certitudes or, in other words, conformity. The fables are quite eloquent and are the result of a systematic provocation of guilt feelings for attending to anything that is not mainstream.

But sometimes the situation is reversed: Hidden beneath strange appearances, heresy—or at least marginal thought—breaks the surface and acquires new powers. Numerous seemingly harmless folk tales are updated versions of ancient beliefs, thereby attesting to the fact that popular memory never forgets.

This is the case of the well-known story of Beauty and the Beast. Depending upon the region in which it appears, its color and detail can vary, but the basic framework remains the same. It is a tale of a young girl who, to save the life of her father, must overcome her repugnance and marry a Beast. If she succeeds at this trial, she will one day see that the Beast she has wed is in reality a very handsome prince who had been under a spell.

However, things do not always run smoothy and happily. Sometimes the young girl cannot overcome her repugnance, and the Beast is condemned to wait longer for the act of salvation that will restore him to his previous appearance. Or the young girl breaks a prohibition by asking a forbidden question or surprising the Beast when he thinks he is alone. The Beast is then forced to leave and the young girl sets off in quest of him, which generally involves a very long journey. To find her destined companion she is forced to wear out three pairs of iron shoes.

The symbolism of this story is quite simple. The Beast, or the prince under a curse, is an angel imprisoned by Satan who, after the fall, found himself in a physical body that was particularly hideous. The sole hope the angel has of recovering his primal nature is to inspire the true love of a young girl. What's fully involved here is the basic Cathar concept: The world is imperfect and devoted to evil because it lacks charity—perfect love. By reintroducing perfect love into this world, evil is driven off and the caged souls become free. The concept is quite attractive and the advantage of the story is that it transmits this message with no need for explanation and no need to resort to logic. It is through such images, addressed to sensibility rather than intellect, that the Cathar spirit survives.

Another story known the world over and generally called something like "The Body without a Soul" also attests to the survival of this spirit. We have numerous variations of this tale, notably in the Basque region and Armoricain Brittany, where this theme seems to be given a particular emphasis.

This story involves a monstrous individual who behaves like a devil. Endowed with a ferocious, cannibalistic appetite, he wears the guise of an ogre and commits the worst kinds of unjust acts, among which is that he demands a young girl of the region, generally a princess, be handed over to him each year. An audacious young man (though he is sometimes middle-aged) decides to vanquish this "body without a soul," and to do this he works to gain the complicity of the wife of the monster. She warns the brash hero that his efforts to kill the monster will be futile, but she nonetheless arranges circumstances so that he can learn the monster's secret. In this version told in upper Brittany she induces the monster to speak and tricks him into revealing why he is invulnerable:

I cannot die because my soul is not in my body, though it is well-guarded. It can be found in the thirteenth egg of a partridge who lives inside a hare that no hunter can catch. Furthermore, this hare lives in the belly of a terrible wolf that devours everything he sees. And this wolf is hidden in the belly of a lion that nobody has the courage to face.*

The following is found in the version from lower Brittany:

"I was born from the union of a siren and a werewolf. I am the body without a soul."

"What?" said the Princess, "a body without a soul? How is it that you are able to live?"

"Thanks to a great spirit who gave me a great power. But my

---

* Jean Markale, *Contes populaire de toutes les Bretagne* (Rennes: Ouest-France, 1977), 107.

power is nothing compared with what it could be if I had my soul."

The princess then asked, "So, you do have a soul, but it is just not with you?"

"Unfortunately," the Body confirmed, "it is not with me. If I had it, there would be nothing I could not accomplish. With my soul I could have turned the universe upside down."

"Then it is very difficult to find your soul, or so it would seem?"

"Too difficult, unfortunately. I have searched countless times to find it and have never succeeded. That is the reason I have been placed here, on this island in the middle of the ocean. Any yet my soul is not so far from here . . . about ten leagues away, on another island, which is quite large."*

The clues contained in this story—which, I must repeat, is a folktale from the oral tradition—present what is clearly a Cathar connotation if we use the doctrine of the radical dualists as our guide. According to this doctrine, there are three constituent elements of the being: body, soul, and spirit. The most important distinction to understand is that between soul and spirit; it is the eternal dichotomy of the yin and the yang, the *animus* and the *anima,* the *mens* and *spiritus,* or even the astral body, the subtle body, and the egregore as defined by various occult schools. Until the present no clear understanding of this distinction has been reached, and the Cathars never found a satisfactory explanation. On the other hand, whatever the exact accepted definitions of the terms *body, soul,* and *spirit* may be, the radical Cathars maintained that Satan seduced and perverted only one part of the angels—in other words, their souls and not their spirits. They concluded that in every incarnation (each of which is equivalent to the Fall), the angelic soul left its body in Heaven and Satan then caged the soul within a physical body. But the bond

---

* Jean Markale, *La tradition celtique* (Paris: Payot, 1975).

between body and soul—the mind—is somewhere else, in an intermediate world situated between Earth and Heaven. The spirit hovers in this intermediate world like the Elohim over the primordial waters, searching for the soul it will recognize as its double. When this discovery is made, enlightenment results and the individual becomes cathar, in other words, a Perfect. In short, this spirit is a kind of guardian angel that permits the reunion of the principles dispersed by evil.

Within the specific framework of the story, the birth of the body without a soul is presented as a farfetched event (his parents are a siren and a werewolf, diabolical creatures of fantasy), and the Creator is a great spirit. Would this be God, creator of the soul, or Satan, creator of the body? It is hard to say. But what is sure is that the soul intentionally separated from the body to prevent the character in the story from acquiring his full power and turning the universe upside down. The secret weakness of the body without a soul is a form of punishment or curse that deprives him of his intellectual and/or physical capabilities. It is impossible not to see in this detail the Fall of the angels and their imprisonment in matter. But their soul (or their spirit) keeps its power intact. It is only separated from the body. If the individual manages to recover his soul, he reintegrates it to return to his original state, that of the essence. But this is something the body without a soul in the story feels it is impossible to achieve: "My soul is in an egg the color of fire. This egg is inside a dove, the dove is inside a fox, the fox is inside a wolf, the wolf is inside a boar, the boar is inside a leopard, the leopard is inside a lion, the lion is inside an ogre who is neither man or beast."*

In another folktale, which is also a traditional children's song, a billy goat (or nanny goat) does not want to come out of the cabbage. The goat's owner seeks out a dog to chase the goat, but the dog refuses to obey, and so on. In fact, this tale follows an archaic theme that can be also be recognized in the well-known walnut of the kabbalists: The

---

* Jean Markale, *La tradition celtique en Bretagne armoricaine*, 4th edition (Paris: Payot, 1975), 206.

shell and skin—the exterior packaging—must be stripped away in order to reach the central core, meaning the divine that is hidden within. The soul of the monstrous figure in "The Body without a Soul" is his divine component that was imprisoned inside another body, another material, after the Fall in order to forestall any possibility of reunion. Only the intervention of a hero or heroine can allow access to this soul caged inside an egg, which is itself inside a dove (a highly significant detail on its own). But in this case the hero or heroine simply breaks the egg. The soul flies away and the body can no longer live, for the two were somehow subtly connected.

This story is a fine example of the permanence of a Cathar theme in oral folk tradition, and quite a few others could be cited, all of which depict symbols commonly used by Albigensian theologians. We have to believe that, following their disappearance, the Perfects tried to leave their message for future generations, but they took care not to carve it in stone or entrust it to writing. The oral path is still the surest and most apt at transmitting something on every level without drawing the wrath of the censors. Art or everything that can be classified as artistic, the oral tale for example, has a totally innocent appearance. It is a game. Its express purpose is to amuse or charm. But if we look at the meaning of *charm*, we understand that magic does not consist so much of uttering words that are incomprehensible to ordinary people; it is the art of transmitting something under the cover of a game.

And what better game than the theater, especially when word is combined with music there? We now know, or guess, what may have been the real meaning of a opera like Mozart's *Magic Flute*. Without too much trouble we can find the underlying messages in a complex work like Wagner's *Parzival* and its obvious connections with the Cathars through the intermediary of Wolfram von Eschenbach. So let us look at another work of this nature, a very strange one that bewilders more than it enlightens: *Pelléas and Mélisande* by Maurice Maeterlinck and Claude Debussy.

It is certainly an initiatory drama presented as a theatrical and

musical game whose intricacies express in the noblest manner possible
the Cathar problem of the angelic soul. Because it is an acknowledged
symbolist work it necessarily contains symbols that are quite apparent;
they are right there on the surface. But others exist in the work, less
detectable but equally effective. These primarily involve the central
character of Melisande, who has brought so many audiences to tears.
We should always be suspicious of tragic heroines who inspire tears
with their poignancy, for this kind of heroine is generally hiding something. Isn't Racine's "sweet" and "gentle" Andromacha in reality a for-
midably intelligent and calculating woman, an actress ready to do anything to ensure her triumph and that of her son?

So who is Melisande? She wanders in the darkened castle and large
park where Arkel rules, continuously passing from darkness into light
and light into darkness, and we learn practically nothing about her.
Prince Golaud encounters her at the edge of a fountain where she was
weeping. But she is no Melusine who lies in wait for Raymond in order
to offer him, along with herself, wealth and power. Melisande expects
nothing; she is devastated. Where did she come from? From "somewhere else," but we are never too sure where this imprecise "somewhere else" is. All we know is that a crown is gleaming in the water,
"the crown that he gave me," she says. We do not know who "he" is.
Golaud wishes to fish out the crown, but Melisande refuses to allow
him to do this just as she refuses all contact with Golaud: "Don't touch
me or I will cast myself into the water!"

But Golaud drags her off with him and marries her. So we find
Melisande in the strange kingdom of Arkel. This kingdom has a name:
Allemonde, which is a play on words, of course, for it vaguely resembles Allemand,* or even a word in Franglais, *all le monde,*† or even,
thanks to the Celtic root *all* (other), a veritable Other World. The

---

* [Allemand = German. —*Trans.*]

† [Franglais is the term for recent English words incorporated whole into the French language; in this case *all le monde* would be the Franglais equivalent of *tout le monde,* literally all the world or "everybody." —*Trans.*]

symbolist poets have done far worse. But why couldn't it be *Ah! Le monde!,** touched with a hint of the disdain that is so characteristic of the Cathar doctrine's view of the material world? After all, Golaud is a kind of devil. In fact, he is the very image of the Cathar Satan who imprisons the soul of the fallen angel (Melisande) in matter (marriage). Melisande is a captive of the world of Satanic illusions, but perhaps she in some way looked for this to happen by refusing to allow the crown to be rescued from the water and accepting marriage to the tyrant Golaud, who had in fact usurped the power that belonged rightfully to Arkel, his grandfather.

Arkel's name is similar in sound to the word *archangel* as well as to the name of the village of Arques in the Razès. And isn't the name Golaud reminiscent of the Golem of occult tradition? Or to the Breton word *golo,* meaning "light"? Could Golaud also be the Fallen Light, meaning Lucifer, after his rebellion and descent into the abyss? But Lucifer retains his essential nature as the light, although he strives to plunge other beings into darkness.

Melisande apparently plays Golaud's game. She is the perfect example of the perverse adolescent. She lies, and she decieves Golaud but never admits it, allowing doubt and uncertainty to hover around him continuously. She is an excellent student of Satan, and she is perfectly aware of what she is doing when she sets her heart on Pelleas, Golaud's younger brother, and drags him to his ruin.

Pelleas bears a familiar name. It is spelled the same way as Pelleas the Fisher King in the English text by Malory. In Celtic mythology Pelleas is Pwyll, a kind of deity from the Other World, husband of the goddess Rhiannon, whose name means "great queen" and who often appears in the form of a mare. Maeterlinck's choice of the name Pelleas is not accidental, and the reference to the Fisher King is quite clear. Isn't Pelleas's father mysteriously ill and invisible, always on death's door but transfixed in his bed of pain?

---

* ["Oh! The World!" —*Trans.*]

Pelleas is seduced by Melisande just as, according to Wagner, Anfortas was seduced by Kundry the sorceress. Melisande—whose name is evocative of Melissende who appears in the chronicles of the Crusades as well as the woman snake Melusine—is also Kundry, the accomplice of Klingsor, who confines the knights in his garden of delights, thanks to the charms of his "flower girls."

But remember: The perverse adolescent Melisande, along with Kundry and, according to Chrétien de Troyes, "the hideous maiden on the mule," is also the messenger of the Grail, which provides the pivotal point in Maeterlinck's and Debussy's lyrical drama. Melisande will show Pelleas a path he can barely make out on his own. By playing with her ring at the edge of the fountain, Melisande frees herself from Golaud while elsewhere at this precise moment, Golaud falls from his horse for no apparent reason. When he sees that Melisande has lost the ring, he forces her to search for it immediately, but Melisande has lied: She claims she lost it in a cave by the sea—which is where she dragged Pelleas. The symbols of both the ring and the cave are quite eloquent here, for henceforth Melisande and Pelleas are bound. Golaud is fully aware of this and tries to frighten Pelleas by leading him through dark underground corridors stinking of death.

The drama in the story lies in the fact that Pelleas, who has still not understood the meaning of Melisande's mission, wishes to leave, and leave alone. Melisande then draws him into a farewell scene, but she knows Golaud is spying on them. Golaud kills Pelleas, but the spirit of Pelleas will not leave. Then, freed in spite of himself from his physical envelope at the very moment he is declaring his love for Melisande, he is once more penetrated by the divine light and returns to the original kingdom. Eventually Melisande, after giving birth to a young girl who will carry all the sorrow of the world, dies in her turn and rejoins Pelleas in the light they have found again.

The Grail was within reach for each of them. Golaud did not find it because he is "like a blind man who seeks his treasure at the bottom of the sea." And Arkel can only repeat, "If I were God, I would have pity in my heart for men." A pretty turn of speech. Arkel is himself piti-ful. But only complete love, in other words pure charity, can awaken the submerged souls. Golaud remains far from that sublime love. He is a violent man, a hunter and a killer. He spills blood because he can feed only on blood to give his body the appearance of life. He is one of the living dead, a kind of vampire. He is illusion, Satan the deceiver, Klingsor. But he still holds the dreadful power of imprisoning souls in his fairyland garden that is far too dark to be paradisical.

For the soul, according to the most ancient traditions, is bonded to blood. "You will not eat meat with its soul, meaning in its own blood" (Genesis 4:4). The Cathars knew this full well, which is why the perfecti forbade the eating of all bloody food. And when the Grail is described, in the Cistercian versions, as holding the blood of Christ, it simply means that it holds the divine soul, the one found in the core of the walnut, in the egg, or contained in the dove, that same dove who places a sacra-mental host on the Grail Stone.

The Cathars, in one way or another, are closely connected to the legend of the Grail—the Holy Grail. Or the Royal Blood.

The perfecti are the sacred lineage of the Grail, those who have awakened to the light that comes from on high. Melisande has carried its message. Through her perversity and ambiguity, this mysterious young woman from somewhere else is one of those bird women of ancient legend. She has delivered her message to the fallen angels, who can be delivered only by one of their own because they were perverted by one of their own. But Melisande, like Galahad, is not destined for a long life. She flies away in the form of a dove, but not until she has given birth to a young girl who will perpetuate the message at the heart of the sacred lineage of Grail guardians.

The Grail guardians are those in whom flows the royal blood, meaning the luminous divine soul that shone in the eyes of the perfecti on March 16, 1244, beneath the pog of Montségur, when a demonic pyre was being lit that has not yet finished burning.

Index